THE
W

Henry's Wars and
Shakespeare's Laws

Henry's Wars and Shakespeare's Laws

Perspectives on the
Law of War
in the Later Middle Ages

THEODOR MERON

CLARENDON PRESS · OXFORD

*This book has been printed digitally and produced in a standard specification
in order to ensure its continuing availability*

OXFORD
UNIVERSITY PRESS

Great Clarendon Street, Oxford OX2 6DP

Oxford University Press is a department of the University of Oxford.
It furthers the University's objective of excellence in research, scholarship,
and education by publishing worldwide in

Oxford New York

Auckland Bangkok Buenos Aires Cape Town Chennai
Dar es Salaam Delhi Hong Kong Istanbul Karachi Kolkata
Kuala Lumpur Madrid Melbourne Mexico City Mumbai Nairobi
São Paulo Shanghai Singapore Taipei Tokyo Toronto
with an associated company in Berlin

Oxford is a registered trade mark of Oxford University Press
in the UK and in certain other countries

Published in the United States
by Oxford University Press Inc., New York

ISBN 0- 19- 825811- 9

Jacket illustration: *Triumph of Maximillian*, by Albrecht Dürer. Reproduced by permission of the
Mary Evans Picture Library

For Monique

it was her idea

Preface

I acknowledge with thanks the helpful comments made on drafts of this study by John Baker, Luigi Condorelli, Yoram Dinstein, Gerald Harriss, Peter Haggenmacher, Graham Hughes, Colin Kidd, Peter Lewis, Andreas Lowenfeld, Aryeh Neier, David Norbrook, Ashley Roach, Donna Sullivan and Malcolm Vale. In addition, for their important help, I thank my research assistants David Berg, Joni Charme, Maria Chedid, Jenny Edelstein, and Audrey Schaus, and my Secretaries Marianne Martin, Isabelle Gerardi, and Doreen Ryan.

I owe a deep debt of gratitude to Maurice Keen and other Oxford medieval historians for their invaluable advice and guidance, so generously given.

I wish to express my appreciation to the Filomen D'Agostino and Max E. Greenberg Research Fund of New York University Law School, the Fellows and the staff of All Souls College, Oxford, where, as a Visiting Fellow in 1989 and 1991 I did much of the research for this study. I also thank the Graduate Institute of International Studies, Geneva, for its support, the *American Journal of International Law* for permitting me to use throughout this book sections of my article 'Shakespeare's Henry the Fifth and the Law of War', which appeared in the January 1992 issue of the *Journal*, and to the *Journal*'s Associate Editor Anna Ascher for her outstanding editing of that article.

Finally, I am grateful for the help and courtesy of the staff of the Clarendon Press, and particularly for the encouragement offered by Richard Hart, Senior Law Editor.

Contents

Abbreviations

Ayala   Balthazar Ayala, *Three Books on the Law of War and on the Duties Connected with War and on Military Discipline*, Carnegie edn., trans. John Pawley Bate (1582) (vol. ii) (1912).

Bouvet   Honoré Bonet [otherwise known as Bouvet], *The Tree of Battles*, ed. G. W. Coopland (1949). Coopland's edn. is a translation of the Ernest Nys edn. of 1883. See further Ch. 2 n. 5 and Ch. 5 n. 3.

CW   William Shakespeare, *The Complete Works*, ed. Stanley Wells and Gary Taylor (Compact edn., 1988). See further Ch. 1 n. 2.

Gentili   Alberico Gentili, *De jure belli libri tres*, Carnegie edn., trans. John C. Rolfe (1933). See further Ch. 2 n. 17 and Ch. 3 n. 80.

Gesta   *Gesta Henrici Quinti*, ed. Frank Taylor and John S. Roskell (1975).

Grose   Francis Grose, *Military Antiquities* (vol. i, 1786; vol. ii, 1788).

Grotius   Hugo Grotius, *De jure belli ac pacis libri tres*, Carnegie edn., trans. Francis Kelsey from 1646 edn. (1925). See further Ch. 2 n. 19.

Hall   Edward Hall, *Hall's Chronicle: Containing the History of England, during the Reign of Henry the Fourth, and the Succeeding Monarchs, to the End of the Reign of Henry the Eighth* (1809; repr. 1965). Original title (1548): *The Union of the Two Noble and Illustre Famelies of Lancastre & Yorke*. See further Ch. 1 n. 7.

Holinshed   Raphael Holinshed, *Holinshed's Chronicles*, ed. R. S. Wallace and Alma Hansen (1923; repr. 1978). See further Ch. 1 n. 6. Text of 2nd edn. (1587).

Legnano   Giovanni da Legnano [John of Legnano], *Tractatus de bello, de represaliis et de duello*, ed. Thomas Erskine Holland (1917). See further Ch. 3 n. 83.

LW   Maurice H. Keen, *The Laws of War in the Late Middle Ages* (1965).

Pisan   Christine de Pisan, *The Book of Fayttes of Armes and of Chyvalrye*, trans. William Caxton, 1489; ed. A. T. P. Byles (1932).

Suárez   Francisco Suárez, *Selections from Three Works*, Carnegie edn., trans. Gwladys L. Williams, Ammi Brown, and John Waldron (1944). See further Ch. 2 n. 18 and Ch. 3 n. 73.

Vitoria   Franciscus de Vitoria, *De Indis et de iure belli relectiones*, Carnegie edn., trans. John Pawley Bate, ed. Ernest Nys (1917). See further Ch. 3 n. 77.

1
Introduction

William Shakespeare (1564–1616) wrote during the Elizabethan Renaissance, a period of revived and intense interest in history.[1] *The Life of Henry the Fifth*, written in 1599,[2] one of Shakespeare's histories, is a patriotic, epic portrayal of a phase in the bloody Hundred Years War (1337–1453) between England and France. In contrast to some of his other histories, internal power struggle is not a central theme in *Henry V*, which concerns a conflict with an enemy from without.[3] It describes a medieval campaign led by a chivalrous and virtuous king, who could perhaps do wrong but not a great deal of wrong, and in which the few acting in a just cause defeat the many. In this play, Shakespeare relives past glories.

King Henry V (1387–1422) succeeded to the throne of Henry IV in 1413 and two years later invaded France. The play telescopes the phase of the Hundred Years War that started in 1415, with the landing of Henry's army near Harfleur and its victory at

---

[1] Lily B. Campbell, *Shakespeare's 'Histories': Mirrors of Elizabethan Policy* (1947), 18–20.

[2] William Shakespeare, *The Complete Works*, ed. Stanley Wells and Gary Taylor (Compact Edn., 1988), 567. Unless otherwise indicated, all plays of Shakespeare will be cited from this edition (hereafter *CW*). The editors drew on the 1600 quarto text of *Henry V* rather than on the text printed from Shakespeare's papers in the 1623 folio, 'in the attempt to represent the play as acted by Shakespeare's company'. Gary Taylor, ibid. 567. They believe that the theatrical versions of Shakespeare's plays come closest to their 'final' versions. Editors' General Introduction at p. xxxvi. Wells and Taylor regard the differences between the quarto and folio texts of *Henry V* as minimal. For a more extreme statement of the differences which still remain open, see Annabel Patterson, *Shakespeare and the Popular Voice*, (1989), 71–92. Among the explanations offered by her for these differences appears the conflict between Elizabeth and the earl of Essex. Ibid. 81–7.

[3] Jan Kott, *Shakespeare Our Contemporary*, trans. Boleslaw Taborski (1974), 8. It has been suggested that in *Henry V*'s treatment of the French side Shakespeare showed a strong patriotic bias. Beverley E. Warner, *English History in Shakespeare's Plays* (1894), 158. Gary Taylor writes that the play has 'aroused accusations of jingoism, but the horrors of war are vividly depicted', *CW* 567.

Agincourt, and ended in 1420 with the conclusion of the Treaty of Troyes, which pronounced Henry the heir to the French throne. The treaty seemed to mark the ascendancy of England— until Joan of Arc's rallying of the French in 1429 sparked a turning-point that eventually led to the defeat of England. The play demonstrates Shakespeare's extraordinary ability to condense history. As Kott observes, 'Shakespeare can contain years in a month, months in a day, in one great scene, in three or four speeches which comprise the very essence of history.'[4]

The play is an ideal vehicle for consideration of the late medieval rules and practice of warfare, for two major reasons. First, it narrates a wide range of relevant events, including assertion of the just cause of the war, issuance of an ultimatum or declaration of war, episodes showing the conduct of the war and negotiation of the treaty of peace. It thus 'presents the anatomy of a war'.[5] Second, it is not an imaginary tale but, on the whole, a rather close reflection of the sixteenth-century chronicles that were its principal sources, those of Raphael Holinshed (1498–c.1580)[6] and Edward Hall (or Halle) (c.1498–1547).[7] As

---

[4] Kott, *supra* note 3, at p. 14.

[5] Alexander Leggatt, *Shakespeare's Political Drama* (1988), 114.

[6] Richard Hosley, (ed.), *An Edition of Holinshed's Chronicles* (1968), Intro., p. xvii. The text of this edn. is that of the 2nd edn. of Holinshed's *Chronicles* (1587), which more than any other source guided and inspired Shakespeare (Campbell, *supra* note 1, at 72). Unless otherwise indicated, the 1587 edition will be referred to in this book in the Greenwood Press reprint (1978) of Raphael Holinshed, *Holinshed's Chronicles*, ed. R. S. Wallace and Alma Hansen (1923). Hereafter Holinshed. References to the unabridged works of Holinshed will be to the same 1587 edition, as printed in London, vol. ii in 1807 and vol. iii in 1808. The 1587 edition that Shakespeare used was prepared by Holinshed's assistants and printed after his death. Fred Jacob Levy, *Tudor Historical Thought* (1967), 185. Holinshed's work, however, should not be regarded as the effort of a single historian. It was rather a 'group project [of which in 1573] Holinshed became . . . the co-ordinator', Campbell, *supra*, at 72. Phyllis Rackin observes that '[i]t is customary to speak of Shakespeare's sources by the names of individual authors (Hall, Holinshed, etc.), even though the chronicles included the work of many writers—predecessors whose work was incorporated, successors who augmented the narratives after their authors' death, and collaborators at the time of their production.' Phyllis Rackin, *Stages of History* (1990), 23.

[7] Richard Grafton posthumously published Hall's *Chronicle* in 1548. Campbell, *supra* note 1, at 67. The 1809 edn., which collates the edns of 1548 and 1550, is the version I shall cite: Edward Hall, *Hall's Chronicle: Containing the History of England, during the Reign of Henry the Fourth, and the Succeeding Monarchs, to the End of the Reign of Henry the Eighth* (1809; repr. AMS Press 1965, hereafter

Fred Jacob Levy noted, Holinshed was far from being the best available source, but he was an excellent source for playwrights.[8]

Even more than the play, the campaign itself is an excellent frame for examination of medieval law of war issues, such as the treatment of the population of occupied territories, truces, the status of rebels, ordinances and practice of war, and rules of chivalry—the law on the books and the law in action. Although Shakespeare's play provides the principal framework for the selection of issues for my discussion, the focus of much of the book must necessarily be the law of war issues which were implicated in the war, but not reflected in the play.

My purposes in this book are, first, to provide a commentary on the law of war issues arising in Henry's French campaigns and to show that attitudes towards some of these aspects of the law of war have remained much the same, while other aspects may have changed since Henry's times and Shakespeare's times, and thus to illustrate the law's evolution. My second aim is to provide an international lawyer's commentary on the play itself, by examining how Shakespeare used international law for his

Hall). The original title (1548) was *The Union of the Two Noble and Illustre Famelies of Lancastre & Yorke.*

The playwright's close attention to these chroniclers gives his play a historical basis, but it also means that Shakespeare probably did not know about some of the events they did not mention. Consequently, at times, events of great dramatic potential were overlooked; for example, the real Henry's challenge to the Dauphin (see Ch. 7), after the conquest of Harfleur, to decide the conflict by single combat (a similar opportunity, the trial by combat between Mowbray and Bolingbroke in *Richard II*, I. iii, was provided by Holinshed's account of that monarch's reign).

[8] Levy observes that 'Holinshed's wide reading in the sources of English history was used not to determine the truth in matters doubtful but merely to add more and more detail. All the old legends were included. . . . The result of this accumulation was that there was virtually no attempt to find the cause of events; without saying so, Holinshed leaves us with the impression that establishing causality is also the task of the reader. In a way, this made him the ideal source for the playwrights; everything needful (and a great deal more) was included, but the "construction," the ordering of events, was left to others, who thus could make of the multitudinous facts what they would. When there was any selection at all, it was not based on matters of evidence but on morality.' Levy, *supra* note 6, at 184. Because poets and playwrights were limited in the 'space they had available, [they were] forced by the nature of their craft to find some sort of unity in the jumbled incidents of the past. . . . They had to see the past as a kind of drama, filled not only with incidents but with characters, and thus they had, perforce, to learn the lesson of selection.' Ibid. 235–6.

dramatic ends; to compare his version with its principal sources, the chronicles of Holinshed and Hall,[9] and frequently with other historians' views as to what transpired during the reign of Henry V; and to assess Shakespeare's text in the light of fifteenth- and sixteenth-century norms of *jus gentium*.

Hall and Holinshed were not the only sources Shakespeare used. As Bullough points out, Shakespeare must have been influenced by an anonymous play, *The Famous Victories of Henry the Fifth*.[10] While there are several significant resemblances between the plays, *Famous Victories* has only a few lines on the siege of Harfleur and none on the killing of French prisoners at Agincourt,[11] or on the pyx incident. Indeed, although it employs the expression 'the law of Armes' (Scene ix), *Famous Victories* contains little on law of war issues. However, because the full text of *Famous Victories* is not available (only a shortened text was published in 1598), 'we cannot tell how much [Shakespeare] depended on it,'[12] or on other contemporary plays, now lost.[13] Inevitably, much of the material common to both plays was based on the chroniclers,[14] and although Shakespeare mostly fol-

---

[9] Shakespeare's histories actually 'reproduc[e] thousands upon thousands of [Holinshed's] words', Hosley, *supra* note 6, at xviii. The notion of plagiarism in the Renaissance was limited: 'the imitator was free to borrow as long as he added to what he borrowed', Richard A. Posner, *Law and Literature* (1988), 346; see also Theodor Meron, 'Common Rights of Mankind in Gentili, Grotius and Suárez', 85 AJIL 110, 112 n. 18 (1991). Plagiarism was also common among medieval writers. The important author and compiler (1408–9) of the laws of war and customs of chivalry, Christine de Pisan, vigorously defended liberal use of others' writings: *The Book of Fayttes of Armes and of Chyvalrye* trans. William Caxton, 1489; ed. A. T. P. Byles, (1932), 190; hereafter Pisan.

Both Holinshed and Hall were writing 'to show the significance of the facts and to establish by them general moral and more especially general political laws', Campbell, *supra* note 1, at 75. As a result, Holinshed's account emphasizes the morals of the Tudor era (ibid. 74) rather than those of the Middle Ages, and Hall's work has even been described as a work of propaganda (ibid. 68, citing W. Gordon Zeeveld). Holinshed and Hall wrote some 100 years after the real events, describing them often in the light of 16th-c. attitudes and assumptions that were not always quite those of Henry's own time.

[10] For a comprehensive discussion of the sources Shakespeare used in writing *Henry V*, see Geoffrey Bullough (ed.), *Narrative and Dramatic Sources of Shakespeare* (1962), iv. 347–75. For the text of *The Famous Victories of Henry the Fifth*, see ibid. 348–9, 299. In the wooing scene, Shakespeare draws on *The Famous Victories*. See Rackin, *supra* note 6, at 242.

[11] *Famous Victories*, *supra* note 10, at 364.

[12] Note by the editors, *supra* note 2, at 453.   [13] Ibid. 567.

[14] Bullough, *supra* note 10, at 348.

lowed Holinshed, who himself followed Hall, Shakespeare did use both chroniclers and 'may have had them both open by his side as he wrote some parts of his play'.[15]

Although there is considerable speculation about parallels between some sections of *Henry V* and several fifteenth-century sources, such as the *Gesta Henrici Quinti*, Shakespeare probably did not know these sources directly, as most of them were still in manuscript form in the sixteenth century.[16]

My tasks have been made easier by the works of modern writers on medieval and Renaissance law such as Maurice Keen, on whom I often draw. Some of my other legal sources are reviewed in Chapter 2. I shall frequently refer to *Gesta Henrici Quinti*,[17] whose anonymous author was a royal chaplain attached to the court,[18] because it provides the only eyewitness account of Henry V's French expedition of 1415, and because it was written very soon after the events it describes (1416–17).[19] Proper weight must, however, be given to the fact that the *Gesta* was a work of propaganda, rather than a chronicle. It was written largely to justify Henry's policy domestically in England and externally in the Council of Constance, as well as to enhance Henry's public relations vis-à-vis foreign powers, and especially Emperor Sigismund. As the Editors of the *Gesta* write, its purpose was to present Henry as 'unjustly denied his right to the crown of France and his ancestral territories there [and] to justify Henry in his policy, in both diplomacy and war'.[20] Although Henry is represented as a peace-loving prince, the peace he desired was 'peace with justice, justice implying, of course, restitution to the crown of its rights and inheritance in France'.[21]

Among French chroniclers, I shall frequently refer to the Religieux de Saint-Denys, a contemporary of Henry V and Charles VI, for his chronicle of Charles VI. The Religieux's objectivity, fairness, culture, depth, and style give his writings added importance. Anonymous until recently, it is now suggested

---

[15] Ibid. 351–2. The author of *Famous Victories* attributed to Canterbury the advice to go to war against France, but his Archbishop, unlike Shakespeare's, advocated that Scotland, an ally of France, be conquered first (Sc. ix).

[16] Ibid. 353.

[17] Trans. and ed. Frank Taylor and John S. Roskell (1975); hereafter *Gesta*.

[18] Ibid., Introduction by the Editors, p. xviii.   [19] Ibid., pp. xviii, xxiv.

[20] Ibid., p. xxiii.   [21] Ibid., p. xxix.

that he was Michel Pintoin (1350–1421), chronicler and cantor of the abbey of Saint-Denis.[22]

[22] Nicole Grévy-Pons and Ezio Ornato, 'Qui est l'auteur de la chronique latine de Charles VI, dite du Religieux de Saint-Denis?', 134 Bibliothèque de l'école des chartes 85, 100 (1976).

2
The Legal Environment

By the time of Henry's invasion of France, and of course even more when Shakespeare wrote about that campaign, a considerable body of law applicable to the conduct of war was already established, as described in the writings of several prominent publicists, and applied by courts, princes, and senior military officers with jurisdiction over military offences. In addition to various local customs, this body of law consisted of the customary rules of chivalry, the 'written' rules of civil law and canon law, as well as the ordinances of war, issued by the kings of England—as they were by the rulers of others countries—'concerning the conduct of both armies and individual combatants in time of war'.[1] Despite the critical role of such courts and authorities, it appears that a particularly effective sanction ensuring compliance with the rules of *jus armorum* was the knight's fear of dishonour and public reprobation. Such dishonour was associated with the reversal (placing upside down) of a knight's coat of arms (*subversio armorum*), a measure frequently imposed for breach of promise to pay ransom.[2] Chivalry, closely associated with war, was a way of life, involving not only critical economic interests of the knightly class through booty and ransom, but also what Maurice Keen calls 'a social mystique associated with the

---

[1] Christopher T. Allmand, *The Hundred Years War* (1988), 113.

[2] Maurice H. Keen, *The Laws of War in the Late Middle Ages* (1965, hereafter *LW*), 20; id., 'The Jurisdiction and Origins of the Constable's Court', in John Gillingham and J. C. Holt (eds.), *War and Government in the Middle Ages* (1984), 159. The Ordinances of War attributed to Henry V are discussed in Chs. 6 and 8 infra. On courts of chivalry, see *LW* 23–59; G. D. Squibb, *The High Court of Chivalry* (1959), 1–28; Christopher Allmand and C. A. J. Armstrong, *English Suits before the Parlement of Paris 1420–1436* (1982); A. Rogers, *Hoton v. Shakell: A Ransom Case in the Court of Chivalry, 1390–5*, ed. Lewis Thorpe, Nottingham Medieval studs. 6 (1962), 74. For an illustration of a contested case of *subversio armorum*, see Pierre-Clement Timbal, *La Guerre de cent ans vue à travers les registres du Parlement (1337–1369)* (1961) 307–13.

conduct of war',[3] including ceremonial knightings before battles and the formal ennoblement of common men who showed particular courage. Chivalry emphasized the notions of duty, honour, and glamour, and involved such humane and noble principles as aid for the weak and the helpless.[4]

Holinshed's *Chronicles* of the reigns of medieval English monarchs—which informed Shakespeare's histories—contain many references to such chivalric practices as trial by combat and letters of defiance (a medieval form of declarations of war) and they are occasionally reflected in those histories. On the basis of Holinshed, Shakespeare's French King Charles VI commands his herald, Montjoy, to 'greet England with our sharp defiance' (*Henry V*, III. v. 37) and Montjoy accordingly tells Henry: 'Thus says my King: ". . . To this add defiance, and tell [Henry] for conclusion he hath betrayed his followers, whose condemnation is pronounced"' (III. vi. 119–35).

Medieval kings of England, including Henry V, occasionally promulgated ordinances governing the conduct of war and severely punishing violators (Chapters 6 and 8 below). Through Holinshed's *Chronicles*, Shakespeare learned about Henry V's proclamations of rules of war. Holinshed explicitly mentions these proclamations and they are reflected in the play. Thus, when told about the likely execution of a soldier for having robbed a church, Shakespeare's Henry declares: 'We would have all such offenders so cut off, and we here give express charge that in our marches through the country there be nothing compelled from the villages, nothing taken but paid for, none of the French upbraided or abused in disdainful language' (III. vi. 108–12).

This proclamation, which anticipated the modern law of war, is explained by Shakespeare on grounds of effectiveness rather than abstract humanity, in much the same way as is taught by modern academies of military law: 'For when lenity and cruelty play for a kingdom, the gentler gamester is the soonest winner' (ibid. 112–14).

Medieval jurists recognized the existence—in Bouvet's words—

---

[3] Maurice H. Keen, 'Chivalry, Nobility, and the Man-at-Arms', in Christopher T. Allmand (ed.), *War, Literature, and Politics in the Late Middle Ages* (1976), 32, at 40.

[4] This element is highlighted in 'The Othes of Heraudes', repr. in Travers Twiss (ed.), *The Black Book of Admiralty*, Monumenta Juridica, i. (1871), 297, 298.

of a law 'which we call in Latin the law of nations, *jus gentium*'.[5] For Bouvet, that law covered 'everything which is according to reason in general. Canon law and civil law can also be called the law of nations.'[6] In an excellent analysis of the medieval law of nations, Maurice Keen points out that medieval lawyers tried to follow Roman lawyers' conception of *jus gentium*, namely law common to all men, or the elements of law common to all known legal systems.[7] Based on natural reason, it was an extension to human affairs of natural law or *jus naturale*.[8]

A glance at the titles of the principal works of jurists of Henry's time—such as *Tractatus de bello, de represaliis et de duello* by Giovanni da Legnano (completed in 1360 and first published in 1477), *The Tree of Battles* (composed *c*.1387) by Honoré Bonet (or Bouvet, as he is now known) and *Book of Fayttes of Armes and of Chyvalrye* by Christine de Pisan (written in 1408-9)—suffices to demonstrate that at the time of Henry V the bulk of *jus gentium* was the law relating to war, that is, the law of arms or *jus armorum*, '*droit coutumier international des chevaliers*',[9] though there were also rules of canon and civil law pertaining to soldiers.[10] The law of arms, based on canon and civil law, was the special law of the knightly class paralleling such special laws as the law merchant and the law of the sea. It was a part of the law of nations, *jus gentium*.[11] The law of nations addressed not only chivalric rules concerning such matters as the conduct of hostilities, ransom, and the division of spoils of war (the law of arms), but also such subjects as just causes of war, the privileges of ambassadors, and the law of treaties.

The customary rules of *jus armorum*, or *jus militare*, regulated the conduct of soldiers within Christendom,[12] but not between Christians and Muslims or other non-Christians. *Jus armorum* was not, it must be stressed, a body of law governing the relations between contending nations, but a body of norms

[5] Honoré Bonet, *The Tree of Battles*, ed. G. W. Coopland (1949), 126; hereafter Bouvet (composed *c*.1387; Coopland's edn. is a translation of the Ernest Nys edn. of 1883.)

[6] Ibid.   [7] *LW* 11.   [8] Ibid. 14.   [9] Timbal, *supra* note 2, at 269.

[10] On the nature of the medieval law of war, see Peter Haggenmacher, 'La Place de Francisco de Vitoria parmi les fondateurs du Droit International', in François Rigaux (ed.), *Actualité de la pensée juridique de Francisco de Vitoria* (1988), 27, 77–80; Peter Haggenmacher, *Grotius et la doctrine de la guerre juste* (1983), 626.

[11] *LW* 14–15.   [12] Ibid. 17.

governing the conduct of warring men.[13] The law of arms was in fact the law of chivalry applicable to knights and to nobility, that is, to those who had the right to bear arms and to make war,[14] regardless of their nationality.

In *Henry V*, Shakespeare wrote of a late medieval war fought between Catholic kings who were committed, at least in principle, to the medieval chivalric law of arms. Despite those constraints, which called for a modicum of humane conduct, this war was both cruel and bloody.

In contrast to the dramatist's familiarity with Holinshed and Hall, '[i]t cannot be maintained that Shakespeare even knew of the works'[15] of the various contemporary writers on *jus gentium*.[16] These include the Spanish Dominican Francisco de Vitoria (1480–1546), who in 1532 delivered his famous lectures *De Indis et de jure belli hispanorum in barbaros*; Alberico Gentili (1552–1608), Shakespeare's contemporary in England;[17] and Francisco Suárez (1548–1617), the Spanish Jesuit scholar.[18] The best-known Renaissance writer on international law, the Dutchman Hugo Grotius (1583–1645), wrote somewhat later (his magisterial *De jure belli ac pacis* appeared in 1625,[19] after Shakespeare's death).

---

[13] *LW* 133. Peter Haggenmacher, 'Grotius and Gentili: A Reassessment of Thomas E. Holland's Inaugural Lecture', in Hedley Bull, Benedict Kingsbury, and Adam Roberts (eds.), *Hugo Grotius and International Relations* (1990), 133, 159.

[14] *LW* 19. Keen points out that a peasant could not claim rights to ransom in an enemy prisoner under the law of arms, because that law did not apply to him.

[15] George W. Keeton, *Shakespeare's Legal and Political Background* (1967), 82.

[16] Because of the dates when the works of Gentili and Suárez were completed, it is nearly impossible to find any reflection of their work in either Holinshed or Hall. That is not necessarily true of Vitoria, but his special interest in the law concerning colonization and wars with 'barbarians' was one with which the English were not yet significantly concerned.

[17] Keeton, *supra* note 15, at 80. See generally Theodor Meron, 'Common Rights of Mankind in Gentili, Grotius and Suárez', 85 AJIL 110 (1991). Gentili, an Italian Protestant, took refuge in England and in 1587 became the Regius Professor of Civil Law in Oxford (the Regius Chair was first established in 1546). Gentili's Oxford lectures appeared in book form in 1588 under the title *Prima commentatio de jure belli* and were republished, in considerably expanded form, in 1598 as *De jure belli libri tres*.

[18] Suárez's *De legibus, ac deo legislatore* (Treatise on Law and God the Legislator) was published in 1612. The law of war was the subject of *De triplici virtute theologica, fide, spe, et charitate* (The Three Theological Virtues, Faith, Hope, and Charity), published posthumously in 1621.

[19] Hugo Grotius, De jure belli ac pacis libri tres (Carnegie ed., Francis Kelsey trans. 1925) (1646). Hereafter cited as Grotius. Kelsey translated the 1646 edition

There is no evidence that the sixteenth-century writers on *jus gentium* influenced Shakespeare either directly or indirectly. However, their work, and sometimes that of earlier, medieval writers, reflects the legal environment of the era.

The fact that Shakespeare preceded the birth of modern international law does not mean that no broadly recognized rules applied, at least in principle, to nations' conduct of war. Indeed, much as in the Middle Ages, most rules of *jus gentium* formed part of the law of war and there was hardly any discrete law of peace.[20] The law of peace was largely limited to rules dealing with the termination of war and the conclusion of peace. Sixteenth-century treatises on the law of war often failed to distinguish among strategy, military discipline, and legal rules governing warfare.[21] Not surprisingly, the lack of clarity regarding these distinctions also characterizes Shakespeare's histories.[22] Although Shakespeare's frequent use of legal phrases was probably not based on a deep knowledge of the law,[23] his use of legal phraseology, especially in matters pertaining to *jus armorum*, was remarkably accurate.

rather than the first, 1625, edition. The principal work on Grotius is Peter Haggenmacher, *supra* note 10.

[20] Haggenmacher, *supra* note 13, at 157.

[21] George W. Keeton, *Shakespeare and his Legal Problems* (1930), 59. Consider e.g. the title of Balthazar Ayala's work *Three Books on the Law of War and on the Duties Connected with War and on Military Discipline* (1582).

[22] Shakespeare tends to refer to the law of arms, disciplines of war, etc. In *Henry V*, Captain Fluellen regards the law of war sometimes as a purely military discipline and sometimes as normative. His plea for silence in the proximity of the enemy ('I warrant you, that there is no tiddle-taddle nor pibble-babble in Pompey's camp') relies on 'the true and ancient prerogatifs and laws of the wars' as a military discipline (IV. i. 68–72). But the law of arms is invoked by Fluellen in the strictly normative sense in his famous condemnation of the French attack on the English encampment (see Ch. 9 below). Shakespeare, or perhaps John Fletcher, also refers to the normative significance of the laws of war in *Henry VIII (All is True)*: 'Nay, ladies, fear not. | By all the laws of war you're privileged' (I. iv. 52–3) (see the note by the editors, *CW* 1193; *1 Henry VI*, 'I crave the benefit of law of arms' (IV. i. 100); and *King Lear*: 'by the law of arms thou wast not bound to answer' (V. iii. 143).

[23] Arthur Underhill, 'Law', in *Shakespeare's England* (1917), 381. The use of legal terms and allusions was not confined to Shakespeare's plays. Clarkson and Warren demonstrated that several Elizabethan playwrights used legalisms even more extensively than Shakespeare. They argued that 'legal locutions as part of the idiom of the stage [were] common to all playwrights', that 'the Elizabethan was an amazingly litigious age', and that there was a 'close relationship between the playwright and the Inns of Court'. Paul S. Clarkson and Clyde T. Warren, *The Law of Property in Shakespeare and the Elizabethan Drama* (1942), 285–6.

Rules of chivalry, civil law, and canon law formed the law applied by courts of chivalry, admiralty courts, and such prestigious tribunals as the Parlement de Paris,[24] in matters typically involving rights over prisoners, entitlement to ransom and goods seized in time of war, and armorial bearings.[25] The English court of chivalry or *curia militaris*,[26] presided over by the Lord High Constable and the Earl Marshal, the highest English military officers, also had some criminal jurisdiction for the trial of cases of treason and homicide committed abroad.[27] The court thus 'took cognisance of appeals, principally of treason, in which battle was offered by the appellor'.[28] The Lord High Constable and the Earl Marshal, and lower constables and marshals, had jurisdiction derived from ordinances of war to enforce those ordinances.[29] The functions of the 'Office of the Conestable and Mareschalle' were thus described: 'In the time of werre is to punysh all manner of men that breken the statutes and ordonnaunce by the kynge made to be keped in the oost in the said tyme, and to punysh the same accordyng to the peynes provided in the said statutes'.[30]

The law of chivalry could be enforced by courts of chivalry, which routinely handled disputes between knights of different nationality (such as the courts held by such *magistri militum* as the Constable and the Marshal in England, the courts of the Constable and the Marshal of France, and, with broader jurisdiction, the French Parlement de Paris). Maurice Keen demonstrated that the jurisdiction of the court of chivalry and of the constable's court ('courts in the hosts') were largely concurrent, and that under the authority granted the constables by the ordinances of war, they could enforce also those provisions of the ordinances which concerned rights in prisoners and ransom. In addition, they settled disputes concerning armorial bearings.

---

[24] Allmand, *supra* note 1, at 112.   [25] Squibb, *supra* note 2, at 1–7.

[26] *Miles* meant 'knight' in English medieval Latin; ibid. 2.

[27] When such cases could not be proven by evidence, they would be decided upon in a trial by battle; ibid. 22–3. See also Ch. 7 below.

[28] Keen, 'The Jurisdiction and Origins of the Constable's Court', *supra* note 2.

[29] Ibid. 3.

[30] Repr. in Travers Twiss (ed.), *The Black Book of Admiralty*, Monumenta Juridica, i. (1871), 281. According to this definition, in a part not cited here, the constable also had the power to consider matters arising overseas in which aliens might be parties. Keen, 'The Jurisdiction and Origins of the Constable's Court', *supra* note 2, at 160.

Because the powers of a commander would lapse after a campaign had ended, 'the real difference between the Court of Chivalry and the courts in the hosts [was] that the one exercised a constant, the others a temporary jurisdiction, not that they were concerned with different types of cases.'[31]

The case-law of the Parlement de Paris shows considerable sophistication, as can be demonstrated by these illustrative cases:

The Bruges Prize Case (1361)

This case concerned the right to seize enemy property at sea. A group of merchants from Bruges claimed that privateers from Boulogne had captured certain vessels moored outside the port of Ostend, and seized their cargo, which was destined for Nieuport. The merchants presented themselves as neutrals, victims of an act of piracy, and argued that, being originally from Italy, they were not enemies of the King of France, and should therefore be allowed to trade freely, without having to suffer the consequences of acts of war.

The captains of the vessels in question had, however, already admitted that their cargo was English, as indicated by the charterparties that they produced. These admissions were accepted despite the merchants' protests that the captains' statements had been obtained by force and that, as a widespread wartime measure of protection, the captains carried two sets of charterparties in order to protect themselves from the privateers of the two warring parties.

Once it was established that the cargo in question was indeed English, the privateers' action, which had received the French Admiral's stamp of approval (according to the ordinances in force, the Admiral was entitled to one-tenth of the value of the prize), could hardly be contested, as it was generally accepted that when a state of war existed between two sovereigns, their subjects were entitled to seize enemy property, on land or at sea. The privateers' seizure was thus deemed entirely legitimate, for the merchandise in question was English, destined for England, and the plaintiffs were in fact Englishmen domiciled in Bruges.[32]

---

[31] Keen, 'The Jurisdiction and Origins of the Constable's Court', *supra* note 2, at 164.

[32] Timbal, *supra* note 2, at 263–4.

The Jean de Melun Case (1368)

The French knight Jean de Melun was taken prisoner in 1359 by an English squire, Henri Poinfroit. A ransom was agreed upon, and Jean de Melun immediately paid a part of it. However, upon his release he still owed his captor a sum of money. Melun delivered promissory notes to Poinfroit for the remaining sum, and agreed to pay either Poinfroit or the holder of the notes the week after the following Christmas, or else to return to captivity. Two other knights guaranteed the payment. As sanction for default, Melun further agreed that, should he renege on his promise, the consequence would be *subversio armorum*, the public turning upside down of his coat of arms.

After a failed attempt to arbitrate, Poinfroit turned to the Court of Marshals (*tribunal des maréchaux*), which decided that Melun must execute the promissory notes. Melun refused to comply, and obtained royal permission to bring the case before the Parlement de Paris, which upheld Melun's refusal. The notes were not executory because they lacked a royal seal and the knight's seal they did carry had not been recognized.

In fact, Melun contested not only his duty to pay the remaining ransom, but the validity of his entire promise, which, he claimed, had been obtained 'through threats and fraud' (*vis, metus, turpis causa*). Furthermore, he argued that he had been taken prisoner during a truce (when all acts of war were prohibited). Finally Poinfroit, being himself a prisoner of a French captor at the time of Melun's capture, could not, according to *jus armorum*, 'acquire' his own prisoners. Melun thus maintained that, his promise being void, not only had he no duty to pay the remainder of the ransom, but Poinfroit should reimburse him the sum already paid. Melun also sought reparation for the *subversio armorum*, to which he had been subjected by Poinfroit. Indeed, once Melun realized that there was a good chance his promise would be judged void, he abandoned his initial argument that by carrying out the *subversio* Poinfroit had forfeited his right to the ransom, and now claimed damages for the 'gratuitous insult' constituted by the *subversio*.

The court held that Melun's promise was indeed void, and ordered Poinfroit to reimburse the sum he had already received, to pay a fine, and to carry out an *erectio armorum* wherever the *subversio* had taken place. Poinfroit was to be imprisoned until full execution had taken place.

The judgment was handed down in 1368. Twelve years later, Poinfroit had not executed the court order, and was still in prison.[33]

The Simon Burley Case (1371)

While a certain Lord of Dampierre was being held prisoner in England, the King of France entrusted the Lord's wife with the custody of a captured English knight, Simon Burley, on the condition that she not ransom him without the King's consent.

Although Burley swore he would not attempt to flee, he did escape. He was, however, recaptured by Raoul de Renneval, Lady of Dampierre's cousin, after she had made public a description of the fugitive and the promise of an award for his recapture and return to her custody. Renneval and his *socius in armis*, Enguerran d'Endin, informed the Lady of Dampierre that they considered they had no obligation under *jus armorum* to return the prisoner, as he had fled because of mistreatment, in which case the escape was lawful, and he could be taken prisoner by his new captors. They did, none the less, agree to sell Burley to the Lady of Dampierre, who paid a part of the sum agreed upon immediately, promising by sealed letters delivered by three knights to pay the remainder. She then appealed to Charles V to recognize that the contract was void, her consent having been obtained 'through threats and fraud' (*turpis aut saltem injusta causa*). The King ordered Renneval and d'Endin to return both the sum already paid and the sealed letters.

The dispute was brought before the Parlement, where Renneval and d'Endin argued that Burley's escape was legal (*debite et licite*), for he had been subjected to ill treatment (*mauvais traitements*) by the Lady of Dampierre. She had, therefore lost all right to recover her prisoner, and Renneval and d'Endin had the right under *jus armorum* to recapture Burley, as well as to sell him for a reasonable price.

After some hesitation and consultations with the Great Council and even the King, the court ruled that the allegation of

---

[33] Timbal, *supra* note 2, at 307–8, 312–13.

mistreatment had not been proven, and that Burley therefore remained the Lady's captive. It ordered Renneval and d'Endin to return both the money and the sealed letters to her.[34]

The Duke and Duchess of Anjou Case (1365)

In this case, the Duke and Duchess of Anjou sued for recovery of goods taken from them by an armed 'compagnie navarraine', but in the possession of another armed band at the time of the suit. The latter had seized the goods from the former and claimed before the court that their seizure of the goods was an act of war, and that they therefore benefited from the rule of *jus armorum* exempting them from any duty to return the goods to their original owner.

The Duke and Duchess argued that they had been the victims not of an act of war, but of a common-law crime perpetrated by pillagers, who could not claim to have acted for the King of Navarre because at the time of the taking a state of truce existed between him and the King of France. Their suit thus was an ordinary claim for recovery of stolen property from third-party holders.

The court considered the suit admissible, and called for an investigation.[35]

---

[34] Timbal, *supra* note 2, at 327–9.   [35] Ibid. 494–5.

3

The War of Rights: Just War—Jus ad Bellum *and* Jus in Bello

The Hundred Years War was a war of rights.[1] Although the conflict concerned *Realpolitik* aims of both England and France, and as in most wars 'rights and advantages, principle and interest were mingled . . . it remains that [in the Hundred Years War] it was in terms of right that the . . . arguments [of the adversaries] and their minds were cast'.[2] The King of England claimed either the throne of France or his French inheritance to hold in full sovereignty.[3] Under Henry V, legalism in negotiations, in propaganda, and in the councils of state, always self-serving and often hypocritical, reached its climax. Henry's war was not only about territory, marriage, and dowry, for through negotiations he could have gained a large measure of his territorial claims, the hand of Charles VI's daughter Catherine, and a very generous dowry. With considerable justification, the French Ambassador (the Archbishop of Bourges) protested before Henry's Chancellor Beaufort that 'l'histoire ne fournit pas d'exemple d'une fille de roi ou d'empereur qui ait quitté le palais de son père avec une

---

[1] The principal causes, though certainly not the only causes of the Hundred Years War (1337–1453) were disputes concerning the feudal relationship between the King of France and his vassal the Duke of Aquitaine (King of England) and the English kings' dynastic claims to the crown of France. In 1328, Charles IV of France died leaving no direct heir. His sister Isabel had married Edward II of England. Their son Edward III, who had ascended to the English throne in 1327, had therefore a claim to succeed his uncle Charles IV as king of France. The French nobility decided, however, to choose as king one of their own, Philip of Valois, rather than Edward. The Hundred Years War broke out in 1337 following abortive negotiations and Philip VI's declaration that because of Edward's disobedience the duchy of Aquitaine was confiscate to the French crown. Christopher Allmand, *The Hundred Years War* (1988), 9–11.

[2] Peter S. Lewis, *Later Medieval France* (1968), 42.

[3] Ibid. 42–3. For a discussion of the origins of the dynastic dispute, see W. M. Ormrod, *The Reign of Edward III* (1990), 8–10.

pareille somme d'argent.'[4] It was Henry's legal claims to the throne of France that made compromise impossible and the resumption of war inevitable.

The French and English royal courts well before Henry's era, however, sought to ground positions in law and articulate claims in terms of legal principle. This may be seen, for example, in the consideration by the French Conseil d'Etat, assembled in parliament in May 1369, of the rejection of Edward III's ultimatum, a rejection which led to the end of the Treaty of Brétigny and the resumption of the war. Guillaume de Dormans (the brother of Jean de Dormans, Cardinal of Beauvais and Chancellor of France) argued that while the King of France had observed to the letter the clauses of the treaty of peace, the King of England, by tolerating the excesses of the companies, had not ceased violating the provisions of the Treaties of Brétigny and Calais.[5]

The controversy regarding the right of Charles V to receive in his court Edward III's Aquitaine subjects and to accept their appeals deserves comment. From the English perspective, by so doing Charles V violated the Treaty of Brétigny and resorted to what in modern times would be considered illegal intervention in the affairs of another country. The French perspective on this question differed entirely. Taking advantage of the fact that the Treaty of Brétigny contained no provision concerning sovereignty over Aquitaine, Charles V, after taking learned legal advice from prominent jurists,

was able to claim in 1369 that, since he had never renounced sovereignty in Aquitaine, he was entitled to hear in his court the complaints of the Gascon lords against their seigneur, the Black Prince. Because it was a fact that, since the sealing of the treaty, Edward III had ceased to use the title of King of France and also that the French king had ceased to exercise sovereign rights in Aquitaine, there was a delicate legal question in issue here.[6]

The Treaty of Brétigny did provide for the surrender of Aquitaine in sovereignty to Edward III,[7] but the Aquitaine clause

---

[4] *Chronique du Religieux de Saint-Denys*, ed. and trans. L. Bellaguet, Collection de documents inédits sur l'histoire de France, ser. 1 (1844), v. 517.

[5] Roland Delachenal, *Histoire de Charles V* (1928), iv. 140.

[6] Maurice H. Keen, 'Diplomacy', in Gerald L. Harriss (ed.), *Henry V* (1985), 181, 183–4.

[7] See Ormrod, *supra* note 3, at 26.

of the treaty was detached from the treaty itself, for future implementation, and never in fact ratified.[8] Not surprisingly, therefore,
in the French Conseil d'Etat Guillaume de Dormans argued that
Charles's acceptance of the appeals was both his right and his
duty. All of the assembled councillors agreed that if Charles's
action led Edward to make war, that war would be both unjusti-
fied and without cause.[9] Taking the floor himself, Charles contended that everything that was done on his behalf in Guyenne
and in Ponthieu was done 'par voie de justice et selon le traité de
la paix', while the King of England and the Prince of Wales
'procédaient par voie de guerre et de fait'.[10]

The tension between *voie de justice* and *voie de fait* was of considerable importance in medieval discourse. The first concerned
the legal resolution of disputes by courts of chivalry or arbitration; the second involved resort to war, dishonour, or reprisals.[11]
As Philippe Contamine put it, for people in the Middle Ages
'[t]oujours . . . la "voie de droit" devait l'emporter sur la "voie de
fait", et il leur paraissait indispensable . . . de recourir à un
"montage" juridique, voire théologico-philosophique, susceptible
de les persuader que les faits s'accordaient au droit, à la raison et
à la justice.'[12] Of course, what for one prince was *voie de justice*
was for another *voie de fait* or *voie de guerre*. Only the more
powerful prince, or at least the prince who believed in the probability of his victory, had the luxury of insisting that *voie de justice*
be followed, thus placing the responsibility for the war on the
other party. ('Le Roi [Charles V] tenait donc pour certain que,
s'il avait la guerre, ce serait au grand tort de ses ennemis et qu'il
aurait pour lui le bon droit.'[13])

---

[8] Ormrod observes that both parties used the treaty as a respite before the
renewal of the war, and that neither intended to honour it. 'Both were eager to
withdraw from the main treaty the special clauses requiring Edward's repudiation
of the French royal title and the handing over by the Valois of those territories
now to be recognized as English possessions.' Ibid. 27. William Longman, *Edward
the Third* (1869), ii. 55–61. Nevertheless, in 1362 Edward bestowed on his eldest
son (the Black Prince) the title of Prince of Aquitaine. The latter's presence and
methods of administration as resident lord of Aquitaine aroused the hostility of
its independent lords. Ormrod, *supra* note 3, at 28.

[9] Delachenal, *supra* note 5, at 140–2.   [10] Ibid. 143.

[11] *LW* 172–3, 45–59.

[12] Philippe Contamine, '"Le Royaume de France ne peut tomber en fille":
Fondement, formulation et implication d'une théorie politique à la fin du Moyen
Age', *Perspectives Médiévales*, 13 (1987), 67, 70.

[13] Delachenal, *supra* note 5, at 143.

The use of such code terms as *voie de justice* has continued to this day. When various Arab countries, for example, refer to a solution of the Middle East conflict on the 'basis of justice and law', they mean complete Israeli withdrawal from lands occupied in June 1967.[14] When Israelis claim territorial rights over the West Bank, they too invoke various 'legal' entitlements.

In June 1369, in reaction to the French replies to his ultimatum, Edward announced in Parliament that he was retaking the name and the title of the King of France, thus renewing the dynastic struggle. Delachenal commented that by approving the necessary funds the Parliament acted not only to fund the war but to reclaim the succession of the last Capetians.[15]

Basing the rejection of Edward III's ultimatum on his tolerance of the free companies' excesses made good sense in contemporary legal theory. Honoré Bouvet maintained that in such circumstances going to war was not only a prince's right but a duty as well:

[The king of France] could not abstain from making war against the king of England without mortal sin, for if he were to allow his men to be killed and pillaged, and his kingdom to be robbed and destroyed, who would pardon such negligence? So I conclude that he must break the truce, and can do it without falling into sin, since the other King has begun.[16]

Bouvet regarded war as 'not as an evil thing, but [as] . . . good and virtuous', because it sought to 'set wrong right'. Its aim was 'to wrest peace, tranquillity and reasonableness, from him who refuses to acknowledge his wrongdoing'.[17] War derived from divine law and from God because, as in the case of the biblical Joshua, God not merely permitted war but ordained it. It was also justified by *jus gentium*, including canon law and civil law, and by the law of nature.

Concern about innocent victims of war was not enough to restrain resort to war. Bouvet maintained that the evil things that happen in war are caused not by war, but by abuse, as in the case of a soldier raping a woman or setting fire to a church.[18]

---

[14] Y. Ibrahim, 'Hassan Portrays Bush as Avowed Friend of Arabs', *International Herald Tribune*, 27 May 1992, 1, col. 1.
[15] Delachenal, *supra* note 5, 144–5.   [16] Bouvet, 192.   [17] Ibid. 125.
[18] Ibid.

Where not attributable to 'false usage',[19] the hardships of war should be regarded as the inevitable collateral effects of an intrinsically positive act.[20]

By justifying war, Bouvet, one of the great writers on chivalry, was serving the interests of the knightly class and the nobility, for whom war was both a way of life and the very *raison d'être*. War afforded them an opportunity to gain glory on the battlefield and to acquire wealth through pillage and ransom.

Justifications such as those proposed by Bouvet, which not only permitted but required war as an instrument for remedying wrongs, together with frequent invocations of the Old Testament, could be used and abused by every prince claiming to wage a just war. Henry's and every other prince's war was just, at least from their own perspective. Indeed, Henry may well have believed that the assertion of his rights to the throne of France was his duty.[21]

By focusing on English sources represented by the *Gesta* and Henry's correspondence with Charles VI, and French sources reflected by the Religieux de Saint-Denys, I shall show how Henry V used legal arguments to justify both his claims on France and his waging of the war.

The *Gesta* attributes the failure of negotiations to the French, who could not be induced by any equitable means 'to accept . . . peace without immense injury to the crown of England and perpetual disinheritance of the same in certain of the most noble parts of it belonging to us in that kingdom'.[22] The campaign was designed 'to recover [Henry's] duchy of Normandy, which belongs to him entirely by a right dating from the time of William the first, the Conqueror, even though now, as for a long time past, it is thus withheld, against God and all justice, by the violence of the French'.[23] Following the precedent set by Charles V, Henry resorted to what would now be regarded as an act of legal propaganda to demonstrate the wrongs of the French, and the reasons that compelled him to raise his standards against the 'rebels'. He ordered the transcription by a notary, under the seal of the Archbishop of Canterbury, of 'the pacts and covenants not

---

[19] Ibid.
[20] Ibid. ('if, in the waging of war, the good have to suffer for the bad, it cannot be otherwise, for indeed, war is to be compared to a medicine').
[21] Charles Lethbridge Kingsford, *Henry V* (1901), 110–11.
[22] *Gesta*, 15.   [23] Ibid. 17.

so long ago entered into between [Henry IV] and certain of the great princes of France on the subject of his divine right and claim to the duchy of Aquitaine',[24] to be presented to the Council of Constance and to Emperor Sigismund. In the course of the July negotiations, the King's Chancellor, Bishop Beaufort, read to French envoys a declaration stating that unless the French gave up certain territories, Henry would recover them by sword, 'calling God to witness that this course was forced upon him by the long delays and by the denial of justice'.[25]

The invocation of the Bible as both divine law and a part of Henry's positive law arsenal, as exemplified by Henry's letter to Charles of 28 July 1415, merits comment. In this letter, Henry invoked the 'law of Deuteronomy':

as the law of Deuteronomy commands that whoever appears in arms before a town, should offer it peace before it is besieged, we have, even up to the present time, done all which our rank allows peaceably to recover the possession of that which belongs to us by legitimate succession, and to reunite to our crown that which you wrongfully and by violence possess; so that from your refusing justice, we may justly have recourse to the force of arms.[26]

The *Gesta*'s frequent emphasis on the law of Deuteronomy is significant in that it gives 'Biblical justification for the severity of a conqueror to the inhabitants of a city which has refused his offer of peace'.[27] Standing before the walls of Harfleur, Henry 'offered, in accordance with the twentieth chapter of the Deuteronomic law, peace to the besieged if, freely and without coercion, they would open their gates to him and, as was their duty, restore that town, which was a noble and hereditary portion of his crown of England and of his duchy of Normandy'.[28]

---

[24] *Gesta*, 17 and editors' n. 3. The *Gesta* refers to the agreement concluded at Bourges and ratified in London on 18 May 1412. Regarding the skilful use by Charles V of opinions of prominent jurists as erudite propaganda to support his challenge against the Treaty of Brétigny and his claims against England, see Keen, 'Diplomacy', *supra* note 6, at 181, 183–4.

[25] James Hamilton Wylie, *The Reign of Henry the Fifth* (1914), i. 491. Henry's letter to Charles of 28 July 1415 was regarded as a letter of defiance. Ibid. 493–4.

[26] Trans. by Harris Nicolas, repr. in H. Nicolas, *A History of the Battle of Agincourt*, (2nd edn., 1832), app. 1, 5.

[27] *Gesta*, Intro. by the editors, p. xxx.

[28] Ibid. 35. See Deuteronomy 20: 10–14: 'When thou comest nigh unto a city to fight against it, then proclaim peace unto it. And it shall be, if it make thee answer of peace, and open unto thee, then it shall be, *that* all the people *that* is

He warned the defenders of Harfleur 'of the penal edicts contained in the aforesaid law which it would be necessary to execute upon them as a rebellious people should they thus persist in their obstinacy to the end'.[29] The *Gesta* claims that in deciding to surrender the inhabitants were moved by their fear 'of the punishments of the law of Deuteronomy'.[30]

In the Middle Ages, as in the present era, the exhaustion of peaceful settlement procedures before resorting to self-help or counter-measures was expected (see Chapter 4 below), both as a moral imperative and as a legal requirement,[31] and often for public-relations and propaganda reasons. However, the *Gesta* and *The First English Life*[32] wrongly suggest that Henry resorted to military preparations only from the failure of negotiations.[33] The truth is that Henry's preparations for war started 'almost from the first intimation of his design'.[34] These preparations were accelerated as early as the period after August 1414.[35] Well before the Bourges embassy reached England, the King's Chancellor, Bishop Beaufort, informed the great council that the King had decided 'to cross the sea to recover his heritage'.[36] It is difficult to believe that Henry conducted the negotiations in good faith; it is indeed impossible to regard them as more than perfunctory. This may be seen by the scope of the demands presented by Henry's ambassadors in March 1415: 'We sought, first, from his cousin of France the crown and kingdom of France,

---

found therein shall be tributaries unto thee, and they shall serve thee. And if it will make no peace with thee, but will make war against thee, then thou shalt besiege it: And when the LORD thy God hath delivered it into thine hands, thou shalt smite every male thereof with the edge of the sword: But the women, and the little ones, and the cattle, and all that is in the city, *even* all the spoil thereof, shalt thou take unto thyself; and thou shalt eat the spoil of thine enemies, which the LORD thy God hath given thee.'

[29] *Gesta*, 37.   [30] Ibid. 49.

[31] See generally Gaetano Arangio-Ruiz, *Fourth Report on State Responsibility*, UN Doc. A/CN.4/444 (1992).

[32] *The First English Life of King Henry the Fifth Written in 1513 by an Anonymous Author Known Commonly as The Translator of Livius*, ed. Charles Lethbridge Kingsford (1911), 24–7.

[33] *Gesta*, 15 and editors' n. 2.

[34] Ibid., intro. by editors, p. xliii.

[35] Ernest F. Jacob, *Henry V and the Invasion of France* (1947; hereafter *Henry V*), 76–7. See also Kingsford, *supra* note 21 at 117.

[36] Jacob, *Henry V*, *supra* note 35, at 73.

with all the rights and appurtenances belonging to it, to be effectually restored and handed over.'[37]

When it became clear that the French would not accept these proposals, the English ambassadors sought that at least there might be 'restored . . . other rights, inheritances, and lordships belonging to him'. These included Normandy, Touraine, Anjou and Maine, Brittany, Flanders, Aquitaine, all other duchies which by the treaty of peace between Edward III and John II the Good were assigned to Edward, possessions between the Somme and Gravelines, and half of the county of Provence with Beaufort and Nogent, as well as 1,600,000 crowns for the outstanding ransom of King John and 2,000,000 crowns for the dowry of Catherine.[38]

Rights were the focus of the correspondence between Henry V and Charles VI.[39] Although the story of negotiations told by the

[37] 'Final Demands of Henry V's Ambassadors, March 1415', *English Historical Documents 1327–1485*, ed. A. R. Myers (1969), 209. For the complete original Latin text, see Thomas Rymer, *Foedera* (The Hague, 1740), iv. pt. 2. 106.

[38] 'Final Demands', *supra* note 37.

[39] Letter from Henry dated 7 April 1415:
'our intention is to propose to you two things; the first is, to do justice to us of the rights to us, and to our crown belonging for so long a time, that we could say that it is entire ages that we have been deprived of them. The other concerns our marriage with our dear cousin Katherine, your daughter, for which all that is wanting is her consent and yours. . . .
[Threatening not to renew the truce that was about to expire, Henry continued:] The time of the truce being nearly at an end, we shall truly be compelled by the good will which it is our duty to maintain, and for the welfare of our people, to attend to their interests, and to acquit ourselves of the oath by which we are bound. . . . Render us a compensation proportionate to the loss which we suffer. . . . We shall have to answer before God for that which we retain by force of the property of another, and more particularly for the prevention of this peace.'
(Translation from French by H. Nicolas, repr. in Nicolas, *supra* note 26, App. I, at 1–2, from texts in Le Laboureur (ed.), *Histoire de Charles VI* (1663), ii. 993–4.)

Letter from Henry to Charles VI dated 15 April 1415:
'we have shortened [the period of the safe conduct for your ambassadors], not believing that so many days were required; but if on their arrival they bring us good news, if they proceed frankly and if we find . . . their powers sufficiently ample upon the two principle [*sic*] points of justice which we have asked from you, and of the alliance which we have proposed, we will extend it as far as shall be necessary. . . .
We shall propose nothing to you, which we have not a right conscienciously to demand.'
(Nicolas, *supra* note 26, App. I at 3; Le Laboureur, *supra*, at 994–5.)

Letter from Henry V to Charles VI dated 28 July 1415:
'we have on our part employed prayers and promises to persuade you [of peace], even by giving up the possession of a State which belongs to us by hereditary right, and which nature would oblige us to preserve for our posterity. . . . we are

French chronicler the Religieux of Saint-Denys differs in various respects from the version presented in the English official correspondence, it too highlights the legal arguments contained in the French negotiating positions.[40] On 4 July Henry demanded that the *voie de justice* be given priority in the negotiations ('il remit en avant la question de la voie de justice'), which prompted the Archbishop of Bourges to make additional concessions.[41] On 6

resolved at last to fight with all our strength, even to death. . . . do us justice. . . . To avoid a deluge of human blood, restore to us our inheritance which you unjustly detain, or render us at least that which we have so many times demanded by our ambassadors.'
(Nicolas, *supra* note 26, App. 1 at 5–6; Le Laboureur, *supra*, at 1000–1.)

Letter from Charles VI to Henry V dated 24 August 1415 (after the landing of Henry's troops near Harfleur):
'you have occasioned us great surprise . . . by having hostilely invaded our kingdom with an armed force, and thus destroying the hopes of peace, to the great sin of your party. And as we never did refuse justice, nor shall we, if it please God, to all who may demand it of us; as it is lawful for every Prince in his just quarrel to defend himself, and to oppose force by force; and as none of your predecessors ever had any right, and you still less, to make the demands contained in certain of your letters . . . it is our intention with the assistance of the Lord, in whom we have singular trust, and especially from the justice of our cause . . . to resist you in a way which shall be to the honor [*sic*] and glory of us and of our kingdom.'
(Nicolas, *supra* note 26, App. 1 at 6–7. Original text in Jean Juvenal des Ursins, *Histoire de Charles VI*, ed. J. A. C. Buchon (1838), 291.)

[40] Statement by the Archbishop of Bourges (2 July 1415) before Chancellor Beaufort: 'Le roi notre maître, dit-il, prend à témoin toute la chrétienté, qu'ill a toujours souhaité la paix, et qu'il a cherché à y parvenir par la voie de justice, en offrant de démembrer du royaume et de céder au roi d'Angleterre plusieurs villes importantes de l'Aquitaine, plusieurs comtés et domaines d'une valeur presque inappréciable, et en lui accordant la main de son illustre fille, madame Catherine, avec une dot de huit cent mille francs d'or. . . .
Les Anglais répondirent que leur roi n'entendait rien retrancher de ses premières demandes, et que, dans le courant de l'année mil quatre cent quatorze, son cousin de France lui avait écrit qu'il lui enverrait une ambassade pour traiter-avec lui de la voie de justice, de l'alliance et du mariage à conclure.'
Chronique du Religieux de Saint-Denys supra note 4, at v. 517.

[41] 'A l'honneur de Jésus-Christ, roi des rois, je déclare ici que notre sérénissime roi, ayant par vos lettres l'assurance et la certitude que vous désirez la paix et son alliance au moyen d'un mariage entre vous et son illustre fille, madame Catherine, et connaissant les qualités recommandables qui distinguent votre personne, a lui-même un vif désir de conclure cette paix, et d'établir entre vous, par voie de parenté et de justice, une alliance durable, dans l'intérêt de vos deux royaumes. Nous avons été chargés, si nous vous trouvions bien disposé à cet accommodement, de vous offrir, outre les quinze villes, comprenant sept comtés et plusieurs sénéchaussées, qui vous ont été proposées auparavant, la ville, le château et toute la sénéchaussée de Limoges, de laquelle dépendent les deux villes populeuses de Limoges et du Tulle, et d'ajouter encore cinquante mille écus d'or aux huit cent mille qui ont été promis pour la dot de madame Catherine.' Ibid. 519–21.

July Beaufort gave the French ambassadors Henry's answer. Satisfaction of Henry's hereditary claim to the crown of France must be given priority over the question of marriage.[42] Emphasizing that over a period of time Edward had enjoyed peaceful possession of the territories transfered to him by a definitive treaty, Beaufort concluded that Henry suffered a denial of justice that he might be forced to redress by other means.[43]

In invading France in 1415, Henry hoped not only to recover lost territory but, far more important, to reactivate the English claim to the French crown that had been asserted—though never pursued in such earnestness—since the beginning of the Hundred Years War. That claim derived—as I have already mentioned—from Isabel, the mother of his great-grandfather Edward III, the daughter of French King Philip IV and the wife of Edward II. In *2 Henry VI*, Shakespeare's Duke of York thus explains Henry V's family tree:

[42] 'Messieurs les ambassadeurs, leur dit-il, nous nous souvenons que naguère encore quelques-uns d'entre vous conseillaient à notre roi de renouveler avec votre maître, dans l'intérêt de la paix, les liens d'alliance et de parenté qui existaient entre eux, en contractant mariage avec l'illustre madame Catherine de France. Quelque honorable que cette union parût à notre roi, il a cru cependant qu'il était de son devoir et de sa dignité de demander auparavant satisfaction au sujet de ses droits sur le royaume et la couronne de France, qui lui appartiennent à titre héréditaire, et qu'on retient injustement depuis tant d'années.' Ibid. 523.

[43] 'Attendu donc que les ambassadeurs et envoyés de notre sire le roi ont bien voulu, sous de certaines réserves, ne pas insister sur de grandes, importantes et notables choses, telles que la couronne et le royaume de France, les duchés de Normandie et de Touraine, les comtés d'Anjou et du Maine, la suzeraineté de la Bretagne et celle du comté et pays de Flandre, à la possession desquels il a plu au Très-Haut de confirmer jadis nos droits par d'insignes et notables événements; attendu qu'ils se bornent à réclamer pour leur maître et en son nom des choses de moindre importance, dont le roi Edouard de vénérable mémoire, l'un des ancêtres de notredit sire, a obtenu la paisible possession, en vertu d'un traité définitif, et dont il a joui tranquillement et sans conteste pendant quelque temps; attendu, d'autre part, que les ambassadeurs de France n'ont offert qu'une petite partie desdites choses, et n'ont pas voulu déclarer de quelle manière notredit sire le roi devrait les posséder, il lui a paru évident que sondit cousin de France n'a point l'intention de travailler sincèrement et réellement à la paix, en la façon et aux conditions qu'il avait fait espérer par ses lettres. C'est pourquoi il faut que notredit sire, avec l'aide et l'assistance de la justice divine, ait recours à d'autres remèdes, prenant à témoin Dieu, les anges et les hommes, le ciel et la terre, et toutes les créatures qui s'y trouvent, qu'il est contraint à ce faire par le déni de justice ou les ajournements qu'il a éprouvés de la part de sondit cousin; car il n'a jamais tenu et il ne tiendra jamais à notre sire le roi, que la paix si long-temps désirée ne s'établisse entre les deux royaumes par tous les moyens licites et honorables, selon ce que le temps et les circonstances demanderont et exigeront.' Ibid. 525.

Edward the Third, my lords, had seven sons:
The first, Edward the Black Prince, Prince of Wales;
The second, William of Hatfield; and the third,
Lionel Duke of Clarence; next to whom
Was John of Gaunt, the Duke of Lancaster;
The fifth was Edmund Langley, Duke of York;
The sixth was Thomas of Woodstock, Duke of Gloucester;
William of Windsor was the seventh and last.
Edward the Black Prince died before his father
And left behind him Richard, his only son,
Who, after Edward the Third's death, reigned as King
Till Henry Bolingbroke, Duke of Lancaster,
The eldest son and heir of John of Gaunt,
Crowned by the name of Henry the Fourth,
Seized on the realm, deposed the rightful king,

> .   .   .   .

Harmless Richard was murdered traitorously.
WARWICK   . . .
Thus got the house of Lancaster the crown.

(2 Henry VI, II. ii. 10–24, 27, 29)

In Shakespeare's *Henry V*, Henry is anxious to have the Archbishop of Canterbury reassure him that the Salic law,[44] which disqualified women and the female line from succession to the crown of France, does not bar his claim. He commands the Archbishop to give him an objective and balanced opinion:

---

[44] White writes: 'The code of laws known as the *salic law* is a collection of the popular laws of the Salic or Salian Franks, committed to writing in barbarous Latin, in the 5th century. Several texts of this code are in existence, but because of the dark ages in which it had its origin, more or less mystery surrounds it. The code relates principally to the definition and punishment of crimes, but there is a chapter . . . relating to the succession of salic lands, which was probably inserted in the law, at a later date. *Salic lands*, or *terra salica*, came to mean inherited land as distinguished from property otherwise acquired, but even in the 15th century . . . there was but little known as to the origin or exact meaning of this law. It was by a very doubtful construction that the salic law in the 14th century was held to exclude the succession of females to the throne of France, but on the accession of Phillip the Long, it was given this interpretation, and the fact that Edward III rested his claim to the throne on female succession no doubt led the French to place this meaning on the law.' Edward J. White, *Commentaries on the Law in Shakespeare* (1913), 283–4 (footnotes omitted). On Salic law and just war, see also Judith Marie O'Malley, *Justice in Shakespeare: Three English Kings in the Light of Thomistic Thought* (1964), 42–5; George W. Keeton, *Shakespeare and his Legal Problems* (1930), 64.

KING   Why the law Salic that they have in France
Or should or should not bar us in our claim.
And God forbid, my dear and faithful lord,
That you should fashion, wrest, or bow your reading . . .

The Archbishop reassures the King that his claim to the throne
of France is just.

There is no bar
To make against your highness' claim to France
But this, which they produce from Pharamond:
'*In terram Salicam mulieres ne succedant*'—
'No woman shall succeed in Salic land'—
Which 'Salic land' the French unjustly gloss
To be the realm of France, and Pharamond
The founder of this law and female bar.
Yet their own authors faithfully affirm
That the land Salic is in Germany,
Between the floods of Saale and of Elbe

    .   .   .   .   .   .

Then doth it well appear the Salic Law
Was not devisèd for the realm of France.
Nor did the French possess the Salic land
Until four hundred one-and-twenty years
After defunction of King Pharamond,
Idly supposed the founder of this law

    .   .   .   .   .   .

So that, as clear as is the summer's sun,
King Pépin's title and Hugh Capet's claim,
King Louis his satisfaction, all appear
To hold in right and title of the female;
So do the kings of France unto this day,
Howbeit they would hold up this Salic Law
To bar your highness claiming from the female

    .   .   .   .   .   .

KING   May I with right and conscience make this claim?
CANTERBURY   The sin upon my head, dread sovereign.
For in the Book of Numbers is it writ,
'When the son dies, let the inheritance
Descend unto the daughter.'

(I. ii. 11–15, 35–100)

The modern reader cannot but marvel at the craftsmanship of
Canterbury's legal arguments: territorially, Salic land does not

mean France but a specific area in Germany. The law had been wrongly interpreted as applying to France. Since the Salic lands became a French possession under the reign of Charles the Great, 421 years after the death of the supposed author of the Salic law—the Frankish King Pharamond—its continued vitality is in doubt. French kings themselves have succeeded to the crown through 'the right and title of the female', and are therefore precluded from invoking the law against Henry.[45] Finally, Henry's claim is bolstered by the Old Testament, which explicitly commands that '[i]f a man die, and have no son, then ye shall cause his inheritance to pass unto his daughter.'[46] The biblical argument should not necessarily be viewed as exclusively theological; it may have been presented as the law of nature, or *jus naturale*,[47] which so prominently figures later in the play in Exeter's ultimatum to the King of France (see Chapter 4 below).

It is not clear that, in the period from Hugh Capet to Philip V the Tall, anyone thought the Salic law was relevant to the French royal succession, or knew of its implications. Peter Lewis observes that while the question of succession was complicated by the English claim to the throne of France, '[t]he exclusion of women derived, not from the Salic Law (which was first invoked in its aid in the reign of John II [1350–64]), but from custom.'[48] Charles Wood explains the exclusion of women from rights of succession in France by reference to the adulteries of the daughters-in-law of Philip IV the Fair, which were discovered in 1314.[49] He emphasizes that doubts about legitimacy played an important role in changing the anticipated royal succession and the accession of Philip V, concluding that: '[a]lthough these theories were not to reach full flower until Charles V—or even Charles VII— France was well on its way to inventing the Salic law.'[50] While it was only after their defeat at Agincourt that 'the French

[45] See Peter Saccio, *Shakespeare's English Kings* (1977), 75–7, 79.
[46] Numbers 27: 8. This was the only explicit reference in the play to the Bible and it was based on Hall and Holinshed. Naseeb Shaheen, *Biblical References in Shakespeare's History Plays* (1989), 177. See also Richmond Noble, *Shakespeare's Biblical Knowledge* (1935), 184.
[47] See generally George W. Keeton, *Shakespeare's Legal and Political Background* (1967), 78.
[48] Lewis, *supra* note 2, at 94–5.
[49] Charles T. Wood, *Joan of Arc and Richard III* (1988), 12–14.
[50] Ibid. 26. On the different view in England of legitimacy and succession, see ibid. 14–18.

seriously undertook the extended definition of their doctrine of royal inheritance',[51] it should not be assumed that the Salic law was created to counter the English claims to the crown of France.

First invoked and applied in 1317 to the Valois succession, as a categorical but unexplained customary rule, the Salic law was later 'rationalized' by theological and philosophical arguments, in which antifeminism and nationalism played an important role, and was eventually transformed into a constitutional principle.

Moving beyond purely dynastic and personal considerations, the Chevalier of Le Songe du Vergier (*c*.1376) articulated, in crudely misogynous terms, a rationale rooted in the good of the country for the custom prohibiting the succession of females to the throne of France. He argued that women were unequal to any responsible functions, that they were false, uncertain, rash, and malicious, and less fit to defend the country than men.[52]

Without explicitly referring to the Salic law, Pope Benedict XII mentioned the firm custom of barring succession to the French kingdom through the female line in his letter of 1340 to Edward III, written in support of Philip VI's claim.[53] Honoré Bouvet wrote of this French custom ('car en France n'ont mie coustume que femme doye estre royne') in the context of the claims of Edward III.[54]

The Salic law was first mentioned in explicit terms in 1358 by Richard Lescot and first invoked against the English claims by Jean de Montreuil between 1408 and 1417.[55] Jean de Montreuil argued that succession was governed by the law and custom of the place relevant to succession, that is, France; that custom was superior to law; and that the King himself was 'restrained from acting in derogation of his office by the nature of his very sovereignty'.[56] By comparing the exclusion of women from the papacy to their exclusion from the throne of France, French writers such as Jean de Montreuil were implying that France enjoyed status comparable to that of the Holy Roman Empire.[57] In a book written between 1418 and 1419, *Contra rebelles suorum regum*,

---

[51] John Milton Potter, 'The Development and Significance of the Salic Law of the French', 52 Eng. Hist. Rev. 235, 238. (1937).

[52] Ibid. 241–2. Contamine, *supra* note 12, at 72.

[53] Contamine, *supra* note 12, at 70–1; Potter, *supra* note 51, at 241.

[54] Bouvet, 297. [55] Contamine, *supra* note 12, at 67.

[56] Potter, *supra* note 51, at 247–8. [57] Contamine, *supra* note, 12, at 74.

[58] Potter, *supra* note 51, at 245.

Jean de Terre Rouge further asserted that the custom prohibiting the succession of females was a constituent principle of the kingdom, which the King himself could not alter or abrogate.[58]

The anonymous *Réponse d'un bon et loyal françois au peuple de France de tous estats*, written in 1422 and devoted to challenging the Treaty of Troyes, went beyond the question of succession of females or through a female line and enunciated the constitutional principle that the crown of France could not be translated to foreigners and that the king of France must be French.[59] The doctrine of the inalienability of the crown thus became a potent argument of the French opponents of the Treaty of Troyes.

The ancient Frankish legend of the Salic law, which resembles Hall's–Holinshed's–Shakespeare's version, first appeared in an anonymous work in 1464 under the title *La Loy salicque, premiere loy des françois*.[60]

Shakespeare's account of the exchange between the Archbishop and the King very closely follows Archbishop Chichele's prepared statement ('prepared tale' in Holinshed's words; 'prepared purpose' in Hall's), as reported by Holinshed in his *Chronicles*.[61] The striking legal craftsmanship of Shakespeare's Henry therefore cannot be credited to the dramatist alone. Shakespeare the dramatist must share the credit either with the person who actually voiced these arguments in the court of Henry V in *anno regni* 2 (1414) or with the chroniclers.

The attribution by the chroniclers and by Shakespeare of the above speech to the Archbishop of Canterbury, Henry Chichele is erroneous, however. It would have been more correct to attribute its substance to Chancellor Beaufort.[62] The speech was

---

[59] Ibid. 249.   [60] Ibid. 249–51.

[61] Holinshed, 9–11 (= R. Holinshed, *Chronicles* (1808), iii. 65–6. See also Hall, 49–52. Hall clearly set out the temporal element: Pharamond, the supposed author of the Salic law, could not have created it for a land he neither possessed nor knew of at the time it was issued. The biblical argument, by invoking God's authority, was intended to put to rest any doubts that may have survived the secular reasoning. Hall, 50–1.

[62] Henry Chichele, Archbishop of Canterbury at the time of Agincourt, is perhaps best remembered by international lawyers for the (Oxford) Chichele Chair of Public International Law and for having co-founded in 1438 with Henry VI the All Souls College (the College of All Souls of the Faithful Departed) at Oxford, in memory of those fallen in the wars in France, of which Henry V's campaign was but one segment. See J. S. G. Simmons, *All Souls College: A Concise Account* (1988), 1; J. S. G. Simmons, *All Souls College, the Codrington Library and the Law* (1986), 1. Thus the person to whom Hall (followed by Holinshed)

purportedly delivered at the Parliament of Leicester in 1414, at which time Chichele had not yet been made Archbishop.[63] It was Beaufort who on various occasions, including the November 1414 session of the Leicester Parliament, made statements in support of war against France.[64] In reference to Shakespeare's Canterbury speech (which was made to divert the attention of the Commons from an attack on the property of the Church), Jacob wrote that while 'there may be no evidence that Chichele ever gave such advice . . . it is quite possible for Henry to have felt that, financial aid forthcoming, he could best unify the upper and middle ranks of society by a strong policy in France . . . Chichele did his part in the loans to the king.'[65] Especially as fund-raiser and negotiator, he helped the King in the conduct of the war. But other senior members of the clergy supported the war effort just as vigorously.

In addition to Henry's quest for glory and justice, there were internal reasons for going to war. 'The magnates were heartily tired of internal struggles, and the lull of war with Scots and Welsh gave them the opportunity of turning their arms against the ancient foe.'[66]

Shakespeare's kings understood that foreign wars could serve to divert attention from internal troubles. Henry IV thus told his

erroneously attributed the justification for starting the campaign later founded the memorial to the souls of those who died in it. Saccio, *supra* note 45, at 79, asserts that 'Archbishop Chichele almost certainly never made the speech on the Salic law that is assigned to him.' *The First English Life of King Henry the Fifth* (*supra* note 32) 24–5, does not mention Canterbury's participation in the deliberations of the King's Council, and refers to him as having delivered the King's answer to the French ambassadors. It was Henry's Chancellor, Bishop Beaufort, who appears to have had a leading role in the discussions in Henry's court and with the envoys of France. See also Wylie (*supra* note 25) i. 491; Jacob, *Henry V* (*supra* note 35) 73; William Stubbs, *A Constitutional History of England* (1880), iii. 89–90; E. F. Jacob, *The Register of Henry Chichele* (1943), vol. i, Intro. pp. xxxiv–xxxv; Kingsford, *Henry V* (*supra* note 21), 109–10. The critical role of Beaufort in advocating resort to arms to uphold Henry's just cause is made clear by Gerald L. Harriss, *Cardinal Beaufort* (1988), 71–3, 84–6.

In his 'Apophthegms New and Old', written about a quarter of a century after *Henry V*, Francis Bacon demonstrated England's scepticism regarding the very existence of the Salic law. Francis Lord Verulam Viscount St Albans, *Apophthegms* (1625), no. 184 (32), p. 150.

[63] Kingsford, *supra* note 21 at 109–10.   [64] Harriss, *supra* note 62, at 71.

[65] Jacob, *supra* note 62, at vol. i, pp. xxxiv–xxxv.

[66] Stubbs, *supra* note 62, at iii. 88. Stubbs suggests that the speech attributed to Canterbury bears tokens of later composition. Ibid. 89.

son that he wanted to lead to the Holy Land those he feared
might depose him, and thus advised the future Henry V:

> Therefore, my Harry,
> Be it thy course to busy giddy minds
> With foreign quarrels, that action hence borne out
> May waste the memory of the former days.

(2 Henry IV, iv. iii. 341–4)

And Shakespeare's bishops would promote wars to save Church
lands from encroachments by Parliament, both by providing the
King with a moral–legal validation of a just cause and with
funds:

> ELY   But, my good lord,
> How now for mitigation of this bill
> Urged by the Commons?
>
> .   .   .   .   .   .
>
> CANTERBURY   . . .
> For I have made an offer to his majesty,
> Upon our spiritual convocation
> And in regard of causes now in hand,
> Which I have opened to his grace at large:
> As touching France, to give a greater sum
> Than ever at one time the clergy yet
> Did to his predecessors part withal.

(Henry V, i. i. 70–1, 76–82)

The story wrongly attributing to Henry Chichele the speech
justifying resort to war gained currency through a seventeenth-
century book published by a Fellow of All Souls, Sir Arthur
Duck, first in Latin and then in English.[67] Duck contended that
All Souls College[68] was established by Chichele because he was
'troubled in Conscience . . . [having been] the Author and
Promoter of that War'.[69] While it might be appealing to think
that a person urging the King to wage a bloody war would later
found a college as a place of prayer for the souls of the departed,

---

[67] *Vita Henrici Chichele* (1617); *The Life of Henry Chichele* (1699).

[68] Which had been founded as 'a place of prayer for the souls of Henry V,
Thomas, Duke of Clarence and other captains who had drunk "the cup of bitter
death" in the French wars; as well as for the souls of all the faithful departed'.
Ernest F. Jacob, *The Founder and his College* (1938), 37.

[69] Arthur Duck, *The Life of Henry Chichele*, *supra* note 67, at 170.

the version attributing the foundation of the college to remorse is wholly 'mythical'.[70]

In addition to assuring himself of the legitimacy of his claim, Henry needed to be satisfied that the war that might be necessary to secure that claim (should France refuse to yield) was grounded in a just cause.[71] The question was important for spiritual reasons (the immortality of his soul) and for such secular reasons as the validity of the title that he and his troops would acquire over the spoils of war; their enjoyment of combatant privileges; and their protection by the laws of war. The establishment of a just cause was therefore also significant, in consequence of these secular considerations, for his ability to raise troops and to sustain their morale. Although, as a matter of *Realpolitik*, a victorious prince faced few difficulties in maintaining that his war was just, this could have presented a real difficulty for a knight whose right to ransom or to other spoils of war, which was not levied by a prince (I shall explain later in this Chapter why this would not be a problem in a regular war levied by a prince), was contested before a court of chivalry applying the customary *jus armorum*.

The discussion that follows suggests that contemporary legal doctrine provided ample reason for Shakespeare's Henry to follow a prudent course by attempting to establish as just a cause as possible for the invasion of France. A just cause was essential to avoid responsibility for causing death. In requesting Canterbury's opinion on the justness of his cause, Shakespeare's Henry emphasizes that 'God doth know how many now in health | Shall drop their blood in approbation | Of what your reverence shall incite us to' (*Henry V*, I. ii. 18–20). That spiritual responsibility was critical to Henry is demonstrated by his death-bed speech, as reported by Holinshed in his *Chronicles*,[72] and by the conversation between Shakespeare's Henry and one of his soldiers,

---

[70] Jacob, *The Register of Henry Chichele*, *supra* note 62, at vol. i, p. xxxiv.

[71] On St Thomas Aquinas's views on just war, see George Weigel, *Tranquillitas ordinis* (1987), 36–8; on St Augustine's theory of just war, see ibid. 29–30. See also Thomas M. Franck, *The Power of Legitimacy among Nations* (1990), 80–1.

[72] '[H]e protested unto them, that neither the ambitious desire to inlarge his dominions, neither to purchase vaine renowme and worldlie fame, nor anie other consideration had mooved him to take the warres in hand; but onelie that in prosecuting his just title, he might in the end atteine to a perfect peace, and come to enjoie those peeces of his inheritance, which to him of right belonged: and that before the beginning of the same warres, he was fullie persuaded by men both wise and of great holinesse of life, that upon such intent he might and ought both

Williams (discussed in Chapter 5 below). Although supporting the war in *Henry V*, Shakespeare emphasized the concept of responsibility for the war, which meant not only that the cause of the war must be just, but that peaceful means of settlement had first to be exhausted. The latter theme—which was strongly supported by Christine de Pisan (Chapter 4)—was highlighted also in *King John*:

> CONSTANCE   Stay for an answer to your embassy,
> Lest unadvised you stain your swords with blood.
> My lord Châtillon may from England bring
> That right in peace which here we urge in war,
> And then we shall repent each drop of blood
> That hot rash haste so indirectly shed.
>
> *(King John*, II. i. 44–9)

In *Henry V*, Shakespeare's Henry advocated a just and thus necessarily a victorious war:

> KING   Now lords for France, the enterprise whereof
> Shall be to you, as us, like glorious.
> We doubt not of a fair and lucky war . . .
>
> *(Henry V*, II. ii. 179–81)

Support for a just war was also expressed by Shakespeare's Duke of Austria in *King John*:

> The peace of heaven is theirs that lift their swords
> In such a just and charitable war.
>
> *(King John*, II. i. 35–61)

In the words of Philip the Bastard, France was guided by 'zeal and charity' in entering this 'resolved and honourable war' (*King John*, II. i. 566, 586)

Like some writers on *jus gentium*, Shakespeare alluded, in *Troilus and Cressida*, to the difficulty that arose when both adversaries invoked a just cause for the war:

> TROILUS   O virtuous fight,
> When right with right wars who shall be most right.
>
> (Troilus and Cressida, III. ii. 167–8)

begin the same warres, and follow them . . . and that without all danger of Gods displeasure or perill of soule.' Holinshed, 129–30 (= R. Holinshed, *Chronicles* (1808), iii. 132–3.

Shakespeare certainly was not a warmonger. In his *King John*, especially in describing the siege of Angers, he ridiculed war, and satirically demonstrated its futility (II. i). Even the heroic, patriotic, and just war, which he favoured in his *Henry V*, ends with the Chorus's admission that it was both bloody and futile: the protector of the infant Henry VI 'lost France and made his England bleed' (Epilogue, 12).

Even in those few plays where he supported war because it was just, and certainly in many other plays, Shakespeare's text is replete with references to the brutality, bloodiness, and horrors of war. To illustrate, Shakespeare's heroes spoke of 'poor souls for whom this hungry war | Opens his vasty jaws' (*Henry V*, II. iv. 104–5), and, at the walls of Harfleur Shakespeare's Henry made a terrifying speech about the cruelties of war (Chapter 6, below). Westmoreland's anti-war speech in *2 Henry IV* merits noting:

> Out of the speech of peace that bears such grace
> Into the harsh and boist'rous tongue of war,
> Turning your books to graves, your ink to blood,
> Your pens to lances, and your tongue divine
> To a loud trumpet and a point of war?
>
> (*2 Henry IV*, IV. i. 48–52)

Shakespeare's heroes spoke of 'the bloody course of war' (*All's Well that Ends Well*, III. iv. 8), 'fierce and bloody war' (*King John*, I. i. 17), 'stern tyrant war' (*2 Henry IV*, Ind. 14), 'fearful war' (*2 Henry IV*, IV. i. 63), 'Hydra the son of war' (*2 Henry IV*, IV. ii. 38), 'O, War, thou son of hell, | Whom angry heavens do make their minister' (*2 Henry VI*, v. ii. 33–4), 'He that is truly dedicate to war | Hath no self-love' (*2 Henry VI*; v. iii. 37–8), 'dreadful war' (*3 Henry VI*, I. i. 188), 'fatal instruments of war' (*3 Henry VI*, v. i. 90), 'bloody trial of sharp war' (*Richard III*, v. ii. 16), 'ships, | Fraught with the ministers and instruments | Of cruel war' (*Troilus and Cressida*, Prologue, 3–5), 'wars and lechery' (*Troilus and Cressida*, v. ii. 197), 'Cry "havoc!" and let slip the dogs of war' (*Julius Caesar*, III. i. 276), 'war and confusion' (*Cymbeline*, III. i. 65), 'Religious canons, civil laws, are cruel; Then what should war be?' (*Timon of Athens*, IV. iii. 60–1). Although Stanley Wells, Gary Taylor, and John Jowett suggest that *Timon of Athens* was a product of collaboration between Shakespeare and Thomas Middleton, the preceding and the following passages from that play were probably written by Shakespeare:

> But if he sack fair Athens
> And take our goodly agèd men by th' beards
> Giving our holy virgins to the stain
> Of contumelious, beastly, mad-brain'd war

(Timon of Athens, v. i. 56–9).

Writers on *jus gentium* in Shakespeare's era often linked spiritual and secular elements as components of the just war doctrine. Thus, Suárez advanced a combination of moral, humanistic, and legal considerations as reasons for limiting lawful resort to war to unquestionably just wars. He observed that since 'in war, men are despoiled of their property, their liberty, and their lives . . . to do such things without just cause is absolutely iniquitous, for if this were permissible, men could kill one another without cause.'[73] He also pointed out that aggressive war is frequently waged against foreign nationals ('non-subjects'), who would deserve neither punishment nor subjection to foreign jurisdiction unless they 'have committed some wrong on account of which they render themselves subjects'.[74] Suárez, rather like Sir John Fastolf in 1435 (see Chapter 11 below), appeared thus to suggest a distinction between foreigners, who did not owe loyalty to the prince, and subjects of the prince, who owed him allegiance and deserved, therefore, severe punishment for the breach of the oath.

Of the possible secular causes for a just war, the cause most directly relevant to King Henry was the recapture of the French territory that he considered to belong to England, or to the Lancastrians as descendants of the Plantagenets. According to writers on *jus gentium* contemporaneous with Shakespeare, a war aimed at repossessing property captured by an enemy would be a defensive, not an aggressive, war.[75] '[T]he seizure by a prince of another's property, and his refusal to restore it', was the very first example of a just cause of war given by Suárez.[76] Vitoria, too, regarded a war designed to repossess property as a defen-

---

[73] Francisco Suárez, *Selections from Three Works* [1612, 1613, 1621], Carnegie edn., trans. Gwladys L. Williams, Ammi Brown, and John Waldron (1944), ii. 816. Hereafter Suárez. See *supra* Ch. 2 n. 18.

[74] Ibid. See also Peter Haggenmacher, *Grotius et la doctrine de la guerre juste* (1983), 409–26.

[75] Suárez, 804.

[76] Ibid. 817.

sive, and necessarily just, war.[77] In those circumstances, it was 'permissible to recapt everything that has been lost'.[78]

In reality, of course, the situation was more complex, because each party to the conflict was likely to maintain that its cause was just (*bellum nostrum justum*).[79] Yet, under medieval legal theory, war could be just for one side only. More realistically, and perhaps ahead of his time, Gentili believed that a war might objectively be just on both sides.[80] 'It is the nature of wars for both sides to maintain that they are supporting a just cause.'[81] In most cases, it is difficult to determine on which side justice rests, 'and if each side aims at justice, neither can be called unjust'.[82] Because in the medieval[83] and in the Renaissance[84] legal doctrines many causes justified resort to war, and because there was no clearly established hierarchy between such 'just causes of war', the requirement of having a just cause did not constitute a significant constraint on waging war.[85]

Gentili's view was also taken by another contemporary of Shakespeare, Balthazar Ayala (1548–84), who related the just war doctrine to the duties of the religious man. He believed that a war between legitimate sovereigns, lawfully conducted, might be just for both sides.[86] But Suárez argued that, if purposes such as ambition or avarice were sufficient to justify resort to war, 'any state whatsoever could aspire to these ends; and hence, a war

[77] Franciscus de Victoria, 'The Second Relectio on the Indians, or on the Law of War made by the Spaniards on the Barbarians', in *De indis et de iure belli relectiones*, Carnegie edn., trans. John Pawley Bate, ed. Ernest Nys (1917), 166–7 (1). These lectures were published posthumously in 1557; hereafter Vitoria.

[78] Ibid. 171 (16).

[79] *LW* 71.

[80] Alberico Gentili, *De jure belli libri tres*, Carnegie edn., trans. John C. Rolfe (1933), ii. 31–3. Hereafter Gentili. This is the 1931 translation of the 1612 edition. *Prima commentatio de jure belli* was published in 1588, the second and third parts in 1589. The three books appeared, as a new work, in 1598 under the title *De jure belli libri tres*. See ibid. 14a: Coleman Phillipson, Intro.; Arthur Nussbaum, *A Concise History of the Law of Nations* (1954), 97. See also Haggenmacher, *supra* note 74, at 203–23, 279–311; Yoram Dinstein, *War, Aggression and Self-Defence* (1988), 65.

[81] Gentili, ii. 31.

[82] Ibid. 32.

[83] Pisan, 11–12; Giovanni da Legnano, *Tractatus de bello, de represaliis et de duello*, ed. Thomas Erskine Holland (1917), 292–300, chs. 94–106. (Bologna MS c.1390. Legnano completed his work in 1360, but it was published in 1477 and in better-known editions in 1487 and 1584.) Hereafter Legnano.

[84] Gentili, ii. 53–127.

[85] Dinstein, *supra* note 80.   [86] Nussbaum, *supra* note 80, at 92.

would be just on both sides, essentially and apart from any element of ignorance. This supposition is entirely absurd; for two mutually conflicting rights cannot both be just.'[87] 'Excluding cases of ignorance', the war cannot 'incidentally be just for both sides.' Suárez conceded, however, that a war could be *unjust* for both sides,[88] for example when waged by mutual agreement.[89]

That mere expansionism ('extension of empire') could not be a just cause of war was already suggested by Vitoria. Otherwise, he claimed, 'each of the two belligerents might have an equally just cause and so both would be innocent. . . . [T]he consequence [would be] that it would not be lawful to kill them and so imply a contradiction, because it would be a just war.'[90] Presumably, Henry's counsel would distinguish between recapturing property lost to another prince, which would constitute a just cause of the war, and extension of empire, which would not. Among the causes of a just war, Christine de Pisan thus mentioned recovering 'landes, seignoryes, or other thynges, by other taken & usurped by unjuste cause, whyche to the prince or to the juridicion of the contree or of the subgettes ought to apperteyne'.[91] The King of France, however, would surely believe that Henry was expanding his empire, not reclaiming property lost to France. Was the recreation of the old Angevin possessions a war aim? Some historians believe that Henry's true goal was to go back 'to the brightest days of the Angevin Empire, when the whole of Western France, from the Somme to the Pyrenees was in English hands'.[92]

In such circumstances, the right of every prince to judge whether or not his cause was just appears inherently arbitrary, self-serving, and even hypocritical. Shakespeare's contemporaries

---

[87] Suárez, 816. Vitoria, 177 (32), implied that ignorance may make the war just for both sides. He wrote that '[a]part from ignorance [a war cannot be just on both sides] . . . for if the right and justice of each side be certain, it is unlawful to fight against it.' However, '[a]ssuming a demonstrable ignorance either of fact or of law.' he continued, 'it may be that on the side where true justice is the war is just of itself, while on the other side the war is just in the sense of being excused from sin by reason of good faith, because invincible ignorance is a complete excuse.' Ibid.

[88] Suárez, 850–1. Cf. Abraham Lincoln's statement: 'In great contests each party claims to act in accordance with the will of God. Both *may* be, and one *must* be wrong.' Quoted by William Safire, *Freedom* (1987), 787.

[89] See Haggenmacher, *supra* note 74, at 436–7. [90] Vitoria, 170 (11).

[91] Pisan, 11. [92] Jacob, *supra* note 35, at 67.

were not unaware of these difficulties. They are hardly dispelled by the fact that Shakespeare's King of England, like Holinshed's Henry, defers to the moral and religious authority of the senior English ecclesiastic (the Archbishop of Canterbury) for assurance of the justness of the English cause.

Actually, advancing an idea that had yet to gain acceptance, Vitoria stated that, if there were any competent judge over the two belligerents, he would have to condemn the unjust aggressors and authors of wrong, not only to make restitution of what they have carried off, but also to make good the expenses of the war to the other side, and also all damages.[93] Absent such a third-party determination, 'a prince who is carrying on a just war is as it were his own judge.'[94] '[A] superior judge has competence to mulct the author of a wrong by taking away from him a city . . . or a fortress. . . . [In the same way] a prince who has suffered wrong can do this too, because by the law of war he is put in the position of a judge.'[95]

Suárez appears to have been less troubled by the privilege of every prince to determine the justness of his own cause. In discussing the possibility of a king's claiming a certain city 'as falling newly to him by hereditary right' (such as Henry's claim to France), he wrote that 'when the case of each side contains [an element of] probability, then the king ought to act as a just judge. . . . [I]f he finds that the opinion favouring his own side is the more probably true, he may, even justly, prosecute his own right.'[96]

Just cause concerned not only *jus ad bellum* (the right to resort to war), but also *jus in bello* (the law governing the conduct of war), since it had bearing on the effects of war. Because medieval legal doctrine taught that the lawfulness of the title to the spoils of war turned on the justness of its cause, Henry required a good cause to realize his objectives. Thus Vitoria emphasized that in a just war it was lawful 'to recover things taken from us'.[97] Subject to certain limits which he suggested, 'everything captured in a just war vests in the seizor. . . . This needs no proof, for that is the end and aim of war.'[98]

A much closer link than remains today between *jus ad bellum*

---

[93] Vitoria, 171 (17).   [94] Ibid.
[95] Ibid. 186 (56). See also Haggenmacher, *supra* note 74, at 409–26.
[96] Suárez, 828.   [97] Vitoria, 182 (44).   [98] Ibid. 184 (50).

and *jus in bello* therefore continued into Shakespeare's era. As Keen has pointed out, the first concern of the medieval soldier was to show that 'his booty was *prise de bonne guerre*, that is, taken in just war. If it was not taken in these circumstances, restitution could be demanded.'[99] A just war could legitimize criminal acts and create a legal title to goods whose taking in other circumstances would be considered robbery.[100] Only in a just war could spoils and prisoners be taken lawfully.[101] Whether or not a captor would acquire a property right in the person of prisoners and the consequent right to the payment of ransom hinged on whether or not the war was just.[102]

Cracks already began to appear in this rigid doctrine during the fourteenth and fifteenth centuries. In discussing *jus in bello*, Keen explains that, according to the canonists, rights to the spoils of a public war—that is, a war declared by a prince, waged on his authority, and governed by *jus gentium*—were in theory dependent on the satisfaction of several standards of justice, in addition to that of authority to wage war. However, because there was no superior or third party to judge the justice of the cause, '[i]n practice . . . a just war . . . and a public war meant the same thing.'[103]

The jurists of Shakespeare's time departed even more sharply from the medieval doctrine. Suárez stated that only in a just war may the prince seize cities and provinces,[104] but he conceded that in a war that is unjust for both sides the victor would acquire the property of the vanquished as a result of the agreement to wage war, that is, by a sort of implied contract theory.[105]

Gentili suggested that the belligerents' rights to prisoners and booty do not depend on the war's justness.[106] By insisting, with considerable sophistication, that war may be just on both sides,

---

[99] *LW* 139. See also Haggenmacher, *supra* note 74, at 300–5.   [100] *LW* 65.
[101] *LW* 70.   [102] *LW* 137.
[103] *LW* 71. Keen cites the 14th-c. Batholomew of Saliceto, *Super VIII Cod.*, tit. 51, *l*. 12: 'It is tacitly assumed that it is in the nature of war waged by kings and lords, that it is public and general on both sides,' and the *c.*1396 disputations of Angelus of Perusia, *Disputatio, Inc. 'Renovata guerra'* (printed *c.*1490, unpag.): 'propter dubium ex utroque latere dicere possumus guerram justam.' (Because of the doubt we can call the war just on both sides.) *LW* 71 n. 1. See also *infra* note 138.
[104] Suárez, 850.
[105] Ibid. 851–2. See Haggenmacher, *supra* note 74, at 426–37.
[106] Nussbaum, *supra* note 80, at 97.

he reached the conclusion that the law must be impartial to both sides. He thus paved the way for the uniform applicability of *jus in bello*,[107] an approach inherently less subject to abuse that is characteristic of modern international law. The rights of war, Gentili wrote, belong to both contestants, 'mak[ing] what is taken on each side the property of the captors'.[108]

Because Gentili understood that 'if it is is doubtful on which side justice is, and if each side aims at justice, neither can be called unjust,'[109] and because only infrequently 'injustice is clearly evident on one of the two sides,'[110] Gentili may well have felt that the distinction between just and unjust war was sophistry, at least in many cases. While not unique, he was not typical of his times. Moreover, like Ayala, he wrote about 175 years after the discussion Shakespeare ascribes to Henry and the Archbishop of Canterbury, in which the justness of Henry's cause is so central.

In the same vein, Ayala held that '[n]othing more is needed . . . so far as concerns the legal effects which are produced and the bringing into operation of the laws of war, than that the war should be waged by parties who are within the definition of "enemies" and who have the right to wage war.'[111] Nevertheless, a soldier who is summoned to fight in an unjust war 'has no action at law either for the recovery of pay or for reimbursement of loss, for no right of action is allowed to arise out of circumstances of disgrace (*ex turpi causa nulla datur actio*)'.[112] Since the right of combatants to engage in war and hence to be protected by the laws of war also depended on the justness of the war, demonstrating just cause was important for many practical reasons, including raising troops and maintaining morale.

To give rise to combatant privileges, the war had to be declared by a prince, acting on behalf of the state. A state could wage war if it constituted '[a] perfect State or community . . . [namely] one which is complete in itself, that is, which is not a

---

[107] See generally Haggenmacher, *supra* note 74, at 597–612.
[108] Gentili, ii. 33. See generally Haggenmacher, *supra* note 74, at 74–139.
[109] Gentili, ii. 32.   [110] Ibid. 33.
[111] Balthazar Ayala, *Three Books on the Law of War and on the Duties Connected with War and on Military Discipline* [1582] Carnegie edn., trans. John Pawley Bate (1912), 23. Hereafter Ayala. It follows that things captured in war become the property of the captors, ibid. 35.
[112] Ibid. 25.

part of another community'.[113] According to Suárez, war could be waged only by a power entitled to declare war, that is, a sovereign prince who has no superior in temporal affairs.[114] Indeed, whether war had been declared by a sovereign prince was an important practical test of the justness of the conflict and its public nature.[115]

Because combatants' privileges and, indeed, the application of chivalric rules depended on the war's justness, it was important that the list of those entitled to wage war not be unduly narrow. Perhaps for this reason, Christine de Pisan suggested that those entitled to wage war were 'prynces souerayn lyke as emperours kynges, dukes, & other lordes terryens whiche ben merely princypall heedes of Juredictions temporall'.[116] Maurice Keen comments that '[a]s dukes and other secular lords are not usually without superior, Christine seems to be here extending the meaning of the phrase "sovereign prince" in order to fit the facts of her day.'[117]

Although the wars of the later Middle Ages were often wars between nations, Keen observes that the adjustment had not yet been made to international wars, and that it was difficult to distinguish between an English army and a band of adventurers using the English colours.[118] Keen cites cases suggesting that in an illegal war pursued by the free companies ransom agreements would not be enforced, even when the captor had been given a letter of obligation. Agreements to pay free companies to leave the countryside off which they lived were enforced by the Parlement de Paris, despite their illegality, however, in light of the government's interest in the companies' departure.[119]

Suárez argued that the captured soldiers of a prince who waged an unjust war would not enjoy the protection of the *jus gentium* and could be killed, but he favoured such protection of mercenary soldiers, who were innocent in the sense that they did

---

[113] Vitoria, 169 (7).

[114] Suárez, 805. Gentili criticized Spain for not treating as 'lawful enemies' some Frenchmen captured in a war with Portugal who held letters from a king unrecognized by Spain. Gentili, ii. 26.

[115] *LW* 72.   [116] Pisan, 10.   [117] *LW* 77.   [118] *LW* 116–17.

[119] *LW* 93–6. In some cases the Parlement de Paris appeared to consider as valid the letters of obligations given by captives to members of free companies (*routiers*). Pierre-Clement Timbal, *La Guerre de cent ans vue à travers les registres du Parlement (1337–1369)* (1961), 486.

not know any reasons indicating the justness of the other side's cause.[120] Neither unjust war nor those participating in it had standing in law.[121]

The medieval *jus in bello*, the law governing the conduct of hostilities, was quite rich and often sophisticated.[122] There were, for example, rules governing the question whether attendants or servants assisting the combatants were entitled to the immunities of the combatants,[123] whether mercy should be shown to persons captured in a lawful war,[124] the justifications and the targets of permissible reprisals,[125] the question whether immoveables captured in war became the property of the captors,[126] weapons and methods of warfare,[127] poisoned weapons which were prohibited,[128] mines (tunnels),[129] spies,[130] ambushes,[131] pillage,[132] spoils of war,[133] treatment of prisoners,[134] safe conducts,[135] activities permitted when a truce was in effect,[136] ruses of war ('wile') which were allowed, and perfidy ('treason') which was prohibited.[137]

In contrast to medieval law, modern rules of warfare (for example on requisitioning property and the treatment of prisoners of war and civilians, that is, *jus in bello*) apply equally to a state fighting a war of aggression and to one involved in lawful self-defence. Thus some of the arbitrariness resulting from unilateral and self-serving characterizations of a war as just or unjust are avoided, and a more uniform and objective application of the *jus in bello* is promoted, enhancing the effectiveness of humanitarian principles. Prisoner-of-war status, combatant privileges, and duties of an occupant in modern international law depend,

[120] Nussbaum, *supra* note 80, at 90.
[121] *LW* 65 (citing Nicholas of Tudeschi, who wrote in 1524).
[122] See e.g. Chs. 6 and 9 *infra*.   [123] Legnano, 274, ch. 71.
[124] Ibid., 274, ch. 69.   [125] Ibid., 308–9, ch. 124; 317–22, chs. 135–46.
[126] Ibid. 270, ch. 61.   [127] Pisan, 157–74.   [128] Ibid. 184.
[129] Ibid. 175.   [130] Ibid. 178–9.   [131] Ibid. 214.
[132] Ibid. 217.   [133] Ibid. 218–19.   [134] Ibid. 220–4.
[135] Ibid. 248.   [136] Ibid. 262. See Ch. 4 *infra*.
[137] Pisan, 213–14. Giovanni da Legnano argued that 'trickery . . . breaks the faith, which should be kept even with an enemy', 271, ch. 62. Elaborating on the scope of trickery, Giovanni explained that '[o]ne way is if a false statement is made in order that another may be deceived, or in order that some promise may not be observed, and such a use of trickery is always unlawful; for between enemies there are certain bonds which must be observed. . . . In the other way, a man may be deceived by our words or acts merely because we do not disclose to him our intentions or our secrets. This mode of deceit is lawful.' Ibid.

in principle, on the combatants' conformity with conditions of openness and respect for the laws and customs of war enumerated in Article 4 of the third Geneva Convention of 1949[138] and in Articles 43 and 44 of Additional Protocol I,[139] regardless of the cause of the conflict.[140]

Yet here and there *jus ad bellum* analogies can be discerned, as in the claim that the use of force by states in support of a just cause, as exemplified by wars of national liberation carried out by a people in the exercise of its right of self-determination (*bellum justum*), is allowed,[141] resort to force in self-defence (Article 51 of the United Nations Charter) and action necessary to maintain

---

[138] Convention Relative to the Treatment of Prisoners of War (Geneva Convention No. III), 12 Aug. 1949, 6 UST 3316, TIAS No. 3364, 75 UNTS 135.

Professor Haggenmacher suggests that in contrast to the medieval doctrine of just war, which focused on the justness of the cause of war, the modern law of war, which underlies the Hague Regulations and the Geneva Conventions for the Protection of Victims of War, focuses on whether the war constitutes a 'regular war'. P. Haggenmacher, 'La doctrine de la guerre juste chez les théologiens et les juristes du siècle d'or', in Georges Van Hecke (ed.), *L'Espagne et la formation du droit des gens moderne* (1988), 27, 28–9. The Geneva Conventions apply to all cases of declared war or of any other armed conflict independently of any formal aspects, however. See Common Article 2 of the Geneva Conventions.

In a more recent article, Haggenmacher discusses two competing approaches to war which existed in the medieval law of war: the notion of a just war and that of the regular war. 32 Int'l Rev. Red Cross 434 (No. 290) (Sept.–Oct. 1992).

A clear statement of the irrelevance of the lawfulness of an occupation and the duties of the occupant was made in the Judgment given in 'the *Hostage* case' (also called Hostages by the UN Series), *United States of America* v. *Wilhelm List et al.*: 'At the outset, we desire to point out that international law makes no distinction between a lawful and an unlawful occupant in dealing with the respective duties of occupant and population in occupied territory. There is no reciprocal connection between the manner of the military occupation of territory and the rights and duties of the occupant and population to each other after the relationship has in fact been established. Whether the invasion was lawful or criminal is not an important factor in the consideration of this subject.' 11 Trials of War Criminals before the Nuernberg Military Tribunals under Control Council Law No. 10 at 759, 1247 (1950). This judgment was of course based on the Hague Convention (No. IV) Respecting the Laws and Customs of War on Land, with Annex of Regulations, signed 18 Oct. 1907, 36 Stat. 2277, TS 539, 1 Bevans 631, but the legal position under the Geneva Conventions and Protocols remains the same.

[139] Protocol Additional to the Geneva Conventions of 12 Aug. 1949, and Relating to the Protection of Victims of International Armed Conflicts (Protocol I), opened for signature 12 Dec. 1977, 1125 UNTS 3.

[140] Dinstein makes a strong case in favour of equal and neutral application of *jus in bello*, Y. Dinstein, *supra* note 80, at 145–53.

[141] For a critique of such claims, see ibid. 67–9. See also Franck, *supra* note 71.

international peace and security (Articles 42–3 of the UN Charter).[142] An echo of the medieval doctrine of just war can also be found in the modern principle outlawing the annexation of territory acquired in a war of aggression.[143]

[142] See e.g. James Turner Johnson and George Weigel, *Just War and the Gulf War* (1991).

[143] Dinstein, *supra* note 80, at 157. This doctrine has been applied by the United Nations rather selectively. The General Assembly's Resolution on the Definition of Aggression of 14 Dec. 1974 reaffirms that 'the territory of a State shall not be violated by being the object, even temporarily, of military occupation or of other measures of force . . . and . . . shall not be the object of acquisition by another State resulting from such measures or the threat thereof.' GA Res. 3314, 29 UN GAOR Supp. (No. 31) at 142, UN Doc. A/9631 (1975). See Yoram Dinstein, 'The International Law of Belligerent Occupation and Human Rights', *Israel Y. B. Human Rights*, 8 (1978), 104, 106.

By Resolution 662 of 9 Aug. 1990, repr. in 29 ILM 1327 (1990), the Security Council asserted its determination 'to restore the sovereignty, independence and territorial integrity of Kuwait' and decided 'that annexation of Kuwait by Iraq under any form and whatever pretext has no legal validity, and is considered null and void'. (See also SC Res. 687A of 3 April 1991, repr. in 30 ILM 847 (1991); Oscar Schachter, 'United Nations Law in the Gulf Conflict', 85 AJIL 452, 454 (1991).

In the more general context of the blueprint for settling the Six-Day War between Israel and the neighbouring Arab states, for whose outbreak responsibility has not been authoritatively established, the Security Council emphasized, in Resolution 242 of 22 Nov. 1967, 'the inadmissibility of the acquisition of territory by war'.

On some contemporary aspects of just war, see Dinstein, *supra* note 80, at 66–74; Oscar Schachter, 'In Defense of International Rules on the Use of Force', 53 U. Chi. L. Rev. 113, 142–4 (1986).

4

Declarations of War and Truce Agreements

On the basis of the Archbishop of Canterbury's reassurances about the justness of Henry's cause, the King's ambassador and special envoy to the court of France, the Duke of Exeter, addresses the following ultimatum to the King of France:

> That you divest yourself and lay apart
> The borrowed glories that by gift of heaven,
> By law of nature and of nations, 'longs
> To him and to his heirs, namely the crown,
> And all wide-stretchèd honours that pertain
> By custom and the ordinance of times
> Unto the crown of France.
>
> .   .   .   .
>
> KING   Or else what follows?
> EXETER   Bloody constraint.
>
> .   .   .   .
>
> Deliver up the crown, and . . . take mercy
> On the poor souls for whom this hungry war
> Opens his vasty jaws.[1]

(Henry V, II. iv. 78–105)

Here Shakespeare renders in dramatic form a declaration of war, or an ultimatum that in effect amounted to a declaration of

---

[1] Cf. the final demands of Henry V's ambassadors, Mar. 1415, repr. in A. R. Myers (ed.), *English Historical Documents 1327–1485* (1969) IV, at 209; Holinshed, 12–13 (= R. Holinshed, *Chronicles* (1808), iii. 67). For an English translation of some of the correspondence between Henry V and Charles VI, see Harris Nicolas, *A History of the Battle of Agincourt*, (2nd edn., 1832), app. 1. For the French text of part of the correspondence, see *Chronique du Religieux de Saint-Denys*, ed. and trans. L. Bellaguet, Collection de documents inédits sur l'histoire de France, ser. 1 (1844), v. 507–11, 527–31. For the Latin version, see Thomas Rymer, *Foedera*, (The Hague, 1740), vol. iv, pt. 2, p. 106. See also the self-justifying account of the negotiations in *Gesta*, 14–15.

war, required by the *jus gentium* of the Renaissance period. The message states the claim to the crown of France, the legal basis for that claim *in the law of nature and the law of nations*, and the consequences of non-compliance with its demands, that is, war.

In the Middle Ages, the requirement that a war be publicly declared was commonly met by issuing letters of defiance (*Henry V*, III. vi. 132–3; *King John*, I. i. 21, II. i. 155). Although different in form from formal declarations of war, letters of defiance served the same function.[2] The medieval system of government recognized the need for both internal and external procedures before resort to war could be had. Christine de Pisan wrote that a prince could only take up arms if he had consulted Parliament to ascertain that he had a just cause for war, and—following upon Parliament's consent—offered his adversary a chance to remedy the wrongs which he was alleged to have committed.[3] (This is, however, based on Caxton's English version of Christine de Pisan; parliament would not have meant to her, as a Frenchwoman, what it did to Caxton who has anglicized its sense for English readers.) Internal procedures amounted to an early model of deliberations, consultations, and institutional authorization of war; external procedures served both as exhaustion of

---

[2] On the medieval requirement of declaring wars, see *LW* 70, 72; Bouvet, 128–9; Pisan, 13; Legnano, 232–4, chs. 13–16.

[3] '& for as moche as a iuste prynce shal doo, | felyng hym self wrongyd by an others myght & power, | ought he thenne for to obeye to goddes lawe to deporte & forbere without doyng more therto, | forsoth nay, | for that deffendeth iustyce, | but the faytte requyreth of the trespaas pugnicion & for that werke iustely he shal holde this waye, | he shall assemble grete counseyl of wysemen in his parliament, | or in the counseil of his souerayn yf he be subgette, | & he shal not onely assemble them of his contree, | to thende that oute be put all suspecion of fauour, | but also of strange contrees that may be knowen not adherent to neyther partye, | as wel auncyent, | nobles, | as iuristes & other, | present them self shal purpose or doo be purposed all the trouth & without ony fauour for god may not be deceyued all suche right & suche wronge that he may haue, | & in concludyng shal saye that of all he wyll reporte hym & holde to the determinacion of ryght, | shortly for to saie by this manere, | this thynge put in right wel seen & discuted so & by suche waye that it appere by true iugement that he hath iuste cause. | Thenne he shal doo sommone his aduersarye for to haue of hym restytucion & amendes of thyniures & wronges by hym receyued. | Thenne yf it happene, | That the said aduersarye delyuer deffences & wyll gaynsaye it, | that he be entierly herd without fauour to hym self in ony wise ne propre wyll ne haynous courage. | These thynges & that whiche apperteyneth duely made, | in caas that the said aduersarie be founde refusying to come to right & lawe, | the prynce may Iustely & surely enttrepryse warre, | the whiche ought not be called vengeaunce, | but pure execucion of rightful Iustyce.' Pisan, 13.

peaceful remedies and as an ultimatum equivalent to a defiance or a declaration of war. The principle of prior consultation on war with the lords and with Parliament (which gave considerable support for Henry V's war) was recognized in early fourteenth-century England and steadily extended.[4]

Later Elizabethan doctrine required not only that the cause of war be just, but also that the procedures of war be followed,[5] and, in particular, that resort be made to a formal declaration of war.[6] Accordingly, Queen Elizabeth published, in 1585, A Declaration of the Causes Mooving the Queene of England to Give Aide to the Defence of the People Afflicted and Oppressed in the Lowe Countries and, in 1596, A Declaration of the Causes Moving the Queenes Majestie of England, to Prepare and Send a Navy to the Seas, for the Defence of Her Realmes against the King of Spaines Forces.[7] Shakespeare's Henry faithfully reflects this doctrine in the message carried by the Duke of Exeter to the court of France. The dramatist's version finds support in Hall's *Chronicle*:

The Kyng like a wise prince and pollitique governor, entendyng to observe the auncient ordres of famous kynges and renoumed potentates used aswel among Paynimes as Christians, which is, not to invade another mannes territory without open war and the cause of the same to hym published and declared, dispatched into Fraunce his uncle the duke of Excester.[8]

A similar declaration of war can be found in Shakespeare's *King John*:

KING JOHN   Now say, Châtillon, what would France with us?
CHATILLON   Thus, after greeting, speaks the King of France . . .

.   .   .   .

CHATILLON   Philip of France, in right and true behalf
Of thy deceasèd brother Geoffrey's son,
Arthur Plantagenet, lays most lawful claim
To this fair island and the territories,
To Ireland, Poitou, Anjou, Touraine, Maine;

---

[4] Michael Powicke, *Military Obligation in Medieval England* (1962), 232, 242–3, 250.

[5] Lily B. Campbell, *Shakespeare's 'Histories': Mirrors of Elizabethan Policy* (1947), 287, regards Henry's demand for the surrender of Harfleur, to be discussed further below, as an example of observance of such procedures.

[6] Ibid. 285–6.   [7] Ibid.   [8] Hall, 57.

.   .   .   .

And put the same into young Arthur's hand,
Thy nephew and right royal sovereign.
KING JOHN   What follows if we disallow of this?
CHATILLON   The proud control of fierce and bloody war,
To enforce these rights so forcibly withheld.

                                        (I. i. 1–18)

George Keeton, a modern commentator, believes that in
Shakespeare's times declarations of war were becoming obsolete
and 'nations not infrequently found themselves at war without
any further notification than the appearance of the army of one
belligerent in the territory of another. . . . In the Historical plays,
however, where Shakespeare was following the Chronicles, a formal declaration of war by a herald or ambassador precedes hostilities.'[9] Regardless of the practice in Renaissance Europe,
contemporaneous legal theory clearly articulated the duty to
declare war. Gentili asserted that the 'enemy are those who have
officially declared war upon us, or upon whom we have officially
declared war'.[10] Those who did not declare war would be considered pirates or brigands, that is, non-privileged combatants in
contemporary usage. The 'war on both sides must be public and
official and there must be sovereigns on both sides to direct the
war.'[11] In his 1929 introduction to the Carnegie edition of
Gentili's *De jure belli libri tres*, Coleman Phillipson explains
Gentili's insistence on the obligation to declare war prior to
resorting to hostilities:

[I]n the time of Gentili, though we find a few instances in which heralds
were dispatched to announce the commencement of hostilities, the practice of declaring war was generally falling into disuse; so that Gentili
was performing a great service by protesting so vigorously against its
discontinuance and by demanding a long interval in accordance (in his
view) with the old-established law of nations as well as with Divine
injunctions.[12]

---

[9] George W. Keeton, *Shakespeare's Legal and Political Background* (1967), 89;
see also id., *Shakespeare and his Legal Problems* (1930), 72–3.

[10] Gentili, ii. 15 (citing Pomponius).

[11] '[I]f war is not declared when it ought to be declared, then war is said to be
carried on treacherously; and such a war is unjust, detestable, and savage. [That
is] because it is waged according to none of the laws of war.' Ibid. 140. See also
Suárez, 837–8.

[12] Gentili, ii. 39a.

Grotius stated that '[d]eclarations of war in fact . . . were wont to be made publicly, with a statement of the cause, in order that the whole human race as it were might judge of the justness of it.'[13] Referring to past events that suggested that 'most wars begin without declaration,'[14] Grotius observed:

[B]efore the possessor of sovereign power is attacked for the debt or crime of a subject, a demand for settlement should be made, which may place him in the wrong, and in consequence of which he may be held either to be causing us loss or to be himself committing a crime, according to the principles which have previously been discussed.

But even in case the law of nature does not require that such a demand be made, still it is honourable and praiseworthy to make it, in order that, for instance, we may avoid giving offence, or that the wrong may be atoned for by repentance and compensation, according to what we have said regarding the means to be tried to avoid war. . . .

. . . But by the law of nations a proclamation is required in all cases in order to secure [the] . . . particular effects [of war].[15]

Whatever their normative status, since Henry's era declarations of war have proved remarkably resilient. The question of the duty to declare war may have been rendered moot by the law of the United Nations Charter, with its categorical prohibition of resort to war (subject to the inherent right of individual or collective self-defence). In determining whether the duty to declare war is firmly rooted in customary law, examples of the failure of states to issue declarations of war must be taken into account. As for conventional law, Article 1 of the 1907 Hague Convention (No. III) Relative to the Opening of Hostilities, which is still in force between forty-two states, including all the permanent members of the UN Security Council except China, provides that the 'Contracting Powers recognize that hostilities between themselves must not commence without previous and explicit warning, in the form either of a reasoned declaration of war or of an ultimatum with conditional declaration of war.'[16] At least as between the

---

[13] Grotius, bk. ii, ch. xxvi, pt. iv (7).   [14] Ibid., bk. iii, ch. iii, pt. vi (1).
[15] Ibid. (2)–(3).

[16] 18 Oct. 1907, 36 Stat. 2259, 2271 (pt. 2), TS No. 538, 1 Bevans 619. In a note to the entry on China, *Treaties in Force*, published by the US Department of State, indicates that this Convention is 'applicable only to Taiwan'.

Dinstein observes that most wars were not preceded by declarations of war and that Hague Convention No. III is not declaratory of customary international law. Yoram Dinstein, *War, Aggression and Self-Defence* (1988), 34.

parties to this Convention,[17] the law remains formally as it was during the reign of Henry V.

Shakespeare treats Henry's war as a new war rather than a refusal to extend a truce, perhaps because his references to peace and to truce sometimes overlap, as in *1 Henry VI*. In *Henry V*, Shakespeare makes no references to truces.[18] Shakespeare appears to highlight the temporary nature of truces. Entered into in response to compelling pressures, they are broken at will when the interests of the prince so demand. This is how the dramatist characterizes the French thinking, probably not only with regard to truces but also peace-making in general. Consider the advice given by the Count of Alençon to Charles, the Dauphin and the future King of France (Charles VII), urging him to accept the English offer of a truce:

> ALENÇON   To say the truth, it is your policy
> To save your subjects from such massacre
> And ruthless slaughters as are daily seen
> By our proceeding in hostility;
> And therefore take this compact of a truce,
> Although you break it when your pleasure serves.
>
> (*1 Henry VI*, v. vi. 159–64)

The English side is presented as a tough and uncompromising negotiator, but one that takes seriously the principle of *pacta sunt servanda*:

> WARWICK   Be patient, York. If we conclude a peace,
> It shall be with such strict and severe covenants
> As little shall the Frenchmen gain thereby.
>
> (*1 Henry VI*, v. vi. 113–15)

Even when the English are the defenders and the French the invaders, as in *King John*, Shakespeare presents truce-making as falling far short of the heroic and the noble. Consider the counsel—against the truce—given John by Philip the Bastard:

---

[17] See Lassa Francis Lawrence Oppenheim, *International Law* (Hersh Lauterpacht 7th edn., 1952), ii. 293; [United Kingdom] War Office, *The Law of War on Land, Being Part III of the Manual of Military Law* (1958), 7–8.

[18] References to truces can be found in several other plays: *The Comedy of Errors, King John, Troilus and Cressida,* and *Romeo and Juliet.*

BASTARD   O inglorious league!
Shall we, upon the footing of our land,
Send fair-play orders, and make compromise,
Insinuation, parley, and base truce
To arms invasive?

(*King John*, v. i. 65–9)

Actually, Henry's invasion of France in August 1415 did not start a new war but continued the war that legally was still extant. The Hundred Years War was renewed with the collapse in 1369 of the Treaty of Brétigny (1360) after the rejection, or 'defiance', by France of Edward III's ultimatum. Since then, the conflict had been interrupted only by truces, which, according to medieval doctrine, suspended but did not end the war. Because, as I shall show, truces suspended the fighting for an agreed period of time only, it was not even necessary, as a matter of law, to declare war when they came to an end,[19] and Henry's ultimatums did more that the law required.

Henry's negotiations with France made it clear that additional extensions of the truces depended on the satisfaction of his demands. Indeed, to press for faster negotiations and concessions, Henry refused to extend the passports or safe conducts of the French ambassadors beyond 8 June 1415. The invasion started on 13 August after the expiration on 1 or 2 August of the truce as last prolonged,[20] there being no record of a definitive rejection of the English demands. Such a rejection was contained only in Charles's letter to Henry of 24 August, which followed the English invasion. Although Henry took an uncompromising stand in the negotiations, insisting on 'justice' and the restoration of his right to the French crown rather than on this or that French duchy, he certainly could not be accused of having failed to give ample and public notice of his intention to resume hostilities.

---

[19] On termination of the Treaty of Brétigny, see R. Delachenal, *Histoire de Charles V* (1928), iv. 134–5. On the status of truces in medieval war, see *LW* 206–17.

[20] On the extension of truces in 1415 and their expiration, see Charles Lethbridge Kingsford, *Henry V* (1901), 301–3; James Hamilton Wylie, *The Reign of Henry the Fifth* (1914), i. 444. Henry's dispatch on 28 July of a herald bearing a letter to the King of France 'was no doubt intended as a formal defiance to war, and as such the French accepted it.' C. Kingsford, *supra* at 122; *accord*, Wylie, *supra*, at 493–4. For the text of the letter of 28 July, see Nicolas, *supra* note 1, app. 1, at 5. On the 'ultimatum' of Bishop Beaufort, see Wylie, *supra*, at 491.

Henry's ultimatums, although possibly not drafted in the form of declarations of war, undoubtedly satisfied the requirements of an open and public war.

Truces were of considerable importance in the Middle Ages, especially during the Hundred Years War, most of which was taken up by truces rather than by major military campaigns.[21] Medieval norms governing truces were often quite sophisticated and, in some respects, advanced for their era. There is considerable similarity between some medieval rules on truces and modern law of war rules on cease-fires, truces, and armistices.[22]

Bouvet wrote that truce signified three things: it gave surety to persons and to goods and 'hope of peace, for during the truce ways and means of reconciling and pacifying the two sides are sought'.[23] Negotiations of new truces and of prorogations of existing truces therefore could not always be dissociated from negotiations for peace.[24]

Truces, wrote Ayala, 'do not put an end to the war; for though the fighting stops, the war continues'.[25] Similarly, Gentili stated that '[t]ruces do not break off a war . . . but only bring hostile acts to an end.'[26] Grotius defined a truce agreement as one 'by which warlike acts are for a time abstained from, though the

---

[21] Kenneth Fowler observes: 'Apart from nine years of incompletely ratified peace between 1360 and 1369 [Treaty of Brétigny], England and France were in a state of either war or truce from 1337 to 1492. More than half of the 116 years between 1337 and 1453 were taken up by periods of general truce. In the 83 years down to the treaty of Troyes in 1420 there were 55 years of general truce, while major campaigns occupied little more than 25–6 years, during which the fighting was often intermittent.' 'Truces', in Kenneth Fowler (ed.), *The Hundred Years War* (1971), 184. Peter Lewis similarly remarks that war in the 14th c. consisted of short campaigns 'set against a constant background of negotiation', characterized by frequent, sometimes long, truces. Peter S. Lewis, *Later Medieval France* (1968), 43. During the reign of Henry V the pattern of the war changed, with the English forces more actively investing Normandy: 'The diplomatic negotiations continued; but in the intervals of truces the conquest of Normandy steadily continued.' Ibid. 45.

[22] See Oppenheim, *supra* note 17, at ii. 546–56; UK *Manual of Military Law supra* note 17, at 125–33; US Department of the Army, *The Law of Land Warfare* (Field Manual No. 27–10, 1956), 172–5; Convention Respecting the Laws and Customs of War on Land, with Annex of Regulations (Hague Convention No. IV), Articles 36–41, signed 18 Oct. 1907, 36 Stat. 2277; TS 539; 1 Bevans 631.

For an excellent discussion of armistices, cease-fires, and truces in modern law, and on the differences between them, see Dinstein, *supra* note 16, at 42–7, 50–8.

[23] Bouvet, 190.

[24] Ibid. See also *Chronique du Religieux de Saint-Denys* (*supra* note 1) v. 511; Wylie, *supra* note 20, at i. 444.

[25] Ayala, 79.   [26] Gentili, ii. 187.

state of war continues'.[27] It follows, therefore, that when the period of truce has expired, there is no need for a new declaration of war.[28] Gentili was of the same opinion: 'it is not necessary to declare war when such truces come to an end.'[29]

Subject to the Charter of the United Nations, modern international law rules pertaining to the termination of an armistice (or cease-fires or truces) are much the same. Article 36 of the Hague Regulations provides that

An armistice suspends military operations by mutual agreement between the belligerent parties. If its duration is not defined, the belligerent parties may resume operations at any time, provided always that the enemy is warned within the time agreed upon, in accordance with the terms of the armistice.

If the duration of the armistice is fixed, hostilities may be commenced without previous notice.[30]

A truce could be abrogated for material breach. 'If the good faith of the truce has been violated by the one party, it should not be doubted that the party injured is free to take up arms even without declaring war,' wrote Grotius.[31] The importance attributed to medieval truces can be demonstrated by the fact that such leading writers as Ayala and Gentili found it necessary to dispute seriously the view of those commentators who argued that truces were more inviolable than treaties of peace, and that because truces were concluded for a fixed period only, the injured party could not terminate a truce in response to a breach but must, instead, await the truce's expiry before resorting to vengeance.[32] Gentili, like Ayala, concluded that a truce was a contract and 'should not be kept with those who do not . . . observe [it]'.[33] Reciprocity was therefore inherent in agreements establishing truces, as in other contracts. As Keen observes in his excellent analysis of truces, contracts were binding even on the enemy, but were not binding on one party if the other broke its word.[34] Thus the maxim *inadimplenti non est adimplendum* was fully applicable to truce agreements.

---

[27] Grotius, bk. III, ch. xxi, pt. i.   [28] Ibid. pt. xiii.   [29] Gentili, ii. 187.
[30] UK *Manual of Military Law, supra* note 17, at 129.
[31] Grotius, bk. III, ch. xxi, pt. xi.   [32] Ayala, 69–71.   [33] Gentili, ii. 189.
[34] *LW* 212–13.

In reality, the determination of breach was difficult,[35] especially in cases where the violators were individuals rather than
the parties collectively. Keen goes on to cite Baldus's view that if
private individuals violated a truce, the other party remained
bound by it, but public and flagrant violations by the party itself,
especially on a large scale, would void the truce agreement. But
Ayala drew attention to the public-relations advantages of
restraint; there was no blame in not retaliating to breach 'with
the idea of throwing on the enemy all the disgrace of breaking
faith'.[36]

The distinction between the violation of a truce by individuals
subject to the jurisdiction of a party and by the parties themselves is still a part of conventional as well as customary international law. The first triggers a right to compensation; the latter,
in case of serious violations, allows the injured party to denounce
the armistice agreement and even to recommence hostilities.[37]

Although there was some controversy among the medieval and
the Renaissance writers on *jus gentium* as to the types of acts that
were not specifically mentioned by the truce agreements and that
could be lawfully carried out by the parties during the truce, the
basic principle was quite clear: status quo must be preserved.
This, as Keen put it, was 'the most striking fact about a medieval
truce'.[38] Limitations on changes did not however, govern the
whole territory of the adversaries. They applied to the lines of
confrontation between the contesting parties, but not to the *hin-
terland*. Henry's preparations for the invasion of France could
not, therefore, have been construed as a breach of the Anglo-
French truce.

Because truce brought about a general suspension of the war,
parties were not allowed to build or repair forts or to move
troops within a certain distance of the lines.[39] Keen considers this
prohibition a reflection of the medieval conception of war as a
lawsuit, where the reopening of the proceedings should occur at
the exact point 'where previously the advocates closed their
debate'.[40] Perhaps it also mirrored the principle of chivalry that

---

[35] Fowler, *supra* note 21, at 200 (breaches during the Hundred Years War were
the norm rather than the exception).
[36] Ayala, 71.   [37] See Hague Regulations, *supra* note 22, Arts. 40–1.
[38] *LW* 207.   [39] *LW* 207–8.   [40] *LW* 208.

did not allow a party to a duel to change its position when the duel resumed following a pause.

The obligation to maintain the status quo, though often violated, was taken quite seriously. Thus occasionally inspection teams were even used to assess the strength of a besieged garrison in time of truce, so that the status quo could be restored when the period of the truce expired.[41] In this respect, modern armistices are quite different. Except for measures explicitly mentioned, only acts of hostility are normally suspended and prohibited. The US Army Field Manual thus provides that

In the absence of stipulations to the contrary, each belligerent is authorized to make movements of troops within his own lines, to receive reinforcements, to construct new fortifications, installations, and bases, to build and repair transportation and communications facilities, to seek information about the enemy, to bring up supplies and equipment, and, in general, to take advantage of the time and means at his disposal to prepare for resuming hostilities.[42]

The British *Manual of Military Law* similarly prohibits the parties from taking any offensive measures during an armistice, but allows them to do anything that will tend to improve their situation after the expiry of the armistice.[43] Oppenheim wrote that '[e]verybody agrees that belligerents during an armistice may, *outside the line where the forces face each other*, do everything and anything they like regarding defence and preparation of offence.'[44]

Truces could be general, binding all subjects of the prince, or particular or local,[45] binding only in a certain locality or even only particular categories of persons (for example, *trèves marchandes*).[46] The area over which a truce applied was considered neutral or *hors de guerre*. Like other chivalric commitments, the promise to keep the truce implicated a knight's honour,[47] and dishonour constituted an important element of deterrence.

Enforcement was both difficult and elusive. Each party would

---

[41] Fowler, *supra* note 21, at 189.   [42] *Supra* note 22, at 174.
[43] *Supra* note 17, at 129.   [44] Oppenheim, *supra* note 17, at 551.
[45] Cf. Art. 37 of the Hague Regulations: 'An Armistice may be general or local. The first suspends the military operations of the belligerent States everywhere; the second only between certain fractions of the belligerent armies and within a fixed radius.'
[46] *LW* 209–10.   [47] *LW* 211.

appoint 'conservators' empowered to enforce compliance with the truce and normally endowed with criminal jurisdiction over violators.[48] Conservators judged complaints for alleged breaches committed by the subjects of their prince and submitted by the subjects of the adversary. Conservators must be distinguished from another category of officials, the so-called commissioners, who performed the role of diplomatic agents, empowered to deal with public liabilities of the parties rather than with the transgressions of individuals.[49]

The frequency of breaches was, however, such that 'most conservators and even some commissioners were more inclined to defend the interests of their party than to indemnify injured enemies or aliens.'[50] To promote greater impartiality, joint commissions of both adversaries were occasionally formed to act as tribunals with jurisdiction over complaints and disputes between persons of the two allegiances.[51] However, by far the most imaginative and impartiality-enhancing method of resolving disputes over breaches was by the appointment of independent third parties to supervise the conservators and judge disputes over breaches. Maurice Keen observes that the position of a third-party adjudicator or a joint independent commission of both parties was akin to that of a modern international court,

resting on the agreement of the powers involved to be bound internally and externally by their decisions. They gave judgments, therefore, but they did not execute them; and in order to obtain execution our plaintiff would have to refer to his adversary's officials, who were bound by the terms of the truce to implement the conservator's judgments.[52]

The non-self-executing character of the judgments of the third-party adjudicators, and the necessity for the plaintiff to turn to the officials of his adversary for enforcement, weakened the system's efficacy. These weaknesses did not, however, destroy its historical significance for the shaping of the future rules of international law pertaining to impartial third-party adjudication.

Henry himself was aware of the importance of curtailing breaches of truces. With regard to breaches of truces at sea, he appointed in every port a 'Conservator of Truces and Safe-Conducts'. Under the Statute of Truces, every breach of truce or

---

[48] *LW* 37.   [49] *LW* 215.   [50] Fowler, *supra* note 21, at 202.
[51] *LW* 38.   [52] *LW* 38-9.

attack upon holders of safe conducts would be considered an act of treason and punished accordingly.[53] But even this law was seldom enforced effectively.[54]

Of particular interest are Henry's conditions for the general truce agreement with Charles VI, as defined in October 1419 in Gisors and Mantes when England's victory was clear and negotiations of the peace treaty were already under way.[55] In these circumstances, Henry could, and did, dictate the terms of the truce. The very title of the conditions, 'Conditions granted by the King of England for a truce with the King of France',[56] demonstrated the obvious inequality in the position of the parties. These conditions excluded a number of regions and their inhabitants from the general truce, particularly those supporting the Armagnacs and the Dauphin. The King of England would be allowed to make war on them without being considered in breach of the truce, while the King of France would be prohibited from hindering his pursuit of the war.[57] The captains of the localities where

[53] Wylie, *supra* note 20, at i. 330–1. For the Statutes of Truces, see 2 Hen. V, Stat. 1, c. 6.

[54] *LW* 206.

[55] For a brief account of the negotiations, see James Hamilton Wylie and William Templeton Waugh, *The Reign of Henry the Fifth* (1929), iii. 190–1. Cf. US Army Field Manual, *supra* note 22, at 172: '[g]eneral armistices are usually of a combined political and military character. They usually precede the negotiations for peace, but may be concluded for other purposes.'

[56] For the Latin text of these conditions, see Paul Bonenfant, *Du meurtre de Montereau au traité de Troyes* (1958), 203. I am grateful to Professor Peter Haggenmacher for translating this text for me from its original Latin.

[57] '1. First, that there be a general truce equally observed on both sides under the conditions set out hereafter, viz. including on the part of the lord king all and each of his vassals and subjects, as well as all and each of the cities, towns, boroughs, castles, lands, countries and dominions lying in the kingdom of France, under the obedience of the said lord king of France; and that it similarly include on the part of the said cousin of France all and each of his vassals and subjects as well as all and each of the cities, towns, boroughs, castles, lands, countries and dominions lying in the same kingdom of France and being currently in fact under the obedience of the said cousin; except the towns and castles hereafter mentioned, that is, Meulant, Poissy, Montjoie, Saint-Germain-en-Laye and Conflans near Pontoise, which are not included in the present truce any more than the persons currently dwelling therein, as well as the persons favouring that party in the kingdom of France called the Dauphin's or the Armagnacs, and the towns and boroughs, castles and places occupied by them in the kingdom of France; so that, if the aforesaid lord king should happen to move and make war on the aforesaid persons, towns, boroughs, castles or places not included in the present truce, this present truce should not be deemed for this reason to be broken and violated, nor should in this respect the aforesaid cousin of France and those

the truce was to apply, subject to the authority of either Charles or Henry, were to swear to observe the truce and cause others to observe it.[58] While passing through the territories subject to the obedience of the King of France in order to make war on the Dauphin or the Armagnacs, or to lay siege to towns or places not included in the truce, the English forces would be allowed to requisition supplies from the inhabitants but only against payment. The following provision resembles Article 52 of the Hague Regulations:

it shall be understood that the said lord king's men may, while marching forth or back, or during the siege of such enemies, receive in the places subject to the said cousin [King of France] victuals or food in reasonable and moderate quantities, either for themselves or their animals, provided they do not take such victuals from those who offer them for sale without paying such price as may be reasonably agreed between them.[59]

Although the conditions established a date *ad quem* for the expiry of the truce, the possibility of an extension was envisaged, should negotiations prove promising.[60] Violations of the truce by individuals subject to the jurisdiction of either party would call for immediate reparation:

Item, should it happen that anything be done or attempted in violation of the truce, the party whose subjects so attempted, whatever may have been thus attempted, shall make immediate reparation.[61]

under his obedience thwart and hinder the aforesaid lord king or his men in any such expedition during this truce.'

[58] Para. 3.   [59] Para. 4.

[60] '5. Item, the aforesaid truce shall last from the day on which it has been agreed and concluded until the eleventh day of the month of November next, that day included; the aforesaid lord king has also agreed, provided that proceedings in other respects are effective and fair, to extend the truce according to the needs and requirements of the negotiations; and the subjects of both parties shall not be allowed, during the present truce, to trespass on the bounds of the other party's obedience as defined in the preceding article.'

[61] Para. 6. Cf. the UK *Manual of Military Law*, *supra* note 22, at 131: 'Violation of the terms of an armistice by individuals acting on their own initiative does not entitle the injured party to do more than demand the punishment of the offenders and compensation for the losses sustained, if any. . . . There is no justification in any such circumstance for a renewal of hostilities, unless the behaviour of these individuals is approved of or sanctioned by their superiors.'

Of even greater interest was the explicit statement that the truce agreement would remain in force whatever violations were committed by the subjects of either party:

Item, the present truce shall not be deemed broken by any such attempt or enterprise made by subjects of either side against the above stipulations, and it shall nevertheless remain in force and vigour; but all misdeeds of this kind shall be repressed and redressed by the conservators and commissioners to be named on both sides, inasmuch as they can lay hand on such individuals.[62]

Because of this clause, which amounted to an irrebutable presumption of the truce agreement's continued validity, opponents of the treaty of peace would not be allowed to derail the course of negotiations by causing the truce to collapse. Henry would therefore continue to enjoy both the advantages of a truce with Charles VI and the right simultaneously to continue waging war against his enemies, the Dauphin and the Armagnacs.

The general truce agreement signed by the commissioners of both parties at Rouen on 24 December 1419 was largely based on Henry's conditions as defined in October.[63] The terms of the truce provided that

[62] General truce agreement, *supra* note 56, at para. 7.

[63] See documents in Thomas Rymer, *Foedera* (London, 1729), ix. 818–24. I express my deep gratitude to Professor John Baker for translating for me the text of these documents from Latin.

Although Rymer's text contains recitals of several instruments, it represents a single document, copied from the Patent Rolls of Normandy, in the form of letters patent issued under the seals of King Henry V's five commissioners (Philip, Bishop of Worcester; John, Bishop of Rochester; Henry, Lord Fitzhugh, the Lord Chamberlain; Walter Hungerford, Master of the Household; John Tiptoft, steward of Aquitaine) on 24 Dec. 1419:

The patent recites the commissioners' royal appointment to treat and conclude with the Burgundian ambassadors (named), as commissioners of King Charles of France, upon those matters which concern the public good, and especially truces and abstentions from wars, as appears from the commission. It then recites the commission from Henry V, given at his castle of Rouen on 21 December 1419, whereby Henry appointed the said commissioners and any four or three of them as ambassadors, envoys (*nuncii*) and commissioners to treat with the King of France or his ambassadors and to conclude truces etc. and to give and take various forms of surety in that behalf; with promise to ratify whatever they should do.

It further recites the commission (in French), from the Duke of Burgundy, in turn reciting a commission—given at Troyes on 7 November 1419 from King Charles of France—stating Charles's intention to make a treaty with the King of England, and giving authority to the Duke of Burgundy, *doyen* of the peers of France, or his commissioners, to make truces etc. This was followed by a

(1) the truce and abstention from war[64] should be general (*per terram*), and should include all the subjects of King Charles and all the cities, towns, castles, and fortresses etc. in the kingdom of France and elsewhere under his obedience, outside the duchy of Normandy, and all the subjects of King Henry, and all the cities etc. both in France and England under his obedience, so that neither of the kings should make war against the subjects etc. of the other or besiege or take the cities etc. of the other party included in this truce.

(2) Excluded from this truce were the persons and cities etc. of Dauphiné or Armagnac. Either king was granted a right of armed passage through the lands obedient to the other party, in case they could not go through their own lands to make war in Dauphiné or Armagnac.

While so going and coming they were allowed to take reasonable and moderate amounts of victuals and food for themselves and their animals, provided that they paid a just price and did not take the victuals violently from those transporting them for sale from place to place.

(3) It was to be lawful for the subjects of King Charles to carry victuals by land (*per terram*) with animals and vehicles through the lands obedient to King Henry, paying any usual customs and duties; provided that they did not enter castles or fortresses without leave of the captains thereof; and provided also that they had letters certifying that they were subjects of the King of France and intended to travel to transport victuals. A similar provision was made for Henry's subjects.

(4) Captains of cities, towns, and castles, especially those situated on the frontiers, were to promise and swear faithfully to keep and observe the truce.

commission, given at Arras, on 7 December 1419, from the Duke of Burgundy appointing his commissioners (eight by name) in pursuance of the royal commission of 7 November.

After these recitals, the patent states that because, for the sake of a final peace, it appeared to the English ambassadors and the Burgundian ambassadors to be expedient to conclude a truce or general abstention from wars, the English ambassadors record that they have made and agreed with the Duke of Burgundy etc. on behalf of King Henry a good, firm and inviolable truce throughout the land (*per terram*) to be in effect from 24 December until 1 March next. The terms of the truce are then set out, as summarized in the text above.

[64] The nouns are all plural whenever they occur: 'truces and abstentions from wars'. The numbering of the paragraphs in the summary of the terms of the truce above is my own.

(5) The final agreement maintained the principle, already stated in Henry's terms, that violations of the truce agreement would not lead to its termination:

Item, it is agreed that the present truce and abstention from war should not be deemed to have been broken by any attempt or enterprise made or to be made by the subjects of one party against the subjects of the other, contrary to the terms expressed above, but they shall notwithstanding remain in their force and vigour.

And all such attempts and misdeeds ought to be corrected, emended and repaired, and duly reformed, by the conservators and commissioners deputed and to be deputed by either party, as it should and may concern each of them.

And the conservators of the present truce and abstention from war shall be:

On behalf of our said lord king, in the parts of Picardy the captain of Calais and his lieutenant . . . [and others]. And on behalf of the said most serene prince Lord Charles of France, in the parts of France the provost of Paris . . . [and others]:

which same conservators, and each of them in his march or province, and also those deputed by them or by any one of them, shall have the power of cognizance and determination in respect of such attempts, and of correcting, repairing, and emending whatever should be attempted or wrongly done (forisfactum), by whomsoever, against the tenor of the present truce and abstention, and of punishing all wrongdoers and transgressors, as the case shall demand and require.

5
Responsibility of Princes

On the eve of the Battle of Agincourt, Shakespeare has Henry circulate among his troops in disguise and engage in a conversation with soldier Williams.

KING [*in disguise*] Methinks I could not die anywhere so contented as in the King's company, his cause being just and his quarrel honourable.
WILLIAMS That's more than we know.

. . . .

WILLIAMS But if the cause be not good, the King himself hath a heavy reckoning to make, when all those legs and arms and heads chopped off in a battle shall join together at the latter day . . .. Now, if these mendo not die well, it will be a black matter for the King that led them to it . . ..
KING So, if a son that is by his father sent about merchandise do sinfully miscarry upon the sea, the imputation of his wickedness, by your rule, should be imposed upon his father, that sent him. Or if a servant, under his master's command transporting a sum of money, be assailed by robbers, and die in many irreconciled iniquities, you may call the business of the master the author of the servant's damnation. But this is not so. The King is not bound to answer the particular endings of his soldiers, the father of his son, nor the master of his servant, for they purpose not their deaths when they propose their services. Besides, there is no king, be his cause never so spotless, if it come to the arbitrament of swords, can try it out with all unspotted soldiers. Some, peradventure, have on them the guilt of premeditated and contrived murder; some, of beguiling virgins with the broken seals of perjury; some, making the wars their bulwark, that have before gored the gentle bosom of peace with pillage and robbery. Now, if these men have defeated the law and outrun native punishment, though they can outstrip men, they have no wings to fly from God. . . . Then if they die unprovided, no more is the King guilty of their damnation than he was before guilty of those impieties for the which they are now visited. Every subject's duty is the King's, but every subject's soul is his own. . . .
WILLIAMS 'Tis certain, every man that dies ill, the ill upon his own head. The King is not to answer it.

(*Henry V*, IV. i. 125–86)

The King's exchange with the soldier Williams concerns the spiritual responsibility of princes for the death of soldiers in a just or unjust war.[1] The dialogue explores the King's responsibility both from a Christian perspective, reflecting the doctrine that persons dying without having had a chance to repent are doomed to eternal damnation, and from a legal viewpoint. In considering whether the King should be held responsible for the damnation of soldiers killed in battle with 'many irreconciled iniquities' on their conscience, Henry makes a clear distinction between authorized acts, committed by soldiers in their official capacity, for which the King is indeed responsible ('every subject's duty is the King's'), and private acts, for which he is not ('but every subject's soul is his own').

Modern commentators such as Edward White have observed that Henry's statement is faithful to the basic common-law principle *respondere non sovereign*, an exception to *respondeat superior*.[2] The rule that the principal is liable for the acts of his agents, including negligent acts, performed pursuant to authority or powers delegated to them was thus inapplicable to the King. These rules, of course, govern civil responsibility; penal responsibility in common law is usually personal. Henry's discourse merits consideration not because it is faithful to the common law but because of what it implies about the King's responsibility for the unauthorized or criminal acts of soldiers in war. The emphasis in Act iv, Scene i, on the King's exemption from responsibility for his soldiers' misdeeds such as pillage and murder is unremarkable for an era in which the concept of central authority over the army was still rudimentary.

[1] See generally F. Shelling, *Shakespeare and 'Demi-Science'* (1927), 97; Judith Marie O'Malley, *Justice in Shakespeare: The English Kings in the Light of Thomistic Thought* (1964), 46–7. Rather like the modern defence of superior orders, obedience to the King could transfer to him his subjects' responsibility for involvement in an unjust war: 'BATES . . . If his cause be wrong, our obedience to the King wipes the crime of it out of us' (*Henry V*, iv. i. 131–2). It has been noted that Henry's reaction to Williams and Bates showed how sensitive he was towards the question of responsibility, 'always trying to shift the burden' to others. Alexander Leggatt, *Shakespeare's Political Drama* (1988), 133. Alvis observed: 'The subject owes absolute obedience to the king. What the king owes is unclear.' John Alvis, 'A Little Touch of the Night in Harry: The Career of Henry Monmouth', in John Alvis and Thomas G. West (eds.), *Shakespeare as Political Thinker* (1981), 95, 120. For an interesting discussion of Shakespeare and the common man, see Phyllis Rackin, *Stages of History* (1990), 225–6.

[2] Edward J. White, *Commentaries on the Law in Shakespeare* (1913), 291–2.

Responsibility for the treatment of prisoners depended to a large extent on who held them. In modern law, Article 12 of the third Geneva Convention provides that '[p]risoners of war are in the hands of the enemy Power, but not of the individuals or military units who have captured them'; and that '[i]rrespective of the individual responsibilities that may exist, the Detaining Power is responsible for the treatment given them.' In medieval law, however, it was not always clear whether a prisoner of war 'belonged' to the captor or the prince.[3]

[3] See Convention Relative to the Treatment of Prisoners of War (Geneva Convention No. III), 12 Aug. 1949, 6 UST 3316, TIAS No. 3364, 75 UNTS 135. Compare the conflict between Henry IV and Hotspur over the prisoners that Hotspur took. Shakespeare, *1 Henry IV*, I. i. and iii.

English indentures commonly show the King reserving certain classes of prisoners to himself (e.g. high-ranking officials, members of the opposing royal family). A captor normally owed a share of his ransom money to his captain, and a captain a share to the King. After all, the right to make such captures only arose because the war was 'licensed' by the King and waged on his authority. What Honoré Bonet or Bouvet as he is now known (N. A. R. Wright, 'The Tree of Battles of Honoré Bouvet and the Laws of War', in Christopher C. Allmand, ed. *War, Literature, and Politics in the Late Middle Ages* (1976), 12) said about spoil in his late 14th-c. work is indicative of how difficult the problem was seen to be:

'[T]he law on the matter is . . . by no means clear, and expressed opinion is doubtful. According to one law it is thought that the chattels a man wins should be his, but another law says that if a man comes into possession of chattels in war, he must deliver them to the duke of the battle [i.e., the commander, the prince or the lieutenant]. For my part I say that what a man gains from his enemies belongs to him, if we bear in mind that previously it belonged to his enemies, who have lost their lordship over it; but it does not belong to the captor to the extent that he is not obliged to hand it over to the duke of the battle; and the duke should share the spoils out among his men . . .' Bouvet, 150. More directly, Bouvet's discussion of prisoners points to similar difficulties:

'I ask now, if a soldier has captured [a duke or marshal] . . . to whom should he belong as prisoner, to the soldier, or to that soldier's lord; for according to these laws it would appear that he is the soldier's prisoner because the laws say that the captive is at the disposal of the captor. I assert, however, the contrary; for, if it is the case that the soldier is in the king's pay, or in that of another lord, the prisoners or other possessions acquired should be the lord's in whose pay the soldier is. And with regard to this the decretal says that all the booty should be at the king's disposal, and he should dispose of it at his pleasure to those who, according to his estimation, have helped him to win. And, if anyone said the contrary, he could not maintain it according to written law, for if a prisoner must belong to him who has taken and conquered him, by similar reasoning every strong castle and fortified town should be his if he took them. And it would not be reasonable that at the king's cost and expense he should gain land, for he does all that he does as a deputy of the king or of the lord in whose pay he is. Therefore what he conquers should be his lord's; for what he does he does not by his own industry or his own initiative.'

Bouvet, 134–5, see also *LW* 144–5. While acknowledging that views on this question differed, Christine de Pisan believed that both prisoners and other spoils of war were 'atte wille of the prynce whom apparteyneth to dystrybute them after dyscrecyon', Pisan, 223.

The Ordinances of War issued by King Henry V provided that soldiers pay their captains one-third of war booty ('wynnyng by werr', para. 16). As regards

Contemporary legal doctrine (*respondere non sovereign*) was probably consistent with the denial of responsibility by Shakespeare's King for the improper acts of his troops when acting in their private capacity. Nevertheless, in view of the bastard feudal structure of fifteenth-century armies with their many contractual and mercenary fighters, it would be misleading to regard the fighting men of France and England exclusively as soldiers of the realm whose sole duty of fealty was to their prince. The medieval system was quite different from the absolutist monarchical state later advocated by Jean Bodin.[4] The connection between a soldier and his immediate captain or lord was extremely important; soldiers were thus enmeshed in a web of relationships involving both king and captain. Keen observes that '[a] company was a *societas*, a corporate body of itself; . . . [the captain] was its head. . . . As such he could be held liable for unauthorised pillaging by his men. . . . He might even, by the terms of his contracts with his soldiers, be bound to ransom them.'[5] Although the king could deny responsibility for the improper acts of his soldiers, this was not necessarily true of their captain. The principle that the captain could and should be held criminally responsible for such acts by his men, including illegal pillaging, is manifested by the ordinance issued by Charles VII of France in 1439.[6]

prisoners, the ordinances required that the captor bring his prisoners to his captain or master. The penalty for non-compliance was forfeiture of the captor's part of the ransom to his captain or master. Within 8 days, the captain or the master was to bring the prisoner to the king, constable, or marshal (para. 20). If he failed to do so, he forfeited his share to whoever first gave notice to the constable or marshal. *Ordinances of War made by King Henry V at Mawnt* [Mantes], repr. in Travers Twiss (ed.), *The Black Book of Admiralty*, Monumenta Juridica, i. (1871) 459. Sir Travers believed that these ordinances were probably issued by King Henry V in July 1419, when he was negotiating a treaty with the Duke of Burgundy and the Queen of France. Another text, the Statutes and Ordinaunces to be Keped in Time of Werre, although attributed to King Richard II, is probably a translation into English of a Latin version of Henry's ordinances; this version omits nine of the ordinances found in the Mantes version. See *The Black Book of Admiralty, supra*, at 282 ed. nn. 1 and 2.

   [4] Jean Bodin, *Six Livres de la république* (1577), trans. as The Six Bookes of a Commonweale, ed. Kenneth Douglas McRae (1962; facsimile reprint of Eng. trans., 1606).

   [5] *LW* 150–1 (footnotes omitted).

   [6] See Lettres de Charles VII, Pour obvier aux pilleries et vexations des gens de guerre (Orléans, le 2 Novembre, 1439), in *Ordonnances des Rois de France* (Paris 1782), xiii. 306, 308: '(cl. 18) Item, Ordonne le Roy, que chacun Capitaine ou

Gentili addressed the broader question whether the faults of individuals could be 'charged against a community'.[7] He concluded that, in principle, the act of a private citizen, not necessarily including soldiers, does not involve the entire community, the wrong not being caused 'by act of the state'.[8] But the state may become responsible if it fails to right the wrong. Since the community 'can hold its citizens to their duty, and indeed is bound to hold them, it does wrong if it fails to do so'.[9] The state has a clear duty to prevent wrongs of which it has notice and which it has the power to prevent: 'the state, which knows because it has been warned, and which ought to prevent the misdeeds of its citizens, and through its jurisdiction can prevent them, will be at fault and guilty of a crime if it does not do so.'[10] In language anticipating Article 18 of the UN International Law Commission's draft articles on state responsibility,[11] Gentili observed that 'a state is liable for such offences of its citizens as are not for the moment but are *successive and continuous; but even then, only if it knew of them and could have prevented them.*'[12] Had Gentili applied the same, if not a higher, duty of care to the acts of soldiers and sailors, the king would have been responsible for those wrongs he had known of and could have prevented.

Grotius took a similar approach: 'Kings and public officials are liable for neglect if they do not employ the remedies which they can and ought to employ for the prevention of robbery and

---

Lieutenant sera tenu des excès, maux & outrages commis par ceux de sa compagnie, ou aucun d'eux, en tant que sitost que plainte ou clameur sera faite au Capitaine, de ses gens, ou d'aucun d'eux, d'aucun malfait ou excès, que incontinent il prenne le délinquant, & le baille à Justice pour en estre faite punition, selon son délit, raisonnable, selon ces présentes Ordonnances; & en cas qu'il ne le fera ou dissimulera ou delayera en quelque maniere que ce soit, ou que par négligence ou autrement le délinquant évadera & s'en ira, en telle maniere que punition & justice n'en soit faite, le Capitaine sera tenu du délit, comme celui qui l'aura fait, & en souffrira pareille peine qu'eust fait le délinquant.' See also *LW* 150.

[7] Gentili, ii. 99.   [8] Ibid. 100.   [9] Ibid.   [10] Ibid.
[11] See Art. 18 and Commentary: '[T]hree different cases are treated separately in the three paragraphs mentioned: that of a single State act of a continuing character extending over a period of time (continuing act); that of an act consisting of a systematic repetition of actions or omissions relating to separate cases (composite act); and that of an act consisting of a plurality of different actions or omissions by State organs relating to a single case (complex act). [1976] 2 Y.B. Int'l L. Comm'n, pt. 2 at 88, UN Doc. A/CN.4/SER.A/1976/Add.1 (Pt. 2).
[12] Gentili, ii. 101 (emphasis added).

piracy,'[13] but their responsibility is limited to the punishment and 'surrender' (extradition) of the guilty persons and the confiscation of the plundered goods. He added that if persons authorized to make captures from enemies at sea unlawfully captured the property of friends, a claim for restitution would not be acceptable even if the assertion were made that the rulers 'utilized the services of wicked men, or . . . had not required a bond.'[14] Grotius appears to have distinguished liability for neglect from non-liability for acts disobeying specific orders. As regards the latter, he categorically denied a prince's responsibility under the law of nations for those acts committed by his troops 'contrary to orders': 'this rule has been approved by witness of France and England. The liability of one for the acts of his servants without fault of his own does not belong to the law of nations, according to which this question has to be settled, but to municipal law.'[15]

The principle of the international responsibility of the state for the unauthorized acts of its soldiers is relatively recent. Recognized in international arbitrations,[16] its most authoritative statement is found in Article 3 of the Hague Convention (No. IV) Respecting the Laws and Customs of War on Land.[17] This

[13] Grotius, bk. ii, ch. xvii, pt. xx(1).

[14] Ibid. Roberto Ago observed that the theory that an action committed by an individual can be attributed to the State as a source of international responsibility, provided that other factors were involved in its commission, particularly failure to prevent the act or to react *a posteriori* and that such omissions derived directly from the State, i.e., from its organs. This type of theory derives from Grotius' idea that the collectivity participated in a crime committed by an individual if nothing was done to prevent the crime (*patientia*) or to punish or to hand over the offender (*receptus*). [1972] 2 Y.B. Int'l L. Comm'n 121, UN Doc. A/CN.4/SER.A/1972/Add.1 (1974).

[15] Grotius, bk. ii, ch. xvii, pt. xx(2).

[16] See, e.g. *Jeannaud v. United States*, 3 John Bassett Moore, *History and Digest of the International Arbitrations to which the United States has been a Party* (1898), iii. 3000; *Zafiro* case (*GB v. US*), 6 R. Int'l Arb. Awards 160 (1925). See also Ian Brownlie, *Principles of Public International Law* (4th edn. 1990), 452.

[17] 18 Oct. 1907, 36 Stat. 2277, TS No. 539, 1 Bevans 631. Article 3 provides that a belligerent party 'shall be responsible for all acts committed by persons forming part of its armed forces'. On responsibility of states under Article 3, see *Affaire des Biens Britanniques au Maroc Espagnol* (*Spain v. UK*), Report III (23 Oct. 1924), 2 R. Int'l Arb. Awards 615, 645 (1925).

Article 3, of course, constitutes *lex specialis*. Regarding the general customary law rules on attribution, see Francisco V. García-Amador, Louis B. Sohn, and Richard R. Baxter, *Recent Codification of the Law of State Responsibility for Injuries to Aliens* (1974), 247–9; Theodor Meron, 'International Responsibility of States for Unauthorized Acts of their Officials', 33 Brit. Y.B. Int'l L. 85 (1957).

provision, now accepted as customary law,[18] goes beyond the generally applicable rules governing the international responsibility of states, which are based on the distinction between official capacity and private capacity, to establish a more stringent standard for members of the armed forces. Article 3 constitutes 'a veritable guarantee covering all damage that might be caused by armed forces, whether they had acted as organs [of the state] or as private persons'.[19] This special rule, however, addresses the *consequences* of acts by a particular category of state agents rather than the attribution of their acts to the state.[20] In contrast to the statement by Shakespeare's Henry, Article 3 holds the state responsible for the misdeeds of the members of its armed forces even when their acts cannot be imputed to the state.

The recognition of the leader's penal responsibility for acts committed by members of the armed forces in violation of the law of war came still later with the '*Yamashita* doctrine', recog-

See also Luigi Condorelli, 'L'Imputation à l'Etat d'un fait internationalement illicite: Solutions classiques et nouvelles tendances', 189 Recueil des Cours 9, 147–8 (1984 VI); Gordon A. Christenson, 'The Doctrine of Attribution in State Responsibility', in Richard B. Lillich (ed.), *International Law of State Responsibility for Injuries to Aliens* (1983), 321; Theodor Meron, *Human Rights and Humanitarian Norms as Customary Law* (1989), 155–71. For other scholarly writings on attribution to states of *ultra vires* acts of state organs, see [1975] 2 Y.B. Int'l L. Comm'n 66 nn.71–2, UN Doc. A/CN.4/SER.A/1975/Add.1 (1976).

[18] [1975] 1 Y.B. Int'l L. Comm'n 7, UN Doc. A/CN.4/SER.A/1975 (comments of Prof. Paul Reuter); see also Meron, *Human Rights*, supra note 17, at 161–2.

[19] [1975] 1 Y.B. Int'l L. Comm'n, *supra* note 18, at 16 (comments by Special Rapporteur Roberto Ago). See also i. Lassa Francis Lawrence Oppenheim, *International Law* (Hersch Lauterpacht 8th edn., 1955), i. 363 n. 1. Article 3 was also intended to apply to cases 'in which negligence cannot be attributed to the government itself', i.e. violations committed 'without the knowledge of governments, or against their will'. Yves Sandoz, 'Unlawful Damage in Armed Conflicts and Redress under International Humanitarian Law', Int'l Rev. Red Cross, No. 228 (May–June 1982), at 131, 136–7. See also Frits Kalshoven, 'State Responsibility for Warlike Acts of the Armed Forces', 40 Int'l & Comp. L.Q. 827, 837–8 (1991).

[20] Note the opinion of Professor Brownlie that '[i]mputability would seem to be a superfluous notion, since the major issue in a given situation is whether there has been a breach of duty: the content of "imputability" will vary according to the particular duty, the nature of the breach, and so on.' Ian Brownlie, *System of the Law of Nations: State Responsibility* (1983) Part I, 36 (footnote omitted). See also Gaetano Arangio-Ruiz, 'Second Report on State Responsibility', UN Doc. A/CN.4/425/Add.1, para. 173 (1989) ('in the case of States as international persons a *legal* attribution seems actually to be an error and a redundancy').

nizing a kind of due-diligence principle.[21] Although the *Yamashita* doctrine now can be regarded as a statement of customary law, it is not expressed in the Geneva Conventions of 12 August 1949 for the Protection of Victims of War,[22] and it found explicit recognition in a treaty only in 1977.

[21] In 1946 General Tomuyuki Yamashita, the commander of the Japanese armed forces in the Philippines in 1944–5, voiced a defence that echoed Henry's plea of *respondere non sovereign*. Charged with failing to discharge his duty to control the operations of the persons subject to his command who had violated the laws of war by committing massacres, acts of violence, cruelty, homicide, pillage, and destruction against the civilian population and prisoners of war, Yamashita maintained that the charge did not allege that he personally had either committed or directed the commission of these acts and that he could therefore not be held responsible for any violation of the law of war. On a petition of *certiorari* from a US military commission, the US Supreme Court considered a military commander's criminal liability for such violations and stated that the aim of protecting civilian populations and POWs from brutality would largely be defeated if the commander of an invading army 'could with impunity neglect to take reasonable measures for their protection. Hence the law of war presupposes that its violation is to be avoided through the control of the operations of war by commanders who are to some extent responsible for their subordinates.' *In re Yamashita*, 327 U.S. 1, 15 (1945). Extrapolating from provisions of the Hague Convention No. IV and other treaties, Chief Justice Stone concluded that they 'plainly imposed on petitioner . . . an affirmative duty to take such measures as were within his power and appropriate in the circumstances to protect prisoners of war and the civilian population. This duty of a commanding officer has heretofore been recognized, and its breach penalized by our own military tribunals.' Ibid. 16. See the criticism of this decision by Michael Walzer, *Just and Unjust Wars* (1977), 319–22.

In *United States* v. *Sadao Araki*, the International Tribunal for the Far East followed the *Yamashita* doctrine with regard to the responsibility of members of the Japanese cabinet for mistreatment of POWs, 'even though they delegate the duties of maintenance and protection to others'. US Naval War College, International Law Studies, 60: Howard S. Levie (ed.), *Documents on Prisoners of War* (1979), 437, 438. The Tribunal held that members of the government and military and civilian officials with control over POWs fail in their duty and become responsible for ill-treatment of prisoners if they do not establish and secure the efficient functioning of a system aimed at preventing such treatment. Ibid. 438. Only for the last two centuries, however, have POWs and civilian internees been considered to be in the power of the captor sovereign. Ibid. 437. The principle of the responsibility of the state for the POWs captured by its troops is stated in the 19th- and 20th-c. law of war instruments.

[22] The authoritative Commentary on Article 146 of the Geneva Convention (No. IV) Relative to the Protection of Civilian Persons in Time of War, 12 Aug. 1949, 6 UST 3516, TIAS No. 3365, 75 UNTS 287, prepared by the International Committee of the Red Cross, mentions the guilty verdicts in several cases in Allied courts and observes: 'In view of the Convention's silence on this point, it will have to be determined under municipal law either by the enactment of special provisions or by the application of the general clauses which may occur in the penal codes.' Oscar M. Uhler and Henri Coursier (eds.), *Commentary on the*

This principle of responsibility, *respondere sovereign*, was incorporated into modern international customary and conventional law as necessary to ensure the effectiveness of the law of war.[23] It is a far cry from Henry's statement on his own responsibility in Act IV, Scene i.

Yet in the conversation between Henry and Williams, Shakespeare voiced the concept of the leader's personal responsibility for unjust war, for which he would have to answer before God ('heavy reckoning', 'black matter'), an idea which evolved into the concept of personal criminal responsibility in modern positive international law. Thus the Nuernberg Charter, adopted by the London Agreement of 8 August 1945,[24] establishes individual responsibility for crimes against peace, 'namely, planning, preparation, initiation or waging of a war of aggression, or a war in violation of international treaties', for which there shall be individual responsibility. In its comments (1950) on the 'Formulation of the Nuernberg Principles', the International Law Commission set out its interpretation of what was the understanding of the Nuernberg Tribunal, that the expression 'waging of a war of aggression' referred 'only to high-ranking military personnel and high State officials' in contrast to 'everyone in uniform who fought in a war of aggression'.[25] Indeed, only the most senior leaders were prosecuted for such crimes.

The view, voiced by the soldier Williams, that princes are personally responsible for an unjust war, had already crystallized in the *jus gentium* of the Renaissance period. Grotius insisted that a distinction be maintained between 'those who were responsible for a war and those who followed the leadership of others', and

Geneva Conventions of 12 August 1949: Geneva Convention Relative to the Protection of Civilian Persons in Time of War (1958), 591–2.

[23] Article 86 (2) of Protocol Additional to the Geneva Conventions of 12 August 1949, and Relating to the Protection of Victims of International Armed Conflicts (Protocol I), opened for signature 12 Dec. 1977, 1125 UNTS 3.

[24] 82 UNTS 280 (Art. 6 (a)).

[25] 2 [1950] Y.B. Int'l L. Comm'n at 376, UN Doc. A/CN.4/SER.A/1950/Add.1 (1957). It may be noted that Article 7 of the Nuernberg Charter ('Charter of the International Military Tribunal') provided that '[t]he official position of defendants, whether as Heads of State or responsible officials in Government Departments, shall not be considered as freeing them from responsibility or mitigating punishment.' Agreement for the Prosecution and Punishment of the Major War Criminals of the European Axis, signed 8 Aug. 1945, 82 UNTS 280, 59 Stat. 1544, 145 BFSP 872.

that the latter, the 'innocent populace', be pardoned.[26] As regards those responsible for the war, Grotius distinguished further between wars with obviously unjust causes and wars which although unjust 'still are such that they may deceive persons who are by no means wicked', justifying pardons for those persons.[27]

Preceding Grotius, Gentili devoted an entire chapter to the treatment of the 'captive leaders of the enemy'. He invoked Augustine ('[s]everity must be visited, not upon a multitude of sinners, but upon the sins of a few'), Cicero ('severity against the leaders, but generosity towards the soldiers'), and Thomas More ('causing the death of the leader of the enemy, in order that in this way the harmless multitude may be spared, which is hurried into war, not of its own volition, but driven by the madness of princes'.[28] Gentili reluctantly agreed to the principle that leaders might be killed to spare the lives of soldiers: 'Yet I do not approve the death even of the captured leaders . . . but I merely desire this, that by far the greatest number be spared.'[29] Addressing the immunity of captured leaders, whose supporters argued that 'equal did not have power over equal' (*par in parem not habet jurisdictionem*), Gentili believed that 'by sinning [the leader] deprives himself of his equality'.[30] Gentili lamented the fact that in practice the soldiers are slain, while the wealthy leaders who can afford to ransom themselves are saved.[31]

In modern times, leaders still invoke defences of immunity and of act of state. And although international law may reject such claims,[32] in practice leaders are still virtually never punished even for the most flagrant offences (consider Saddam Hussein or Pol Pot). International law's typical reaction to aggression is still to

---

[26] Grotius, bk. III, ch. xi, pt. v. I am grateful to Professor Howard S. Levie for drawing my attention to this passage of Grotius. Regarding modern law, see generally Yoram Dinstein, *The Defence of Obedience to Superior Orders in International Law* (1965).

[27] Grotius, bk. III, ch. xi, pt. vi (1).

[28] Gentili, ii. 322, 325.   [29] Ibid. 325.   [30] Ibid. 323.

[31] Ibid. 325.

[32] See Article 13 of the Draft Code of Crimes against the Peace and Security of Mankind, provisionally adopted by the International Law Commission: 'The official position of an individual who commits a crime against the peace and security of mankind, and particularly the fact that he acts as Head of State or Government, does not relieve him of criminal responsibility.' *Report of the International Law Commission on the work of its forty-third session*, 46 GAOR Supp. (No. 10) at 243, UN Doc. A/46/10 (1991).

insist on the civil responsibility of the state for reparations, rather than on the individual criminal responsibility of the leaders.[33]

[33] See e.g. UN Security Council Resolution 687 E imposing on Iraq the payment of war reparations for direct losses resulting from the unlawful invasion and occupation of Kuwait. UN Doc. S/RES/687 (1991). See also Report of the Secretary-General, UN Doc. S/22559 (1991). By Resolution 808 (22 Feb. 1992) the UN Security Council decided to establish an international tribunal for the prosecution of persons responsible for serious violations of international humanitarian law committed in the territory of the former Yugoslavia. It is still too early to assess this Resolution's impact on future war crimes prosecutions.

6

The Siege of Harfleur and Treatment of Occupied Territory: The Limits of Protection

AT THE WALLS OF HARFLEUR

KING   How yet resolves the Governor of the town?
This is the latest parle we will admit.
Therefore to our best mercy give yourselves,
Or like to men proud of destruction
Defy us to our worst. For as I am a soldier,
A name that in my thoughts becomes me best,
If I begin the batt'ry once again
I will not leave the half-achievèd Harfleur
Till in her ashes she lie burièd.
The gates of mercy shall be all shut up,
And the fleshed soldier, rough and hard of heart,
In liberty of bloody hand shall range
With conscience wide as hell, mowing like grass
Your fresh fair virgins and your flow'ring infants.
What is it then to me if impious war
Arrayed in flames like to the prince of fiends
Do with his smirched complexion all fell feats
Enlinked to waste and desolation?
What is't to me, when you yourselves are cause,
If your pure maidens fall into the hand
Of hot and forcing violation?
What rein can hold licentious wickedness
When down the hill he holds his fierce career?
We may as bootless spend our vain command
Upon th'enragèd soldiers in their spoil
As send precepts to the leviathan
To come ashore. Therefore, you men of Harfleur,
Take pity of your town and of your people

Whiles yet my soldiers are in my command,
Whiles yet the cool and temperate wind of grace
O'erblows the filthy and contagious clouds
Of heady murder, spoil, and villainy.
If not—why, in a moment look to see
The blind and bloody soldier with foul hand
Defile the locks of your shrill-shrieking daughters;
Your fathers taken by the silver beards,
And their most reverend heads dashed to the walls;
Your naked infants spitted upon pikes,
Whiles the mad mothers with their howls confused
Do break the clouds, as did the wives of Jewry
At Herod's bloody-hunting slaughtermen.
What say you? Will you yield, and this avoid?
Or, guilty in defence, be thus destroyed?
GOVERNOR   . . .
We yield our town and lives to thy soft mercy.
Enter our gates, dispose of us and ours,
For we no longer are defensible.
KING   Open your gates. Come, Uncle Exeter,
Go you and enter Harfleur. There remain,
And fortify it strongly 'gainst the French.
Use mercy to them all.[1]

(Henry V, III. iii. 84–137)

A commentator on the modern law of war would be hard pressed to offer a more terrifying catalogue of violations of the law of war than that contained in the speech by Shakespeare's Henry before the walls of Harfleur, threatening cruel retribution should Harfleur refuse to surrender: denying quarter; killing or wounding an enemy who, having laid down his arms or no longer having a means of defence, has been captured; ignoring the principle of distinction between combatants and civilians; attacking civilians;[2] enforcing collective penalties; resorting to

---

[1] Cf. David M. White, 'Shakespeare and Psychological Warfare', 12 *Public Opinion Quarterly* 68, 70–2 (1948). Cf. Hague Regulations annexed to Convention (No. IV), Respecting the Laws and Customs of War on Land, Art. 23 (c)–(d). 18 Oct. 1907, 36 Stat. 2277, TS No. 539, 1 Bevans 631. In negotiating the terms of surrender of Rone, Henry insisted that 'the gunners that had discharged anie peece against the Englishmen should suffer death.' Holinshed, 69 (= R. Holinshed, *Chronicles* (1808), iii. 99).

[2] Protocol Additional to the Geneva Conventions of 12 August 1949, and Relating to the Protection of Victims of International Armed Conflicts (Protocol I), Art. 51, opened for signature, 12 Dec. 1977, 1125 UNTS 3. Of course there is,

measures of intimidation and terrorism; and engaging in pillaging and rape.[3] Of course, Henry cannot be judged by modern international norms, which in any case are often violated.[4] Rather, the relevant questions are, first, how did the real Henry treat the conquered inhabitants of Harfleur? Did he actually 'use mercy to them all'? Second, to what extent did the speech of Shakespeare's Henry and the conduct of the real Henry's troops comport with the then-prevailing standards? Our discussion will centre on certain key aspects of the late medieval law of war presented in discrete sections, starting with the concept of mercy and ending with the characteristics of the medieval army.

MERCY

Henry's reference to mercy towards Harfleur is not mentioned either by Holinshed or by Hall and is therefore unlikely to have been known to Shakespeare, but other sources suggest that the real Henry may well have mentioned mercy there. When the delegation of Harfleur surrendered itself and the townspeople to the King's mercy, Henry promised the town's spokesman Sire de Gaucourt 'that, although he and his company had, in God's despite and contrary to all justice, retained against him a town which, being a noble portion of his inheritance, belonged to him, nevertheless, because they had submitted themselves to his mercy, even though tardily, they should not depart entirely without mercy'.[5] The King then entertained the delegation and the hostages with a sumptuous dinner. Similarly, Sir Harris Nicolas writes that although King Henry intimated to the French that, unless they would yield at discretion, they must not expect any

in our era, a tremendous gap between the law on the books and the law in action. Consider this comment on the atrocities in Yugoslavia: 'We read of the murder of children, the massacre of unarmed men, the shelling of residential areas. . . . And this is in Europe. Our time, not the past.' Richard Cohen, 'We did Know—but we didn't Care', *International Herald Tribune*, 3 July 1992, 6, col. 3.

[3] Geneva Convention (No. IV) Relative to the Protection of Civilian Persons in Time of War, 12 Aug. 1949, Arts. 33 and 27, respectively. 6 UST 3516, TIAS No. 3365, 75 UNTS 287.

[4] e.g., the treatment of Kuwaiti civilians by Iraq in 1990. See, e.g., SC Res. 674 (29 Oct. 1990), repr. in 29 ILM 1561 (1990); and UN Doc. A/C.3/45/L.90 (27 Nov. 1990).

[5] *Gesta*, 53.

terms.[6] The King is reported to have stated after the surrender that, although Harfleur had defied him, 'in consideration of their having submitted to his clemency, he would not entirely withhold his mercy from them'.[7] After the dinner, the delegation and the hostages were entrusted to the custody of King's officers with the instructions that they were to be treated honourably.[8] It is possible, therefore, that the King's reference to mercy was aimed primarily at the delegation and the hostages, rather than the townspeople as a whole.

Was Shakespeare's reference to mercy, which was obviously intended to present Henry in a positive light, based on some historical or contemporary account which came to his attention? We do not know whether the original text of *Famous Victories*, a play that appears to have influenced Shakespeare,[9] mentioned mercy.[10] Some aspects of Shakespeare's play parallel the *Gesta*,[11] including the mention of mercy. The *Gesta* itself was published in some form in 1417.[12] While a copy could have come to Shakespeare's attention, whether or not it did remains a matter of conjecture. Shakespeare's reference to mercy in Henry's orders to Exeter may be entirely fictitious.

If Henry's speech reflected the medieval norms contemporaneous with the siege of Harfleur, Henry's command to Exeter to 'use mercy' may well have reflected the wide medieval recognition of the injunction to use mercy, a secular counterpart and reflection of the Christian concept of charity or *caritas*.[13] Nevertheless,

---

[6] Harris Nicolas, *A History of the Battle of Agincourt* (2nd edn., 1832), 62.

[7] Ibid. 66.   [8] Ibid.

[9] Geoffrey Bullough (ed.), *Narrative and Dramatic Sources of Shakespeare* (1962). iv. 347–75.

[10] Ibid. 348 for a discussion of the truncated version of *Famous Victories* which has survived.

[11] Ibid. 353.

[12] Intro. to *Gesta* by F. Taylor and J. Roskell, p. xlix.

[13] The word 'mercy' appears four times in Henry's speech. On the concept of mercy, see James Turner Johnson, *Just War Tradition and the Restraint of War* (1981), 6–10 ; Paul Ramsey, *The Just War: Force and Political Responsibility* (1968), 150–1. In discussing war, St Thomas Aquinas cited Augustine: 'Among true worshippers of God those wars are looked on as peace-making which are waged neither from aggrandisement nor cruelty, but with the object of securing peace, of repressing the evil and supporting the good. . . . The craving to hurt people, the cruel thirst for revenge, the unappeased and unrelenting spirit, the savageness of fighting on . . . all these are rightly condemned in wars.' *Summa Theologiae*, vol. xxxv, trans. Thomas R. Heath (Blackfriars edn., 1972):

Shakespeare clearly intended to emphasize Henry's humanity, for the order to use mercy is mentioned neither by Holinshed nor by Hall.[14] Moreover, both the sack of Harfleur and the deportations that followed are passed over in silence in the play, though related by Holinshed (Hall mentioned the sack of Harfleur but not the deportations).

In emphasizing the signal importance of mercy, Shakespeare was close to the medieval convention that regarded justice and mercy as twin attributes of kingship, as of course they were of God himself. St Thomas Aquinas articulated this convention thus:

A king, then, should realize that he has assumed the duty of being to his kingdom what the soul is to the body and what God is to the universe. If he thinks attentively upon this point he will, on the one hand, be fired with zeal for justice, seeing himself appointed to administer justice throughout his realm in the name of God, and, on the other hand, he will grow in mildness and clemency, looking upon the persons subject to his government, as the members of his own body.[15]

Consequences of Charity, Question 40, at 83. See also Question 44, on the commands to love, ibid. 143, 155, 157.

Grotius recognized that history abounded with accounts of 'the destruction of whole cities, or the levelling of walls to the ground, the devastation of fields, and conflagrations. . . . [They were] permissible also against those who have surrendered.' Grotius, bk. iii, ch. v, pt. i. However, both in battle and in a siege, a 'surrender of those who yield upon condition that their lives be spared ought not to be rejected,' ibid. ch. xi, pt. xiv(1) and '[t]he same sense of justice bids that those be spared who yield themselves unconditionally to the victor, or who become suppliants,' ibid. pt. xv.

[14] See Holinshed, *supra* note 1, at 23–5 (= R. Holinshed, *Chronicles*, (1808) iii. 73–4); Hall, 62–3.

[15] See St Thomas Aquinas, *De regimene principum*, ch. 12, in Aquinas, *Selected Political Writings*, ed. A. P. D'Antrèves, trans J. G. Dawson (Basil Blackwell edn., Oxford, 1965), 67; id., *Summa Theologiae*, vol. v, trans. and ed. Thomas Gilbey (Blackfriars edn., 1967): 'God's Will and Providence', Question 21, at 73, 85 ('justice and mercy in God'); ibid., vol. xxxvii, trans. and ed. Thomas Gilbey (Blackfriars edn., 1975): 'Justice', Question 58, at 19 ('justice'); ibid., vol. xxxiv, trans. and ed. R. J. Batten (Blackfriars edn., 1975): 'Charity', Question 25, at 81 ('the objects of charity'), Question 27, at 161 ('the chief act of charity'), Question 30, at 209 ('mercy'). See also Philippe de Meziere, *Le Songe du Vieil Pelerin*, ii. 158 (bk. 3), ed. G. W. Coopland (Cambridge 1969). The theme of the King judging with both justice and mercy is prominent in *Piers Plowman*. See Myra Stokes, *Justice and Mercy in Piers Plowman* (Croom Helm edn. London and Canberra, 1984), 1–2, 154; Anna P. Baldwin, *The Theme of Government in Piers Plowman* edn. D. S. Brewer (1981), 15–16. Later in the 15th c. there is a tract (A Defence of the Proscription of the Yorkists in 1459) dating from 1459 debating whether the treasonous Yorkist lords who had rebelled against Henry VI should be

Some situations called for the exercise of clemency; others for the full rigour of the law. The latter was appropriate for deliberate and hardened sinners, the former for the repentant and the mistaken. The ideal king knew which was appropriate in any situation; the foolish king applied them wrongly, with disastrous results.

The importance attributed by Shakespeare to mercy in *Henry V* was entirely consistent with the esteem the dramatist expressed for mercy in his other plays. Mercy was the highest attribute; it was God's quality, as it was that of kings, the brave and the noble: 'But mercy is above this sceptred sway. It is enthronèd in the hearts of kings; | It is an attribute to God himself' (*Merchant of Venice*, iv. i. 190–2), 'Sweet mercy is nobility's true badge' (*Titus Andronicus*, I. I. 119), 'you have a vice of mercy in you, | Which better fits a lion than a man' (*Troilus and Cressida*, v. iii. 37–8), 'Beyond the infinite and boundless reach | Of mercy, if thou didst this deed of death | Art thou damned' (*King John*, IV. iii. 117–19), 'then let them have | That mercy which true prayer ought to have' (*Richard II*, v. iii. 107–8), 'This offer comes from mercy, not from fear' (*2 Henry IV*, iv. i. 148), 'Wert thou a man | Thou wouldst have mercy on me' (*Antony and Cleopatra*, v. ii. 170–1), 'I do think that you might pardon him, | And neither heaven nor man grieve at the mercy' (*Measure for Measure*, II. ii. 49–50), 'How shalt thou hope for mercy, rend'ring none?' (*Merchant of Venice*, IV. i. 87), 'The quality of mercy is not strained. | It droppeth as the gentle rain from heaven | Upon the place beneath' (ibid. IV. i. 181–3), 'We do pray for mercy, | And that same prayer doth teach us all to render | The deeds of mercy' (ibid. 197–9).

Law could be severe. 'Call him to present trial. If he may | Find mercy in the law, 'tis his; if none, | Let him not seek't of us' (*Henry VIII*, I. ii. 212–14). But mercy mitigated the severity of the law. 'And earthly power doth then show likest God's | When mercy seasons justice' (*Merchant of Venice*, IV. i. 193–4). Shakespeare's Henry refused mercy to the Southampton traitors Richard Earl of Cambridge, Henry Lord Scrope of Masham, and

attainted or not, and the question argued over between the protagonists was whether a prince should be rigorous or clement: 26 *English Historical Review* 512, 514–16 (1911). For an excellent discussion of justice and mercy in the reign of Henry V, see Gerald L. Harriss, 'Introduction: The Examplar of Kingship', in Gerald L. Harriss (ed.), *Henry V: The Practice of Kingship* (1985), 11–13.

Thomas Grey, knight of Northumberland, but only after they favoured denying mercy to a minor offender and thus could not very well appeal to mercy for themselves.

> KING The mercy that was quick in us but late
> By your own counsel is suppressed and killed.
> You must not dare, for shame, to talk of mercy.
>
> (*Henry V*, ii. ii. 76–8)

HOSTAGES

The treatment of hostages merits attention. *Gesta* reported that Harfleur's surrender delegation was accompanied 'by those persons who had previously sworn to keep the agreements',[16] and that the delegation consisted of sixty-six persons, including twenty-four hostages. Hall wrote that when the surrender agreement was reached, 'to performe [the agreement] [Harfleur] delivered into the kynges possession xxx of the beste capitaines and Marchauntes of the toune'.[17] Holinshed, reiterating Hall's version, added that according to other sources only twelve 'pledges' were delivered while thirty 'of the cheefest personages . . . to stand for life or death at [Henry's] will and pleasure' were to be delivered 'if the siege were not raised' by the French King within six days.[18] Although Shakespeare knew about the hostages from Hall's and Holinshed's accounts, he made no reference to them in his play. This omission may be explained by the fact that Holinshed said little about the Harfleur hostages. Moreover, Shakespeare's references to hostages in his other plays were few and brief, perhaps suggesting that he was not particularly interested in hostages.

The real Henry himself was probably aware of the harsh treatment of hostages during the Hundred Years War. When Calais was forced to yield to Edward III after a long siege in 1347, for example, the King demanded, as a condition for accepting the surrender, that 'six of the cheefe burgesses of the towne should come foorth bareheaded, barefooted, and barelegged, and in their

---

[16] *Gesta*, 53. See also ibid. 51–3. According to other sources, there were 64 hostages, ibid. 53 n. 3.

[17] Hall, 62.   [18] Holinshed, 24 (= R. Holinshed, *Chronicles* (1808), iii. 73).

shirts, with halters about their necks, with the keies of the towne and castell in their hands, to submit themselves simplie to the kings will, and the residue he was contented to take to mercie.'[19] When the hostages presented themselves before the King, he ordered that 'their heads should be striken off.'[20] It was only after the Queen, who was expecting a child, 'kneeled downe before the king hir husband'[21] and begged him for mercy, that he relented and turned the hostages over to her.

In theory, hostages were given as a pledge to respect an agreement,[22] and could be killed if that agreement were breached.[23] Despite his predilection for humanitarian principles, Gentili considered the killing of innocent hostages to be justified by the preeminent importance of respecting agreements and by the conviction that the right to punish hostages was implicit in the agreement by which they were delivered. Public good trumped individual rights: 'Every great principle has some element of injustice, in which the loss of the individual is compensated by the public advantage.'[24] Grotius agreed that 'according to the strict law of nations a hostage can be put to death; but that is not also in accord with moral justice, unless there is a fault on the part of the hostage meriting such punishment.'[25] Vitoria tried to temper the severity of the treatment of hostages. He agreed that it was lawful to kill hostages when the enemy did not abide by his commitments, but insisted that an additional condition be satisfied: the hostages should be 'in other respects among the guilty, as, for instance, because they have borne arms'.[26]

The case of Calais demonstrates that considerable ambiguity prevailed in the understanding of the status of hostages and that captors had virtually unlimited discretion. Because no violation of the surrender agreement had been committed in Calais, Edward's order to kill the hostages could not be justified on ground of breach. Rather, Edward appears to have considered the hostages sacrificial lambs, on whom he could vent his fury against Calais. Holinshed's description of the Calais incident recalls the Roman custom of putting to death the commanders of

---

[19] R. Holinshed, *Chronicles* (1808), iii., 647–8.   [20] Ibid. 648.
[21] Ibid.   [22] Gentili, ii. 241.   [23] Ibid. 241–2.   [24] Ibid. 243.
[25] Grotius, bk. iii, ch. xx, pt. liii.
[26] Vitoria, 181–2 (43). Second Relectio on the Indians, or on the Law of War made by the Spaniards on the Barbarians.

the enemy, whether captured or delivered, on the day of Rome's triumph.[27] Presumably, Edward would have defended his order by arguing that the agreement to surrender the hostages to his 'will' gave him absolute discretion over their lives and perhaps that they bore some guilt owing to their leadership role in Calais.

The taking, and particularly the killing of hostages is considered a war crime or grave breach by modern international law.[28] This prohibition reflects the concept of individual responsibility, which prohibits punishing an individual for an offence he or she has not personally committed, and the strict limitations now imposed upon the right to resort to reprisals.

That both the taking and the killing of hostages should be prohibited by modern international law is unremarkable. What might surprise some readers, however, is the fact that in certain circumstances the taking and the killing of hostages was not considered absolutely illegal by some of the post-Second World War war crimes tribunals. During the Second World War, Germany resorted to the killing of hostages on an unprecedented scale. The Germans took hostages not as a pledge for keeping agreements, as during the Hundred Years War, but 'as a means of intimidating the population in order to weaken its spirit of resistance and to prevent breaches of the law and sabotage in order to ensure the security of the Detaining Power.'[29] During the Second World War, the treatment of hostages was governed only by customary law. Although the killing of hostages was both mentioned as a war crime in Article 6 (b) of the London Agreement, and condemned in many cases by war crimes tribunals,[30] this prohibition was not absolute. In the *Hostage* Case, *United States* v. *List*, the US Tribunal established under Control Council Law No. 10 condemned as barbaric the ancient practice of taking hostages to be

[27] Grotius, bk. iii, ch. iv, pt. xii.

[28] See the fourth Geneva Convention, *supra* note 3, Arts. 33–4; Additional Protocol I, *supra* note 2, Art. 75 (2)(c); Protocol Additional to the Geneva Conventions of 12 Aug. 1949, and Relating to the Protection of Victims of Non-International Armed Conflicts (Protocol II), opened for signature 12 Dec. 1977, 16 ILM 1442 (1977), 1125 UNTS 609, Art. 4 (2)(c); Common Article 3 (1)(b) to the Geneva Conventions.

[29] Oscar M. Uhler and Henri Coursier (eds.), *Commentary on the Geneva Conventions of 12 August 1949: Geneva Convention Relative to the Protection of Civilian Persons in Time of War* (1958), 229–30.

[30] The [United Kingdom] War Office, *The Law of War on Land, Being Part III of the Manual of Military Law* (1958), 185–6 and n. 1.

held responsible for the good faith of the persons who delivered them, but insisted that it had to apply the law as it stood:

An examination of the available evidence on the subject convinces us that hostages may be taken in order to guarantee the peaceful conduct of the populations of occupied territories and, when certain conditions exist and the necessary preliminaries have been taken, they may, as a last resort, be shot. The taking of hostages is based fundamentally on a theory of collective responsibility.[31]

The tribunal held that the killing of hostages constituted a war crime, *unless* the following conditions were met: a proclamation must be made notifying the population that upon the recurrence of certain acts named hostages would be shot; and the number of hostages shot must not exceed in severity the offences which the shooting was designed to deter. In addition to these requirements of notice, warning, and proportionality, the tribunal appeared to resurrect the medieval notion of guilt and innocence: hostages could be taken only when 'it can be shown that the population generally is a party to the offense, either actively or passively'.[32] Despite these refinements, the *List* tribunal's questionable law still gave arbitrary powers to the occupying powers and supported the concepts of collective responsibility and collective punishment. The tribunal stated that '[a]s a last resort, hostages and reprisal prisoners may be shot in accordance with international custom and practice.'[33] These concepts are anathema to our modern concepts of human rights and individual freedoms, and to the Geneva Conventions.

Despite its universal condemnation, the taking of hostages is still being used not only by terrorist organizations or other non-state entities in various countries, but, occasionally, even by sovereign states. Most recently, in 1990–1, Iraq resorted to a large-scale hostage-taking,[34] which was condemned by the UN Security Council and by most states.

[31] 11 Trials of War Criminals before the Nuernberg Military Tribunals under Control Council No. 10, at 757, 1249 (1950).
[32] Ibid. 1250.
[33] The *Hostages* case, *United States of America* v. *Wilhelm List et al*, 8 Law Reports of Trials of War Criminals 34, 67 (The United Nations War Crimes Commission 1949).
[34] 'Whatever the purpose, whether for intimidation, concessions, reprisal, or to render areas or legitimate military objects immune from military operations, the taking of hostages is unequivocally and expressly prohibited.' The [US]

HARFLEUR'S SURRENDER

Of considerable legal importance is the fact that, in the negotiations preceding its surrender, the leaders of Harfleur had offered 'to deliver the towne into the kings hands, their lives and goods saved'.' This offer, however, was refused, the King having successfully insisted on 'their bodies and goods to stand at the kings pleasure'.[35] After the surrender, which was achieved by agreement ('composition'),[36] '[t]he souldiors were ransomed, and the towne sacked, to the great gaine of the Englishmen.'[37] The

Department of Defense, Final Report to Congress on Conduct of the Persian Gulf War, Chapters I through VIII, App. O at 04 (April 1992).

The following newspaper report suggests that despite tremendous advances in *de jure* protection, the taking and the killing of hostages is not infrequent in such conflicts as the one in Bosnia-Herzegovina: 'Toward dusk a week ago, a bus carrying 56 Muslims . . . who were being held by Serbian gunmen, halted on a mountain road . . . The hostages, men between 17 and 63, were told . . . that they should lie face down on the floor. . . . According to survivors, the Serbs got off the bus, walked up a hillside, turned and opened fire with a bazooka and automatic weapons. . . . Of the 56 hostages, all but 9 were said to have been killed. . . . The raid was one of a growing number of such attacks across this former Yugoslav republic, which has declared its independence. Some have compared the atrocities to the murder of civilians by the Nazis in occupied Europe.' John F. Burns, 'The Vicious Twist of Death in Bosnia', *International Herald Tribune*, 22 June 1992, 1, col. 1. See also the Report on the Situation of Human Rights in the Territory of the former Yugoslavia submitted by Tadeusz Mazowiecki, Special Rapporteur of the Commission on Human Rights, UN Doc. E/CN.4/1992/S-1/9. The UN Security Council decided (6 Oct. 1992) to request the Secretary-General to establish an impartial Commission of Experts to examine and analyse information on violations of humanitarian law, including grave breaches of the Geneva Conventions (war crimes), in the territory of the former Yugoslavia and especially in Bosnia and Herzegovina. *New York Times*, 7 Oct. 1992, A1, col. 1. By Resolution 808 (22 Feb., 1993), the Security Council decided that such grave violations of international humanitarian law as mass killings and 'ethnic cleansing' in the former Yugoslavia constitute a threat to international peace, that the establishment of an international *ad hoc* war crimes tribunal would contribute to the restoration of international peace, and, therefore, that such a tribunal be established under Chapter VII of the UN Charter.

[35] Holinshed, 23–4 (= R. Holinshed, *Chronicles* (1808), iii. 73). On siege warfare in the modern law of war, see Yoram Dinstein, 'Siege Warfare and the Starvation of Civilians', in Astrid J. M. Delissen and Gerard J. Tanja (eds.), *Humanitarian Law of Armed Conflict: Challenges Ahead (Essays in Honour of Frits Kalshoven)* (1991), 145.

[36] James Hamilton Wylie, *The Reign of Henry the Fifth* (1919), ii. 50.

[37] Holinshed, 24 (= R. Holinshed, *Chronicles* (1808), iii. 73). But see Harold F. Hutchison, *King Henry V* (1967), 14, who argues that Harfleur was not sacked. He explains the deportation order as based on Henry's belief that Harfleur belonged to him, and on his wish to settle Englishmen in place of the deported

wealthy were allowed to pay ransom in return for permission to stay,[38] but 'a greate part of the women and children'[39] were 'expelled out of their habitations . . . parents with their children, yoong maids and old folke went out of the towne gates with heavie harts.'[40] 'The priestes had licence to depart leuyng behinde them their substaunce.'[41] The King then issued a proclamation in England 'that whosoever . . . would inhabit in Harflue, should have his dwelling given him gratis.'[42] Nicolas wrote that according to Henry's proclamation 'whatever tradesman would settle [in Harfleur], should receive a house and household to hold to him and his heirs for ever; in consequence of which, many of the merchants and working classes came over and made it their residence.'[43] Because of his remarkable objectivity, the version presented by the Religieux de Saint-Denys has special credibility:[44]

natives. See also Desmond Seward, *Henry V* (1988), 67–8; and Ernest F. Jacob, *Henry V and the Invasion of France* (1947), 90. Jacob gives the most generous account of Henry's orders: that he prohibited all looting and plundering; that all those willing to swear allegiance to him could retain their goods and possessions; and that burgesses unwilling to submit were to be sent to England until ransom for them were paid. He does, however, mention the deportation of 2,000 of the indigent inhabitants and of women and children. Nicolas wrote that the booty found in Harfleur was distributed among the army, each according to his rank and merits. Nicolas, *Agincourt, supra* note 6, 70–1. Nicolas's version accords with the account in 1513 by the Translator of Livius, according to which all the 'booties and gaine' were 'devided to every man of the King's hoast, after his degree and desert'. Charles Lethbridge Kingsford (ed.), *The First English Life of King Henry the Fifth* (1911), 41. George Makepeace Towle, *The History of Henry the Fifth* (1866), 304, wrote that Henry tried to prevent pillage, but in vain. Despite Holinshed's statement that Harfleur was sacked, historians thus obviously differ on whether it was. Because of his familiarity with Holinshed, Shakespeare must have assumed that Harfleur was sacked.

[38] Hall, 63; Wylie, *supra* note 36, ii. at 58–9.   [39] Hall, 63.

[40] Holinshed, 24 (= R. Holinshed, *Chronicles* (1808) iii. 74.). *The First English Life, supra* note 37, at 41, does not mention the deportation. See also Nicolas, *supra* note 6, at 68–9.

[41] Hall, 63.

[42] Holinshed, 24 (= R. Holinshed, *Chronicles*, (1808), iii. 74). Cf. Geneva Convention No. IV *supra* note 3, Art. 49 (which categorically prohibits deportation of the population of occupied territories and transfer of the occupying power's population to occupied territory). Henry also expelled French population elsewhere, e.g. in Caen. Holinshed, 58 (= R. Holinshed, *Chronicles* (1808), iii. 92). In Rone, however, the terms of surrender included the right of the townspeople to remain in their dwellings.

[43] Nicolas, *supra* note 6, at 71.

[44] See the Intro. by Frank Taylor and John S. Roskell to the *Gesta*, p. xliv.

Il ordonna qu'on épargnât la vie des habitants désarmés; mais il fit conduire les plus riches en Angleterre pour les y retenir captifs jusqu'à ce qu'ils eussent payé rançon. Il laissa les hommes jeunes et valides pour la défense de la ville, en chassa les malades, les pauvres et les vieillards; quant aux femmes, il leur permit, par compassion pour leur sexe, de s'éloigner en toute liberté et sans obstacle avec leurs vêtements et tout ce qu'elles purent emporter.[45]

Although from the modern viewpoint the treatment of the captured Harfleur cannot easily be seen as merciful, more massive violations, particularly widespread killing of the population such as that resorted to by Henry's troops in taking Caen,[46] were avoided. Not surprisingly, Henry's contemporaries, including the French chronicler the Religieux de Saint-Denys, thus considered the treatment of Harfleur lenient.[47]

DEPORTING THE FRENCH AND SETTLING THE ENGLISH

In deciding to resort to wide-scale expulsions, Henry was informed by his conviction that he was retaking possessions that were lawfully his, from which he was merely expelling trespassers, or perhaps even rebels. The *Gesta* thus speaks of the 'lamentation, grief, and tears [of those being expelled] for the loss of their customary although unlawful habitation . . . [and who] by the true judgment of God . . . were proved sojourners where they had thought themselves inhabitants'.[48] Similarly, at the end of the siege of Rouen, Henry told its defenders that the city was not theirs, but his.[49] Henry's belief that he was fighting to retake his lawful property from the rebels was, of course, a constant *leitmotif* in his French campaign, as noted above (see Chapter 3).

---

[45] *Chronique du Religieux de Saint-Denys*, ed. and trans. L. Bellaguet, Collection de documents inédits sur l'histoire de France, ser. 1 (1844) v. 545.

[46] *LW* 121. For the description of the assault on Caen, see Holinshed, 54–5 (= R. Holinshed, *Chronicles* (1808), iii. 90–1).

[47] Wylie, *supra* note 36, at ii. 59. 'Il [Henry V] traita les chevaliers et les écuyers qui avaient été faits prisonniers avec plus de douceur et de générosité qu'on s'y attendait.' *Chronique du Religieux de Saint-Denys, supra* note 45, at v. 545.

[48] *Gesta*, 55. Although, despite these expulsions, Henry treated Harfleur 'fairly humanely', his policy towards the inhabitants was based on his belief that '[i]n resisting him they had rebelled.' Christopher Allmand, *Henry V* (1992) 81.

[49] Jacob, *supra* note 37, at 67–8.

The cruel practices carried out by Henry's ancestors during the Hundred Years War were likely to have been known to him. These harsh precedents may have affected his decisions to deport indigent inhabitants, as in Harfleur, or not to give them quarter, as in Caen, where Henry's men showed no mercy except to women, children, and priests, and where both soldiers and able-bodied inhabitants were put to death.[50]

Among those precedents, two merit attention. First, regarding both deportations of the French and settlement of the English, the case of Calais, which in 1347 unconditionally surrendered to Edward III after a siege, is particularly instructive. It provides both a model for Henry's actions at Harfleur and a reflection of his grand design for French cities. Holinshed reports:

The capteine . . . and all the other capteins and men of name were staied as prisoners, and the common soldiers and other meane people of the towne were licenced to depart and void their houses, leaving all their armor and riches behind them. The king would not have any of the old inhabitants to remaine in the towne, save onlie a priest, and two other ancient personages, such as best knew the customes, lawes and ordinances of the towne. He appointed to send over thither amongst other Englishmen, there to inhabit, 36 burgesses of London, and those of the wealthiest sort, for he meant to people the towne onelie [sic] with Englishmen, for the better and more sure defense thereof.[51]

In addition to settlers brought from England, Henry's officers and soldiers were frequently granted lands in occupied France, creating a base for future settlement. As Curry points out, military settlers were intended to form not only the backbone of the English army in France but also the basis of English settlement. They could ensure the defence of the area, and obviated 'the need for a large, formal, paid army of occupation, not just for financial reasons but also to achieve the desire of just and acceptable possession, in appearance at least'.[52]

---

[50] *LW* 121. On the siege of Rouen, see Christopher T. Allmand, 'The War and Non-Combatant', in Kenneth Fowler (ed.), *The Hundred Years War* (1971), 166.

[51] R. Holinshed, *Chronicles* (1808), iii. 648; Jacob, *supra* note 37, at 90. In Caen the King 'put out fifteene hundred women and impotent persons, replenishing the towne with English people.' Holinshed, 58 (= R. Holinshed, *Chronicles* (1808), iii. 92).

[52] Anne E. Curry, 'The First English Standing Army?—Military Organisation in Lancastrian Normandy, 1420–1450', in C. D. Ross (ed.), *Patronage, Pedigree and Power in Later Medieval England* (1979), 193, 197.

Henry V created in occupied France a system of feudal fiefdoms that was continued for some time after his death by Bedford as regent. Captains who received land grants were supposed not only to accept responsibility for local defence, but also to provide troops to defend other lands held by the English. The eventual failure of this policy of trying to ensure the security of the English conquests through settlements is explained by such factors as intensified resistance by the French population, the pressure from Charles VII, the need for large forces to fight the French, the reluctance of the English settler soldier to fight outside his own locality, and the devaluation (caused by the continuation of the war) of the estates and therefore the increasing difficulty of meeting 'the burden of meeting their feudal obligation[s]'.[53] The need to win Norman support through the return of French estates that had been given to the English settlers prompted the effective termination of the settlement policy after 1435; English captains were thereafter given pensions, rather than land.[54]

SACK AND MASSACRE

The second case, a precedent for sack and massacre, is that of the siege and conquest of Limoges in 1370, led by Edward, the Black Prince (Prince of Wales and Lord of Aquitaine). Because the Bishop of Limoges, who had been Edward's adviser, turned the city over to the French, Edward ordered that it be taken by assault, that terms for surrender be refused, and that quarter be denied.[55] What followed stands out as one of the most horrible slaughters of French civilians, even in the context of the cruel Anglo-French wars. Consider the moving account—with its underlying plea for the principle of humanity and mercy for the human person—by the French chronicler Froissart: 'Nobody was spared. Men, women and children, whatever their age, were all killed by the English. The city was plundered and most of it was burnt and destroyed.'[56] Froissart continued:

Men, women and children threw themselves on their knees before the prince and cried 'mercy, noble lords, mercy!' But he was so incensed by

---

[53] Ibid. 199.   [54] Ibid.   [55] *LW* 1.
[56] Jean Froissart, *Œuvres*, viii. *Chroniques 1370–1377*, ed. Kervyn de Lettenhove (1869), 39. My own translation.

anger that he did not listen to them. The English killed whomever they found, men and women who were not guilty. I do not understand how they did not have mercy of those poor people who were not guilty of any treason. . . . More than 3,000 persons—men, women, and children—were killed that day in Limoges.[57]

By mentioning the innocence of the population at large, especially of the poor and the ignorant who could not have been guilty of any treason, Froissart may have wished to highlight the chivalric principles which required that the lives of the ignorant and the innocent be spared. However, these principles had only a very attenuated relationship to the conduct of a prince who had conquered a town such as Limoges by assault—particularly if he considered the situation to be one of rebellion.

Froissart reported, however, one incident in Limoges which concerned knights and chivalric honour rather than the town's populace, in which the invocation of the law of arms was heeded, resulting in the sparing of human lives. Three French knights surrendered after a long and brave combat and, throwing themselves on the mercy of John of Gaunt and the Earl of Cambridge, asked that their captors comport themselves according to the law of arms: 'Signeur, nous sommes vostres et nous avés conquis; si ouvrés de nous au droit d'armes.' 'Par Dieu, messire Jehan, ce dist li dus de Lancastre, nous ne le vorrions pas faire aultrement, et nous vous retenons comme nos prisonniers.'[58]

The treatment of the Bishop of Limoges (Jean de Cros), who defected from the English to the French side, also merits attention. The Prince of Wales was adamant that the Bishop should be killed.[59] Only the intervention of Pope Urban V, who threatened to declare illegitimate the offspring of the Prince's marriage to the Princess of Kent, spared the Bishop's life and secured his freedom.[60]

Men of the cloth were, as I show later, entitled to immunity from acts of war, which they could lose if they engaged in combat or carried arms. At least, in principle, they could not be deprived of immunity solely because of political leadership. However, the Prince of Wales may have considered the Bishop both a traitor and the leader of a rebellious town.

---

[57] Ibid. (my own translation). According to the historians of Limoges the number was 18,000. Editor's note, ibid. 424.

[58] Ibid. 43.   [59] Ibid. 40.   [60] Ibid. 40, and editor's note, ibid. 424.

Massacres were also perpetrated during Henry's campaigns. In his treatment of Caen, which he captured by assault in 1417, Henry may well have been guided by the example of Limoges. After the English prevailed, they 'slew so manie as they found with weapon in hand, readie to resist them'.[61] Not only was Caen ransacked and the spoils distributed to Henry's soldiers, but 'all the magistrats and governors of the towne [were called] to senat house, where some for their wilfull stubbornesse [in resisting surrender] were adjudged to die, other were sore fined and ransomed.'[62]

PRIVILEGED CATEGORIES OF INHABITANTS AND HENRY'S ORDINANCES

Turning from the historical accounts to the prevailing law, it must be made clear that some norms regulating warfare were agreed upon, at least in theory. The canonistic doctrine of privilege 'was rooted in the notion that the public welfare could be promoted in certain circumstances by granting special rights to groups who served the general interests of the community [such as scholars and clerics]'.[63] The concept of Peace of God,[64] a canonical attempt to humanize warfare, was instrumental in establishing the principle of the immunity of non-combatants, though immunity was frequently disrespected in practice. The latter principle, which was developed considerably earlier,[65] was incorporated into canon law during the papacy of Gregory IX in the thirteenth century. *De treuga et pace* (Of Truces and Peace) listed eight categories of persons 'who should have full security against the ravages of war: clerics, monks, friars, other religious,

---

[61] Holinshed, 54 (= R. Holinshed, *Chronicles* (1808), iii. 90).

[62] Holinshed, 55 (= R. Holinshed, *Chronicles* (1808), iii. 91).

[63] James A. Brundage, *Medieval Canon Law and the Crusader* (1969), 140. The foundations of this doctrine can be found in Gratian's *Decretum*. Ibid. 141. On the latter, see *infra*, notes 65, 68.

[64] Brundage does not appear to distinguish between the Truce of God and the Peace of God. See ibid. 13 n. 40, 161.

[65] For a discussion of Gratian's *Decretum* (*c.*1140), see Frederick H. Russell, *The Just War in the Middle Ages* (1975), 55, 70. Gratian proclaimed immunity from violence for pilgrims, clerics, monks, women and the unarmed poor. Ibid. 70.

pilgrims, travellers, merchants and peasants cultivating the soil'.[66] They were also to be accorded protection for at least some of their property. These classes were composed of persons whose social functions precluded their engaging in war; reciprocity required that war not be waged against them.[67] In elaborating this list, the Church took good care of its own. Strikingly, the classification did not include women, children, and the aged, that is, those physically unable to bear arms.[68] In theory, however, these groups benefited from the parallel, secular code of chivalry, which required the protection of broader categories of persons, defined by weakness and innocence: women, children, the aged, the sick, and other peaceable persons.[69]

Various ordinances of war and admiralty promulgated by the Kings of England in the Middle Ages are also relevant (see Chapter 8 below).[70] Of these, the most comprehensive and important regarding war on land are the Ordinances of War made by King Richard II at Durham (1385)[71] and the Ordinances of War made by King Henry V at Mantes (1419).[72] The latter obviously drew on the former, particularly in the provision that prohibited stealing from the church and killing or raping women.[73] The penalty for violating these prohibitions was death. Apart from military discipline, the ordinances of Henry V imposed such humanitarian measures as prohibiting the taking of children under the age of 14 as prisoners and protecting women confined by childbirth[74] and peasants, whose agricultural tools and work animals were safeguarded from seizure. This was not

[66] Johnson, *supra* note 13, at 127; Peter Haggenmacher, *Grotius et la doctrine de la guerre juste*, (1983), 268–72. The Magna Carta (12 June 1215), Art. 41, repr. in Richard L. Perry and John C. Cooper (eds.), *Sources of Our Liberties* (1959) 11, 17 already recognized, on the basis of reciprocity, the immunity of merchants in time of war.

[67] Johnson, *supra* note 13, at 132.

[68] Women and the unarmed poor, however, were included in the protected categories in Gratian's *Decretum*. Russell, *supra* note 65, at 70.

[69] Johnson, *supra* note 13, at 135–6. Both women and unarmed priests were protected by King Henry V's Ordinances of War.

[70] See generally Travers Twiss, Intro. to The Black Book of Admiralty, repr. in 1 Monumenta Juridica, i. (1871), pp. lviii–lxxvii.

[71] These ordinances (ibid. 453) are in French. See ibid., p. lxxvi. On the official use of French in England in the 13th and 14th c., see ibid., pp. xlv–lvi. For the text of the Ordinances of Richard II, see ibid. 453.

[72] Ibid. 459. These ordinances were probably written in Latin, but there is no complete Latin text extant. Editor's notes, ibid. 282–3.

[73] See *infra* note 188.   [74] See also *infra* note 196.

the first time that Henry had promulgated laws protecting the civilian population of France from the excesses of his soldiery. Soon after reaching Harfleur in 1415, Henry issued a proclamation, mentioned by Holinshed that prohibited under penalty of death such crimes as setting houses on fire and violating churches or the person of women. The proclamation also prohibited violating the person of priests, unless they were armed;[75] in reality, ecclesiastics often engaged in warfare. Henry found it necessary to reaffirm these strictures by issuing a similar proclamation after the conquest of Harfleur, forbidding his troops to devastate the area or to plunder the inhabitants, except for food and other necessities of life.[76] In Chapter 11 we shall see how widely Henry's orders differed from Sir John Fastolf's advice of 1435 for the conduct of war.

Writers on *jus gentium* contemporaneous with Shakespeare recognized several protected categories of non-combatants. Vitoria asserted that even when fighting against Turks it was unlawful to kill children, because they are innocent, and women, because they are presumed innocent.[77] In war between Christians, 'harmless agricultural folk', other 'peaceable civilian population', 'foreigners or guests', 'clerics and members of a religious order', who were all presumed innocent and therefore could not be killed.[78] The presumption of innocence could be rebutted by showing that the person concerned took part in the hostilities. Although Vitoria circumscribed the prohibition on killing innocents by the necessities of war ('when there is no other means of carrying on the operations of a just war'),[79] he articulated a precursor of the modern principle of proportionality:[80]

[75] Nicolas, *supra* note 6, at 52–3. According to Holinshed: 'At his first comming on land, he caused proclamation to be made, that no person should be so hardie on paine of death, either to take anie thing out of anie church that belonged to the same, or to hurt or doo anie violence either to priests, women, or anie such as should be found without weapon or armor, and not readie to make resistance.' Holinshed, 21–2 (= R. Holinshed, *Chronicles* (1808), iii, 72).
[76] Nicolas, *supra* note 6, at 81–2. See also *infra* text at notes 188–199 below; Hutchison, *supra* note 37 above, at 111. Hutchison believes that 'such regulations were common to most medieval armies, and the fact that they were issued at all argues as much for their regrettable necessity as for the mercy . . . of those who made them.' Ibid. Henry issued similar regulations also in Rouen in 1421. See Intro. by Frank Taylor and John S. Roskell to *Gesta*, 26 n. 1.
[77] Vitoria, 179 (36).   [78] Ibid.   [79] Ibid. 179 (37).
[80] See Additional Protocol I, *supra* note 2, Art. 51 (5)(b), which prohibits as indiscriminate an attack 'which may be expected to cause incidental loss of

[If] little effect upon the ultimate issue of the war is to be expected from the storming of a fortress . . . wherein are many innocent folk, it would not be right, for the purpose of assailing a few guilty, to slay the many innocent by use of fire or engines of war or other means likely to overwhelm indifferently both innocent and guilty.[81]

Gentili, for his part, insisted that '[c]hildren should always be spared, and so should women.'[82] '[W]omen, because they cannot handle arms, are treated like the clergy . . . . [T]hey are spared.'[83] He also advocated the protection of farmers, traders and foreigners.[84] Suárez argued that the innocent include children, women, and all those unable to bear arms, by virtue of natural law; ambassadors, by virtue of *jus gentium*; and members of religious orders and priests, by virtue of canon law. All other persons forming part of a hostile state (which excludes strangers and foreigners) are considered enemies.[85] In practice, these rules may have been breached more frequently than respected, as was claimed by the military law expert Ayala, who wrote that the canons requiring that 'clergy, monks, converts, foreigners, merchants, and country folk' be spared had been abrogated by contrary usage.[86]

The 1785 Treaty of Amity and Commerce between the United States and Prussia exemplifies the convergence of the canonical and chivalric lists of protected persons. This treaty, cited by the US Supreme Court in the *Paquete Habana*,[87] reflects the medieval

civilian life, injury to civilians, damage to civilian objects, or a combination thereof, which would be excessive in relation to the concrete and direct military advantage anticipated.'

[81] Vitoria, at 179 (37). See Haggenmacher, *supra* note 66, at 275–6.

[82] Gentili, ii. 251.

[83] Ibid. Gentili believed that women (ibid. 251–4) and clergy (ibid. 427–8) who take up arms lose their immunity. Regarding armed clergy's loss of protection from acts of war, see also Pisan, 235–6, 257, 283.

[84] Gentili, ii. 261–9.　　　　　[85] Suárez, 843.　　　　　[86] Ayala, 45.

[87] 175 US 677, 690–1 (1900). Article XXIII of the Treaty of Amity and Commerce between the United States and Prussia, 9 July and 10 Sept. 1785, provided that in case of war: 'the merchants of either country then residing in the other shall be allowed to remain nine months to collect their debts and settle their affairs, and may depart freely, carrying off all their effects without molestation or hindrance. And all women and children, scholars of every faculty, cultivators of the earth, artizans, manufacturers, and fishermen, unarmed and inhabiting unfortified towns, villages, or places, and in general all others whose occupations are for the common subsistence and benefit of mankind, shall be allowed to continue

concepts of innocence and social function. Modern international law differs in that it is informed primarily by the notions of civilian status and the immunity of civilians from attack, into which the concept of innocence metamorphosed. It focuses on the protection of individual civilians and the civilian population,[88] with the exception of the special protection granted to the Red Cross and other humanitarian organizations.[89] Additional measures regarding children and women are subsumed under the protection of the civilian population. With the exception of the Red Cross and medical and religious personnel, beneficial social function as a criterion for protection has become obsolete.

LOSS OF PRIVILEGED STATUS: WOMEN AND CLERGY

Armed Women

Henry's caveat limiting the immunity of women and clergy to those who were not armed requires comment. The chivalric presumption that women were not strong enough to carry arms and engage in warfare was clearly rebuttable. Women could and in some cases did engage in warfare, usually in the defence of cities under siege. Sometimes, although rarely, women even assumed leadership roles, as did Joan of Arc. In German medieval aristocracy, widows in a number of instances led their deceased husbands' armies into battle. Professor Leyser mentions the case of one such 'bellicose widow, the Welf princess Sophia [who] joined her brother Henry the Proud at the siege of Falkenstein (near Regensburg) with 800 knights in 1129 shortly after the death of her second husband. She could safely be left in charge of the operations when her brother was called away to another and more urgent siege.'[90] Of course, women who engaged in warfare

their respective employments, and shall not be molested in their persons, nor shall their houses or goods be burnt or otherwise destroyed, nor their fields wasted by the armed force of the enemy, into whose power by the events of war they may happen to fall; but if anything is necessary to be taken from them for the use of such armed force, the same shall be paid for at a reasonable price.' 8 Stat. 84, TS No. 292, 8 Bevans 78, 85–6.

[88] See e.g. Additional Protocol I, *supra* note 2, Arts. 50–2.
[89] Ibid., Art. 81.
[90] Karl J. Leyser, 'The German Aristocracy from the Ninth to the Early Twelfth Century', 41 Past and Present 25, 51 (1968).

would lose their immunity.[91] Gentili advocated treating women combatants on the basis of equality with men: 'in so far as women play the part of men they are men and not women. And if that were not so, all places could easily be held by using women as their guards and defenders.'[92] He rejected the view of those who, on the basis of the Old Testament's prohibition of women's putting on the dress of men, contended that because women put on men's attire, they could be treated 'with less respect than the laws of war require'. Gentili condemned as a pretext the invocation of this excuse when Joan of Arc 'was slain by her English enemies'.[93]

Except in their occasional participation in defending besieged towns, women were most typically involved in the life of a medieval army as the wives of soldiers. Francis Grose, extolling the usefulness of army wives, especially for soldiers 'of the lower condition',[94] urged that because they bought victuals, cooked, and laundered (they were sometimes called their 'husbands' mules'), they should not be banished from the armies.[95]

Women prostitutes were frequently involved in the life of the medieval army. To maintain discipline in the army, English kings harshly punished prostitutes who violated bans on entering or remaining in the army's camps. Henry V himself promulgated a barbaric order whereby one of the 'publick and common whore[s]' who remained, after one admonition, in a castle or fortress taken by his troops, was to be punished by 'fracture of the left arm'.[96]

Armed Clergy

In restricting the immunity of the clergy to unarmed churchmen, Henry was simply acknowledging the reality that English kings (including himself) exacted military service from the Church for the defence of the realm. He assumed, of course, that his enemy, the King of France, would do no less. Before the end of May 1415, Henry ordered the bishops to array the forces of the clergy

---

[91] Giovanni da Legnano allowed reprisals against the women soldiers of Bologna, ch. 136, p. 318.

[92] Gentili, ii. 253.   [93] Ibid.

[94] Francis Grose, *Military Antiquities* (1786), i. 261.   [95] Ibid. 261–2.

[96] Grose, ii. 79.

by 16 July. All the clergy were to be armed for the defence of the kingdom.[97] All the tenants-in-chief were convened by the King to hear of his plans to invade Normandy, and to prepare to accompany him.[98] Francis Grose notes that '[a]mong the persons indenting to raise soldiers for King Henry V, are several bishops: and at the battle of Floddon Field, there were slain of the Scots, one archbishop, two bishops and four abbots.'[99]

Among the most enthusiastic bishop warriors was Henry Spencer (or Spenser), the bishop of Norwich, whom Holinshed described as 'a man more fit for the field than the church, & better skilled . . . in arms than in divinitie'.[100] During the reign of Richard II (in 1383) Spenser led to Flanders, and himself commanded, an invading army.[101] Spenser was in fact so anxious to embark on this expedition that he disregarded the King's order to return to the court, claiming 'that the time would not then permit him to staie [in France] longer'.[102] For this act of disobedience Spenser was punished by the King's seizure of his temporalities.[103]

According to McNab, the first writs of array were issued to the clergy by Edward III on 6 July 1368,[104] and subsequent writs followed in 1372 and 1373. Similar writs were issued on several occasions by Richard II and Henry IV, and finally by Henry V in 1415 and in 1418.[105] These writs called for the clergy to be armed as a home guard or militia for the defence of the kingdom.[106] By a specified date, each bishop was to certify to Chancery both the number and the armament of his arrayed clergy.[107]

---

[97] James Hamilton Wylie, *The Reign of Henry the Fifth* (1914), i. 479–80.

[98] William Stubbs, *The Constitutional History of England* (1880), i. 61–4.

[99] Grose, i. 71.   [100] R. Holinshed, *Chronicles* (1807), ii. 745.

[101] Ibid.; see also ibid. 757–8.   [102] Ibid. 758.   [103] Ibid. 762.

[104] A full translation of this writ is given in Grose, i. 67–9. Grose attributes the writ's date to 6 July 1369. The writ, addressed to the Archbishop of Canterbury, invokes the breach of the peace by the French, their entry into Calais, and their threat to invade the Kingdom, to 'cause all abbots, priors, religious, and other ecclesiastical persons . . . to be armed, arrayed, and furnished with competent arms (to wit) every one between the said ages . . . and these to be arranged into thousands, hundreds, and twenties, so that they may be ready and prepared to set forth . . . against our said enemies.'

[105] Bruce McNab, 'Obligations of the Church in English Society: Military Arrays of the Clergy, 1369–1418', in W. C. Jordan, B. McNab and T. F. Ruiz (eds.), *Order and Innovation in the Middle Ages: Essays in Honour of J. Strayer* (1976), 293, 294.

[106] Ibid. 295.   [107] Ibid. 300.

On the whole, the clergy willingly acquiesced in royal demands for military service, perhaps because they were made during a particularly nationalistic period that was characterized by strong anti-French and anti-Scottish sentiments.[108] Of course, under the feudal system, the great clergy owed military obligations to the crown. Although according to the feudal law the King was entitled to the corporal service of all his immediate vassals, including the clerical tenants-in-chief, the practice of commutation of service through the payment of a levy at a uniform rate per knight (scutage) became increasingly common.[109] Under Edward I and later, summonses requiring personal service were usually followed by writs allowing financial substitutions for personal service in certain circumstances, in the form of fines *pro servicio*.[110] It was often true, therefore, as Francis Grose suggested, that 'after all, the . . . summonses [to the clergy] were issued rather with an intent to draw a commutation from their treasury, than to call them to the field.'[111]

Resistance to service and to its commutation into financial payments was relatively rare. A famous example of such resistance was provided by Bishop Hugh of Lincoln. In response to Richard I's order (1196) that a force be mustered for the approaching war with Philip Augustus of France, Bishop Hugh of Lincoln bravely asserted that he owed military service to the King only in England and not abroad (*extra metas angliae*). Richard then ordered that Hugh's possessions, as well as those of the Bishop of Salisbury who agreed with Hugh, be seized by the fisc.[112] From the full execution of the order in the case of the Bishop of Salisbury, Chew drew the conclusion that the claim of the clergy to immunity from service outside England had not been established by 1197.[113]

It should be noted that Hugh admitted that service was owed in respect of the lands of his see, in England, and that it was service of knights that it owed the King. But this is different from

---

[108] Ibid. 313.

[109] Helena M. Chew, *The English Ecclesiastical Tenants-in-Chief and Knight Service* (1932), 37. See also I. J. Sanders, *Feudal Military Service in England* (1956), 16–21, 54–5.

[110] Ibid. 79.   [111] Grose, i. 70.

[112] Karl J. Leyser, 'The Angevin Kings and the Holy Man', in *St Hugh of Lincoln* (1987), 62–3.

[113] Chew, *supra* note 109, at 42–3.

Hugh's admitting that he ought personally to lead his knights into battle. Canonically, it was improper for a bishop, being in priest's orders, so to do, though of course, some did. And some took a leading part in directing a campaign, but took care in the field to confine themselves to a non-combatant or a priestly role (exhorting, praying, etc.).

English clergy served the kings of England in their French wars not merely on the basis of legal duty. Indeed, the Church supported Edward III's military campaigns with enthusiasm and patriotism.[114] Clergy were active in Edward's diplomatic service; graduates in civil or canon law were 'the closest thing to an international lawyer in the fourteenth century'.[115] Clergy served as instruments of propaganda, and in some cases '[t]he lure of war was such that some ecclesiastics even took up arms [and] soldier clerk [including several warrior bishops] was still very much a reality.'[116] It was only later in Edward's reign, when setbacks occurred, that after a long acquiescence some members of the clergy questioned the practicality and the morality of the war.[117]

Francis Grose suggested that, in addition to their love of glory, great ecclesiastics believed that practice in the use of arms would better prepare them for defence against the encroachments by the great barons. Had the great churchmen in fact wholly disliked serving in wars, they could perhaps have had their obligation to serve abrogated, given the power of the Church and the many arguments against the military service by men of the cloth.[118] French abbots frequently impoverished their abbeys by fitting out their equipages for war.[119]

The clergy also assisted the belligerent power through spying, a role facilitated by the clergy's mobility between religious institutions in England and those in France. Faced with the threat of spying, both Edward III and Richard II took measures, including orders issued to heads of monasteries to refuse alien clergy admission to their houses. Henry V went even further, in completely excluding alien clergy from England.[120]

---

[114] W. M. Ormrod, *The Reign of Edward III* (1990), 131.   [115] Ibid.
[116] Ibid. 132.   [117] Ibid. 133.   [118] Grose, i. 71–2.   [119] Ibid.
[120] J. B. Alban and Christopher. T. Allmand, 'Spies and Spying in the Fourteenth Century', in Allmand (ed.), *War, Literature, and Politics in the Late Middle Ages* (1976), 90–3.

Grose complained that the widespread practice of ecclesiastics serving in and sometimes commanding armies clashed with the 'canons, councils, and popes [that] unanimously forbid ecclesiastics of all degrees to use the sword, or engage in any military operations'.[121] In some cases, the clergy's readiness to fight without violating the letter of the law led to disingenuosness and hypocrisy, of which an egregious example is provided by Philip de Dreux, Bishop of Beauvais. As told by Grose,

> to avoid offending the letter of the canon and other regulations, [Philip de Dreux] did not use a sword, but fought with a mace, of which he made so powerful an use, that at the battle of Bovines, he beat down Long Sword earl of Salisbury; how he contrived to avoid the spilling of blood, is not so evident, since it would be next to impossible, to beat out a man's brains, without causing the prohibited effusion.[122]

Medieval and Renaissance writers on *jus gentium* devoted considerable attention to the question of whether clerics had the right, or were under the obligation, to go to war. Giovanni da Legnano allowed clerics summoned by a Pope to go to war, but not those summoned by a secular prince. He permitted the former even to kill, but only in self-defence.[123] More realistically, Honoré Bouvet took account of the feudal obligations of high clergy as holders of fiefs from the King. He thus cited the opinion of those who said that bishops and other clerks who held countries, baronies, castles or fortresses as fief-holders from the King were obliged to accompany him in his wars and battles.[124] Following Bouvet, Christine de Pisan recognized the feudal obligations of clerks as fief-holders from princes, and especially of kings of France, to go to war and to use force in self-defence.[125] She admonished the English clergy for helping the King to pursue the war with their revenues, rents, and counsel, however, without acknowledging their feudal obligations to serve the King.[126] She concluded that if a clergyman, who should attend to his religious and spiritual duties, nevertheless went to war, he did not deserve to be spared and could be put in prison. Her refusal to recognize the obligations of the English clergy can perhaps be explained by her patriotic sentiments toward France.

---

[121] Grose, i. 70.   [122] Ibid.   [123] Legnano, 264.

[124] Bouvet, 144–5. Bouvet does not question the right of a clerk to defend his temporal possessions by force of arms, ibid. 140–1.

[125] Pisan, 283–4.   [126] Ibid. 235–6.

Suárez supported without hesitation the right of those prelates of the Church who were sovereign in temporal affairs to declare a just war.[127] Ecclesiastical law, though not the divine law, forbade clerks to engage in war, but the Pope could grant a dispensation from this prohibition. Highlighting the close link between *jus in bello* and *jus ad bellum* which characterized his era, Suárez believed that in an unjust war all killing, whether by priests or others, was prohibited; in a just war, however, '[i]f a cleric . . . while legitimately a combatant, kills or mutilates some one by his own hand, but does so in absolutely necessary defence of his life, he does not contract an irregularity.'[128] The reality was of course different. Clerics participating in wars seldom hesitated to kill in offensive operations. Holinshed thus reported that 'preests and religious men that were with the bishop [of Norwich during his Flanders invasion of 1383] fought most egerlie, some one of them slaieng sixteene of the enimies.'[129] Lower clerics were not to participate in wars, but if they did, and if the war was just, they committed a sin against religion or obedience, but not against secular justice. The authority which the prince gave them to engage in war sufficed, therefore, to exempt them from making restitution of goods acquired in that war.[130]

The cleric's right to engage in war must, however, be distinguished from the immunity of ecclesiastical persons and property. Suárez stated that if men sought retreat in a church solely to protect their own lives, they should enjoy ecclesiastical immunity, but the use of a church as a citadel or as a defensive camp deprived it of such immunity and made it subject to attack and burning.[131] Henry was therefore within the law in denying immunity to armed French clerics, and to armed women. Similarly, in the modern law of war civilians lose civilian status by taking a direct part in hostilities.

TREATMENT OF CITIES CONQUERED AFTER SIEGE

How, then, can the dire threats of Shakespeare's Henry be reconciled with the existing and emerging norms protecting women

---

[127] Suárez, ii. 810–13.

[129] R. Holinshed, *Chronicles* (1807), ii. 759.

[131] Ibid. 845.

[128] Ibid. 813.

[130] Suárez, 813.

and others from the ravages of war? The distinction in medieval law between the treatment of both combatants and civilians in captured territory or on the battlefield, on the one hand, and their treatment in a besieged city or fortress[132] that was taken by 'assault',[133] on the other hand, suggests an explanation. Unmitigated brutality was reserved for the latter:

In a city taken by storm almost any licence was condoned by the law. Only churches and churchmen were technically secure, but even they were not often spared. Women could be raped, and men killed out of hand. All the goods of the inhabitants were regarded as forfeit. . . . The prospect of this free run of his lusts for blood, spoil and women was a major incentive to a soldier to persevere in the rigours which were likely to attend a protracted siege.[134]

Notwithstanding the importance of such famous battles as Crécy and Agincourt, medieval warfare turned far more on sieges of strongholds than on pitched battles.[135] Only through the conquest of fortresses could a territory be effectively occupied. Resistance therefore was grimly viewed and severely punished. Both the goods and the lives of the inhabitants of a conquered town 'were forefeit [*sic*] for the contumacious disregard of a prince's summons to surrender. . . . [S]poliation was not an act of

---

[132] On sieges, see generally Michael Walzer, *Just and Unjust Wars* (2nd edn. 1992), ch. 10.

[133] i..e., following an unconditional surrender, whether or not the city was stormed. *LW* 122. A city that did not surrender by a treaty (*appointment*) could be taken by assault, ibid. 119. Medieval strategists taught that a fortress could be reduced 'by methods of drought [poisoning or cutting the supply of water], famine [blockade] or fight [assault].' Wylie, *supra* note 36, at ii. 32. The prohibition of starvation of civilians as a method of warfare is of quite recent origin. See Additional Protocol I, *supra* note 2, Art. 54. See generally Dinstein, *supra* note 35, at 145. Siege should not be confused with sanctions or a blockade imposed by the Security Council of the United Nations. Interpreting its Resolution 661 of 6 August 1990, repr. in 29 ILM 1325 (1990), which imposed sanctions on Iraq and prohibited importation of foodstuffs, except in humanitarian circumstances, the Security Council recognized, in Resolution 666 of 13 September 1990 (repr. in 29 ILM at 1330), that foodstuffs might have to be supplied to the civilian population of Iraq or Kuwait to relieve human suffering. See Theodor Meron, 'Prisoners of War, Civilians and Diplomats in the Gulf Crisis', 85 AJIL 104, 107–8 (1991). See also Additional Protocol I, *supra* note 2, at Art. 70.

[134] *LW* 121–2.

[135] Johnson, *supra* note 13, at 133. Keen writes that the 'stories of great sieges . . . loom large in the history of the Hundred Years War; in fact they are its turning points.' *LW* 119. See also Geoffrey Parker, *The Military Revolution* (1988), 7–9; and Malcom G. A. Vale, *War and Chivalry* (1981), 147.

war, but the sentence of justice.'[136] On the authority of Deuteronomy, Vitoria argued that, in a city of the enemy that has been
taken by force, the killing of 'all who have borne arms against
us' was justified.[137] He thus appeared to be advocating particularly severe sanctions against rebels, persons who breached oaths
and joined with the prince's adversaries (as contrasted to foreign
combatants). This question is explored more fully below in
Chapter 11.

In a similar vein, Henry ordered, after the surrender of Loviers
which had resisted him, that 'the gunners that had discharged
anie peece against the Englishmen should suffer death'.[138] A city
such as Harfleur, which 'held out till it had to yield unconditionally was at the mercy of its captor, to be given up to plunder or
ransomed according to his will. Its population [could be] . . . subjected to pillage, slaughter and rape.'[139]

Vitoria's reluctant recognition that the sacking of a city was
legal if it was 'necessary for the conduct of the war or as a deterrent to the enemy or as a spur to the courage of the troops'[140]
indicates that the threats made by Shakespeare's Henry com-
ported with the norms prevailing during the Hundred Years War.
However, because such sacking resulted 'in many horrors and
cruelties, enacted beyond all humane limits by a barbarous soldiery, such as slaughter and torture of the innocent, rape of virgins, dishonor of matrons, and looting of temples',[141] delivering
up a city to be sacked 'without the greatest necessity and weighti-
est reason' was unjust.[142]

These harsh norms, seldom questioned in medieval times, were
challenged by Renaissance writers on *jus gentium*. As was often
the case, Gentili led the way in promoting the humanization of
the law.[143] With eloquence and clarity, he proclaimed that '[t]hese
are called the rights of humanity and the laws of war, which
order the sparing of those who surrender.'[144] If conditions of

---

[136] *LW* 123. While the penalties for holding out against a siege were brutal, a
captain who surrendered a town without siege while there was a chance of
defending it would be guilty of treason toward another prince. *LW* 124–5. See
also Ayala, 233.　　　　　　　　　　　　[137] Deuteronomy 20; Vitoria, 182 (45).

[138] Holinshed, 69 (= R. Holinshed, *Chronicles* (1808), iii. 99).

[139] Edward P. Cheyney, *The Dawn of a New Era: 1250–1453* (1936), 165.

[140] Vitoria, 184 (52).　　　[141] Ibid. 184–5 (52).　　　[142] Ibid. 185 (52).

[143] See also Haggenmacher, *supra* note 66, at 277.

[144] Gentili, ii. 216. Invoking the law of Lycurgus and the Greeks, Gentili wrote
(ibid. 211) that 'when the victory was assured the slaying of the enemy should cease.'

surrender are stipulated, the law of nature requires that they be observed.[145] Even unconditional surrenders, 'surrender . . . at discretion', may not lead to licence with regard to 'property, life, and honour' because discretion ought to be understood as 'the discretion of a good man'.[146]

TREATMENT OF COMMANDERS WHO SURRENDERED TO ADVERSARIES

Given the terrible dangers to which a surrender at discretion or a conquest by assault could lead, the temptation to surrender on terms that would guarantee the lives and the property of the besieged garrison and the population must have been great. But too early a surrender created a countervailing danger, at least for the captain himself. A captain who resisted the command to surrender was treated by the besieging prince as a rebel (the status of rebels under medieval law of arms is considered below in Chapter 11), whose own life and property, as well as the lives and the property of those under his command, including civilians, was at the mercy of the prince. Surrendering, or at least surrendering too early and without overwhelming compulsion (for example, when food and supplies ran out), would prompt his former master, the prince whose domain was now being lost to a new claimant, to view him as a traitor. The captain of a besieged town was thus often faced with an impossible choice: condemning the town to destruction at the hands of the invading prince, or risking harsh treatment and probable execution by his former lord, into the hands of whom he might yet fall.[147]

In important cases, English nobles who surrendered towns or fortresses entrusted to them were tried before the Parliament.[148] Because surrender involved breach of a knight's promise not to deliver the town up to anyone except his prince, or to the prince's heirs or to others duly authorized by him, the captain who surrendered was dishonoured and chivalric rules were breached. It followed that every knight could charge the captain who surrendered with treason before courts of chivalry, or challenge him to a duel, even if the former prince refrained from so

[145] Gentili, ii. 219.   [146] Ibid. 227.   [147] See *LW* 123–8.
[148] Grose, ii. 53 and nn.

doing.[149] In his Chronicle of the reign of Richard II, Holinshed reported one well-known case of such a duel (1380), in which a knight, Sir John Ansley, accused an esquire, Thomas Katrington, of treason for selling the fortress of Saint-Saveur in Normandy to the French, at a time when the men, munitions, and food available to the defendant made the defence of the fortress possible, and 'offered . . . to trie the quarell by combat'.[150] In this case, the accuser ('appellant') had a proprietary claim to the castle, but such challenges could be made on the basis of the challenger's general interest in the upholding of chivalric rules, without a showing of any special interest. Although judicial duels still occurred in the fourteenth century, the Ansley–Katrington combat attracted a crowd 'thought to exceed that of the kings coronation, so desirous men were to behold a sight so strange and unaccustomed'.[151] Sir John Ansley's victory over Katrington was considered proof of the accusation.[152]

The 1377 trials of William de Weston and Sir John de Gomenez before the Parliament, for delivering to the enemies of King Richard II certain castles entrusted to them, illustrate the various legal and factual issues implicated,[153] as well as the policy of exemplary punishment and deterrence which such trials embodied. This policy was reflected in the following statement by the Parliament:

that all such captains as had by their misbehaviour lost or delivered up either castles or towns, might be made to answer for it to this parliament, and according to their desert, be severely punished by the award of the lords and baronage, to prevent the effects of the bad example which they have given to others, who are governors of towns and castles.

The key issue in these trials was whether the captain had no choice but to surrender at the time he did. William, for instance, argued that his requests for reinforcements went unanswered, that he was besieged by a force of several thousand men, assisted by artillery, that he resisted several days of bombardment, and

---

[149] *LW* 127.   [150] R. Holinshed, *Chronicles* (1807), ii. 727.
[151] Ibid.   [152] See *LW* 127.
[153] Rolls of the Parliament, repr. in Grose, ii. App. II. Weston was sentenced to be drawn and hanged for treason, although the crime was not so classified. He obtained pardon. J. G. Bellamy, *The Law of Treason in England in the Later Middle Ages* (1970), 110.

that once there remained of the whole garrison only thirty-eight healthy man, the defence became untenable and he was 'by force obliged to surrender, to save the goods and lives of the men'. However, after surrendering, William sold his supplies to the victors, suggesting to the Parliament that he could have held out longer.[154] Lord John de Gomenez argued in his defence that the

. . . town and castle of Arde were so weak, that he could not keep them against so great a power of the enemies as were there and ready to assaile the said towne and castle, and therefore he caused all the knights, esquires and other inhabitants of the said town, to be assembled, and informed them of the danger of the said town and the force of the enemy, and by the common council and assent of the said knights, esquires and others; he went forth out of the said town to treat with them, in order to save the subjects of our lord the king, within the said town and castle of Arde.

This version was contested in the Parliament by another knight who claimed that he had been present in Arde and that the council had never consented to the surrender, 'but that he was always ready to dye or live on the safe guard thereof'.

The death verdicts handed down by the Parliament in both cases emphasized that the surrenders were not justified by real compulsion or duress, and implicitly acknowledged the possibility of lawful surrenders.[155] To surrender while the supplies lasted,

---

[154] *LW* 125.

[155] The verdict addressed to William thus read: '. . . that you William didst surrender the said castle of Outhrewyk to the enemies of our lord the king aforesaid, without any hardship or defect of victuals, contrary to your allegiance and undertaking aforesaid the lords abovenamed sitting here in full parliament, adjudge you to death; and that you be drawn and hanged.'

The verdict addressed to John read: '. . . and now you John, without duresse, want of victuals, artillery, or other things necessary for the defence of the said town and castle of Arde, without commandement of our lord the king, have in an evil manner delivered and surrendered to the enemies of our lord the king, by your own default, against appearance of right or reason, and contrary to your undertaking before-mentioned; by which the lords aforesaid, here in full parliament do adjudge you to suffer death, and because that you are a gentleman and a banneret, and have served the said [king] in his wars, and are no liege-man of our lord the king; you shall be beheaded without having any other judgement.' Grose, ii. App. II.

Bellamy perceptively analysed the crime of surrendering a fortress to the enemy. While in some cases this crime was treated as treason, in others it was described as treachery and rebellion, or even as negligence, misprision, and trespass. Neither the Parliament nor the crown was interested in permanently classifying as treason the crime of surrendering a fortress to the enemy, which did not

and as long as there were any prospects for help, could be regarded as treason. At the siege of Harfleur, the French surrendered only when it became clear that Charles was unable to relieve the besieged town. Significantly, Henry agreed to the request of Harfleur to defer surrender until the prospects of relief appeared doomed. Shakespeare's Governor of Harfleur gives a realistic expression to the situation of a besieged town which can no longer hope for help:

> GOVERNOR   Our expectation hath this day an end.
> The Dauphin, whom of succours we entreated,
> Returns us that his powers are yet not ready
> To raise so great a siege. Therefore, dread King,
> We yield our town and lives to thy soft mercy.
> Enter our gates, dispose of us and ours,
> For we no longer are defensible.
>
> (*Henry V*, III. iii. 127–33)

Under modern military law of many countries, whether a commander's surrender to an invading army was justified depends on considerations resembling those that informed chivalric customs in the Middle Ages. Military legislators are reluctant to prescribe in detail the circumstances in which a commander may surrender his post to the enemy. As in the Middle Ages, the commander must choose between imminent danger to his own life and the lives of his soldiers, and the more attenuated risk of being tried by a court martial for treason or cowardly behaviour.[156]

---

amount to a wilful support of the king's enemies, and as a military offence was triable in the court of chivalry. It was probably not triable under the common law or the statute of treasons of 1352. Nevertheless such crimes 'were treason in all but name which lay outside the common law, being in fact offences against the king's majesty and prerogatives.' Bellamy, *supra* note 153, at 111.

In the Middle Ages, as Keen points out, it was a common practice in surrender agreements to stipulate that a town be surrendered, if it was not relieved by a date stipulated in the agreement (*LW* 128–9). It was also a not uncommon practice for garrison commanders, in their indentures, to stipulate that if besieged they were only obliged to resist for a stated period, after which, if not relieved, they could lawfully surrender. A variant was that the contracting prince agreed he was bound to relieve his captain if the captain was besieged. Kenneth Fowler, *The King's Lieutenant: Henry of Grosmont, First Duke of Lancaster 1310–1361* (1969), 232 (indenture of war between Edward III and Henry of Lancaster, 13 March 1345), App. IV.

[156] See Art. 99 of the US Code of Military Justice ('Misbehavior before the enemy'), 10 USCA sec. 899 (1983): 'Any member of the armed forces who before or in the presence of the enemy . . . (2) shamefully abandons, surrenders, or delivers

DENIAL OF QUARTER

Three of the elements in Henry's ultimatum merit more detailed comment: the denial of quarter, and the threats of rape and of pillage. The chivalric code of conduct 'required that a knight vanquished in battle be given quarter rather than being killed, that when taken prisoner he must be treated as a gentleman, and that he be ransomed for a reasonable sum not beyond his means to pay'.[157] Of course, a knight who surrendered might refuse to enter into a contract to pay ransom and would be killed or condemned to captivity, or would have to fight on and risk being killed on the battlefield. The latter possibility is heroically depicted by Shakespeare's Henry:

> KING   Herald, save thou thy labour.
> Come thou no more for ransom, gentle herald.
> They shall have none, I swear, but these my joints—
> Which if they have as I will leave 'em them,
> Shall yield them little. Tell the Constable.

(IV. iii. 122–6)

It was unclear, however, to what extent these protective rules applied to 'non-knightly infantry' (commoners and peasants who, not infrequently, were massacred[158]) and to non-Christians.[159] It should not be assumed that only gentlemen were given the chance to ransom themselves. Honoré Bouvet, writing before Agincourt, thus complained that 'excessive payments and ransoms [were demanded] without pity or mercy . . . from the poor

up any command, unit, place, or military property which it is his duty to defend . . . shall be punished by death or such other punishment as a court-martial may direct.' *United States Manual for Courts-Martial* (1984), promulgated by Executive Order 12473. The manual explains that 'surrender or abondonment of a command, unit, place, ship, or military property by a person charged with its defense can be justified only by the utmost necessity or extremity.' Ibid. (c) *Explanation* 2 (d). Cf. this provision: '[w]hosoever yieldeth up any town, fort, magazine, victuals, armes, ammunition, or that motioneth any such thing, but upon extremity, and that to the governor, or in councell, shall be executed as a traitor.' Laws and Ordinances of War issued by the Earl of Northumberland for the army of Charles I (1640), repr. in Grose, ii. 106, 110.

[157] Johnson, *supra* note 13, at 126.   [158] Ibid. 137.
[159] Vitoria, 183 (48). However, even in war with the Turks, it was not lawful to kill women, who were presumed innocent, or children. Ibid. 179 (36).

labourers who cultivate lands and vineyards.'[160] Nevertheless, a lowly prisoner could call upon his lord's duty to him when it came to ransom, which might encourage the captor to treat him kindly.[161]

Even knights could not always rely on an offer of quarter on the battlefield.[162] In his important fourteenth-century work on the law of war,[163] Giovanni da Legnano favoured sparing captured generals but made the grant of quarter subject to the necessities of war:

[Q]uarter should be granted to one who humbles himself and does not try to resist, unless the grant of quarter gives reason for fearing a disturbance of the peace, in which case he must suffer. . . . [Q]uarter is to be granted only when disturbance of the peace is not feared, and otherwise not.[164]

According to the modern historian James Hamilton Wylie, word had circulated among Henry's troops in Agincourt 'that the Frenchmen meant to give no quarter save to the king and his nobles, for whose captivity . . . they had already begun to make arrangements, while the rumour ran that they would cut off every archer's right hand'.[165] The practice of denying quarter even on the battlefield found support among some writers on *jus gentium* in Shakespeare's era. Thus Vitoria stated that '[a]ll the doubt and difficulty [was] . . . to know whether, when we have won our victory and the enemy is no longer any danger to us, we

---

[160] Bouvet, 153.

[161] *LW* 150–1, points out that by the terms of his contracts with his soldiers, the captain might be bound to ransom them. See also Peter J. Lewis, *Later Medieval France* (1968), 212: 'It was possible to get help with one's ransom from one's lord: from the king or from one's commander.'

[162] Bouvet, 152, wrote that 'if a knight, captain, or champion, take another in battle he may freely kill him. . . . [B]ut out of battle no man may kill another save in self-defence.'

[163] Keen regards Legnano and Bouvet as the most famous academic lawyers who wrote about the law of war. *LW* 7. (Actually, Bouvet was a monk rather than an academic lawyer.).Holland describes Legnano's work as 'the earliest attempt to deal, as a whole, with the group of rights and duties which arise out of a state of war.' Intro. by Holland to Legnano, b and pp. xxvii–xxix. Keen observed that Bouvet (or Bonet) largely restated what was previously written by Legnano, and that Christine de Pisan's work was largely copied from Bouvet. *LW* 21.

[164] Legnano, ch. 30, pp. 253–4. See also ibid. ch. 69, p. 274: 'Should mercy be shown to persons captured in a lawful war? We must say that it should, unless by sparing them there is fear of a disturbance of the peace.'

may kill all who have borne arms against us. Manifestly, yes.'[166] He justified this licence to kill on the basis of its promise of future security through the deterrent effect of punishment.[167] He attempted to temper the severity of the law by invoking the need 'to take into account the nature of the wrong done by the enemy and of the damage they have caused . . . and from that stand-point to move to our revenge and punishment, without any cru-elty and inhumanity'.[168] Gentili, however, advocated greater humanity.[169]

In contrast to combat on the battlefield, siege warfare was waged in accordance with the rule of 'war to the death without quarter (though the rule could be waived for anyone, and a pris-oner who could pay a good ransom was likely enough to be spared)'.[170] The rule applied 'not against soldiers only, but against all the able-bodied inhabitants of the town'.[171] Disregarding those cases where the attacking prince insisted on unconditional surrender, Vitoria argued that, if a city surrendered unconditionally without providing in the conditions of capitula-tion for the safety of its inhabitants, it would be permissible, sub-ject to some qualifications, to put 'the more notorious offenders' to death.[172] Nevertheless, guided by his theory of innocence, Vitoria believed that troops engaged in defending or attacking cities, whether in a just or an unjust war, should not be killed if the presumption was 'that they entered on the strife in good faith'.[173] Gentili criticized the denial of quarter more directly. Specifically in the context of siege warfare, he admitted that there might be reasons for refusing to accept a surrender, 'but if there is no such cause, it surely seems right to accept it; otherwise we have a war of extermination.'[174] He regarded an order to kill a

---

[165] Wylie, *supra* note 36, at ii. 154.

[166] Vitoria, 182 (45). Suárez, 845, argued for the protection from killing of innocent persons, even if the punishment inflicted upon their state was insuffi-cient; but he favoured allowing, in these circumstances, the killing of some addi-tional guilty individuals after the war. Ibid. at 841: '[T]he slaying of a great multitude would be thus permissible only when there was most urgent cause, nev-ertheless, even such slaughter may sometimes be allowed, in order to terrify the rest.'

[167] Vitoria, 182 (46).   [168] Ibid. 182–3 (47).
[169] See *supra* text at notes 82–4, 144–6.   [170] *LW* 121.
[171] Ibid.   [172] Vitoria, 183–4 (49).
[173] Ibid. 183 (48).   [174] Gentili, ii. 218.

large number of warriors 'who surrendered themselves and threw down their arms on the ground . . . [as a grave] crime'.[175]

RAPE OF WOMEN

I turn now to the second element specified in Shakespeare's ultimatum: the rape of women. Henry's speech, which implies that violation of women would be inevitable because soldiery could not be controlled in the heat of battle, falls short of the real Henry's severe prohibition of rape,[176] though rape in a town taken by assault following a siege would have been more leniently treated. Here, Shakespeare's Henry may have reflected the difficulties of the real Henry.

No account better demonstrates how difficult it was to enforce the law than the *Gesta*'s statement that when Henry's invasion fleet dropped anchor near Harfleur,

an order was issued throughout the whole fleet that, under pain of death, no one should land before the king, but rather that they should make ready to land early on the following morning when he did, lest, if it were done otherwise, the English in their recklessness, not foreseeing the dangers and coming ashore too soon and at the wrong time, might perhaps scatter in search of plunder and leave the king's own landing too exposed.[177]

Henry's Ordinances of War attempted to protect the non-combatant, but enforcing compliance with the norms was—and remains—a real problem. Keen observes that '[w]hat is important is not that the law of arms tolerated outrages (which it did not do); but that it was not effectively enforced throughout most of the Hundred Years War.'[178] Hence the consistent repetition by Henry V and other kings of England of ordinances on military discipline.

The reality was even grimmer. I have already cited Keen's observation that the licence to rape was considered a major

---

[175] Gentili, ii. 223.   [176] See *infra* note 188.   [177] *Gesta*, 23.
[178] *LW* 192; see also *LW* 190. Cf. Common Article 1 of the Geneva Conventions, which requires the parties 'to respect and to ensure respect for the present Convention in all circumstances'. The authoritative Commentary prepared by the International Committee of the Red Cross to the fourth Convention adds: '[T]he Party to the conflict is responsible for the treatment accorded to protected

incentive for the soldier involved in siege warfare. While urging generals to forbid and prevent rape during the sacking of a city, Vitoria reluctantly admitted the lawfulness of allowing soldiers to sack a city if 'the necessities of war' required it, 'or as a spur to the courage of the troops',[179] even when rape would result. These cruel rules, however, were rejected by Gentili:

Further, to violate the honour of women will always be held to be unjust. For although it is not contrary to nature to despoil one whom it is honourable to kill, and although where the law of slavery obtains it is permitted according to the laws of war to sell the enemy together with his wives and children, yet it is not lawful for any captive to be visited with insult. . . . I make no allowance for retaliation. . . .

At some time the enemy [who allows raping women] . . . will surely render an account to . . . the rest of the world, if there is no magistrate here to check and punish the injustice of the victor. He will render an account to those sovereigns who wish to observe honourable causes for war and to maintain the common law of nations and of nature.[180]

Under modern international law, despite the prohibition of 'all rape' in Lieber's Code of 1863,[181] the protection of women's rights to physical and mental integrity does not appear to have been a priority. The Hague Regulations provide only indirect and

persons. It would not, for example, be enough for a State to give orders or directions . . . It is for the State to supervise the execution of the orders it gives.' *Commentary on the Geneva Conventions of 12 August 1949*, *supra* note 29, at 16.

[179] Vitoria, 184–5 (52). Cf. this recent comment: 'All wars are alike in at least three particulars: death, destruction and rape . . . Serbian commanders [said] that raping Muslim women was "good for raising the fighters' morale".' 'The Rape of Bosnia', *New York Times* editorial, repr. *Herald Tribune International*, 8 Dec. 1992, 4, col. 1. The UN Human Rights Commission (Res. 1992/S–2/1) and the Security Council (S/RES/798 (1992)) have recently condemned the systematic practice of rape in Bosnia and Herzegovina.

[180] Gentili, ii. 257. See also Theodor Meron, 'Common Rights of Mankind in Gentili, Grotius and Suárez', 85 AJIL 110, 115–16 (1991). Although Grotius mentioned the argument that rape should be legal on the ground that 'it is not inconsistent with the law of war that everything which belongs to the enemy should be at the disposition of the victor,' he reasoned that, being unrelated to either security or punishment, rape 'should consequently not go unpunished in war any more than in peace. The latter view is the law not of all nations, but of the better ones.' Grotius, bk. iii, ch. iv, pt. xix(1).

[181] Francis Lieber, *Instructions for the Government of Armies of the United States in the Field*, Art. 44, originally published as US War Department, Adjutant General's Office, General Orders No. 100 (24 Apr. 1863), repr. in Richard Shelly Hartigan, Lieber's Code and the Law of War (1983), 54.

partial protection against rape.[182] The 1929 Geneva Convention on Prisoners of War contained a general provision too vague to afford effective protection to women prisoners.[183] During the Second World War, rape was tolerated and, horrifyingly, was even utilized in some instances as an instrument of policy. Walzer recounts that Moroccan mercenary troops fought with Free French forces in Italy in 1943 on 'terms [which] included [as a spur to masculine courage] license to rape'.[184] In occupied Europe, thousands of women were subjected to rape and thousands more were forced to enter brothels for Nazi troops.[185] Only in the fourth Geneva Convention of 1949 was an unequivocal prohibition of rape established.[186] Even so, infringement of this provision was not listed among the 'grave breaches' of the Convention, which require the imposition of penal sanctions or extradition.[187] The numerous cases of rape committed in recent armed conflicts (Kuwait and Bosnia–Herzegovina) sadly demonstrate the continuing seriousness of the problem.

[182] *Supra* note 1, Art. 46.

[183] (Geneva) Convention Relative to the Treatment of Prisoners of War, 27 July 1929, Art. 3, 47 Stat. 2021, 2031 (pt. 2), TS No. 846, 2 Bevans 932 ('Women shall be treated with all the regard due to their sex').

[184] Walzer, *supra* note 132, at 133–4.

[185] See Françoise Krill, 'The Protection of Women in International Humanitarian Law', *Int'l Rev. Red Cross*, 249 (Nov.–Dec. 1985), at 337; *Commentary, supra* note 29, at 205.

Thousands of Korean women were forced by the Japanese army to work as 'comfort girls' in Japanese army brothels. Only in 1992 did some Japanese leaders apologize for this practice. *New York Times*, 17 Jan. 1992, A 6, col. 3.

[186] 'Women shall be especially protected against any attack on their honour, in particular against rape, enforced prostitution, or any form of indecent assault.' Geneva Convention No. IV, *supra* note 3, Art. 27. For a similar prohibition, see Additional Protocol I, *supra* note 2, Art. 76(1).

[187] Geneva Convention No. IV, *supra* note 3, Arts. 146–7. Rape and enforced prostitution were not included in the list of grave breaches in Art. 85 of Additional Protocol I, *supra* note 2. See generally Krill, *supra* note 185, at 337, 341. 'A useful precedent for the international criminalization of rape as inhuman treatment, or even as torture, was established by the European Commission of Human Rights in *Cyprus* v. *Turkey*, Applications Nos. 6780/74 and 6950/75 (10 July 1976). As regards rape committed by Turkish soldiers and officers, members of the armed forces of an occupying power, the Commission ruled that those acts which could be imputed to the occupying power constituted 'inhuman . . . treatment' in the sense of Art. 3 of the European Convention on the Protection of Human Rights and Fundamental Freedoms, opened for signature 4 Nov. 1950, 213 UNTS 221. Nos. 6780/74, 6950/75, paras. 373–4. The Commission emphasized that '[i]t has not been shown that the Turkish authorities took adequate

PILLAGE AND CHURCH PROPERTY

We return to consideration of a third element in the King's ultimatum, pillage. With the exception of siege warfare, Henry's prohibition of pillage in occupied territories is best reflected by the
previously mentioned incident of the stolen pyx, reported to
Captain Fluellen by Lieutenant Pistol:

> PISTOL　Fortune is Bardolph's foe and frowns on him,
> For he hath stol'n a pax, and hangèd must a be.
> A damnèd death—
> Let gallows gape for dog, let man go free,
> And let not hemp his windpipe suffocate.
> But Exeter hath given the doom of death
> For pax of little price.
> Therefore go speak, the Duke will hear thy voice,
> And let not Bardolph's vital thread be cut
> With edge of penny cord and vile reproach.
> Speak, captain, for his life, and I will thee requite.
>
> 　　　·　　·　　·　　·　　·　　·　　·
>
> FLUELLEN . . . [I]f, look you, he were my brother, I would
> desire the Duke to use his good pleasure, and put him to
> executions. For discipline ought to be used.
>
> 　　　　　　　　　　　　　　　　(*Henry V*, iii. vi. 37–54)

measures to prevent this happening or that they generally took any disciplinary
measures following such incidents.' Ibid., para. 373. See generally Andrew Byrnes,
'The Committee against Torture', in Philip Alston (ed.), *The United Nations and
Human Rights* (1992), 509, 519, and n. 38 ; Charlotte Bunch, 'Women's Rights as
Human Rights: Toward a Re-Vision of Human Rights', 12 Hum. Rts. Q. 486
(1990). Although rape is not explicitly mentioned in Article 147 of the Geneva
Convention No. IV among the enumerated grave breaches, in certain circumstances rape can be considered as the grave breach of 'wilfully causing great
suffering or serious injury to body or health', if not 'torture or inhuman treatment'.

Under the weight of the events in the former Yugoslavia, and especially the inde-
scribable abuse of women in Bosnia–Herzegovina, the reluctance to recognize that
rape can be a war crime or a grave breach has begun to crumble. This development
was aided by the decision of the Security Council (Res. 808) to establish a war
crimes tribunal for former Yugoslavia. Several governments and the International
Committee of the Red Cross have recently confirmed that rape could be a war
crime or a grave breach and, in certain circumstances, also a crime against humanity. See Theodor Meron, 'Rape as a Crime under International Humanitarian
Law', 87 AJIL 424 (1993).

As we have seen, when Fluellen later tells the King about Bardolph's offence and likely execution, Henry endorses the harsh punishment and orders that 'in our marches through the country there be nothing compelled from the villages, nothing taken but paid for, none of the French upbraided or abused in disdainful language' (ibid. 109–12).

Shakespeare based the story of the stolen pyx on Holinshed, who reported that, despite the needs of the English troops, nothing was taken from the local population without payment and no offences were committed

except one, which was, that a souldiour tooke a pix out of a church, for which he was apprehended, and the king not once remooved [did not move at all, halted] till the box was restored, and the offendor strangled. The people of the countries thereabout, hearing of such zeale in him, to the maintenance of justice, ministered to his armie victuals, and other necessaries, although by open proclamation so to doo they were prohibited.[188]

The incident of the stolen pyx is reported by most of the sources, including the *Gesta* ('pyx of copper-gilt' which the soldier stole 'perhaps thinking it was made of gold'),[189] and the *First English Life*.[190] The real Henry indeed ordered that churches and their contents be left unharmed and that no man lay hands on priests or women unless they were actually armed

---

[188] Holinshed 30 (= R. Holinshed, *Chronicles* (1808) iii. 77); see also Hall, 64. According to Wylie, *supra* note 36, at ii. 117: 'A cry was at once raised, the battalion was halted and the king refused to advance till the thief was caught. He was dragged out before the gazing files and hanged on a tree beside the church where the theft had been committed; the pyx was restored.' See also Nicolas, *supra* note 6, at 91–2. The incident of the pyx is also reported in the contemporary account, *Gesta* 69. The hanging of the offender appears to have been consistent with para. 3 of King Henry V's Ordinances of War: '[A]lso, that no maner of man be so hardy to robbe ne to pille holy Church of no goode, ne ornament, that longeth to the Church, ne to sle no man of holy Church, religious, ne none other, but if he be armed, upon peyne of deth, noper that noman be so hardy to sle ne enforce no woman uppon the same peyn. And that noman take no woman prisoner, man of holy Churche, ne none oper religious, but if he be armed, uppon peyn of enprisonement and his body at the Kynges will.' Although these ordinances were promulgated in 1419, the earlier proclamations of King Henry appear to have contained similar prohibitions. See *supra* text at notes 75–6. According to Holinshed, 58 (R. Holinshed, *Chronicles* (1808), iii, 92), Henry found a large amount of money at Caen castle, which he fully restored to the inhabitants.

[189] *Gesta*, 69.

[190] '[A] pixe of sylver', *First English Life*, *supra* note 37, at 44–5.

or planning a violent attack. '[A]ll victuals which might be useful for the support of the army were to be spared from waste and pillage.'[191] These rules did not originate with Henry but preceded him. Christine de Pisan, who compiled the medieval laws of war and customs of chivalry in 1408–9, supported the death penalty for soldiers committing pillage,[192] strongly advocated the protection of non-combatants,[193] and proclaimed prohibitions on the killing of prisoners[194] and the use of poisoned weapons, which she considered so inhumane as to be against the law of war for Christians.[195]

Henry V promulgated ordinances on warfare not only to maintain the necessary discipline among his troops, but also to promote various humane practices.[196] The army, however, disrespected these protective rules to such an extent, particularly through plunder, that six years later they had to be solemnly reissued.[197] Nevertheless, Henry's 'humane intentions . . . had made so deep an impression in France that one of the most high-minded of the French ecclesiastics appealed to him to protect French churches from the plundering violence of their own people.'[198]

This appeal is unsurprising because the French troops appeared to be even less disciplined than the English troops and, according to the French chronicler the Religieux de Saint-Denys, committed more excesses towards the French population than did the English towards those French who accepted the occupation: 'ils [the English troops] montraient plus d'égards que les Français eux-mêmes pour les habitants qui se déclaraient en leur faveur; . . . ils observaient sévèrement les règles de la discipline militaire.'[199] The monk described the French soldiery recruited

---

[191] Wylie, *supra* note 36, at ii. 20–2. [192] Pisan, 44; see also ibid. 217.

[193] Ibid. 224–35.

[194] Ibid. 222, 64–5. Her statement on the use of poisoned weapons anticipates Article 23 (a) of the Hague Regulations. Like writers on modern law of war, Christine de Pisan considered the use of ruses permissible, but not perfidy, 213–14.

[195] Ibid. 184.

[196] e.g., the prohibition against making captives of children under 14, or requiring that an occupied lying-in room be spared. Wylie, *supra* note 36, at ii. 22.

[197] Ibid. 23–4. See also *supra* text at note 76.

[198] Wylie, *supra* note 36, at ii. 24.

[199] *Chronique du Religieux de Saint-Denys supra* note 45, at v. 557.

for the service of the princes, as 'plus avides de pillage qu'accou-
tumés à la discipline militaire'.[200] He graphically depicted the
ruthless pillage and robbery of French inhabitants by those *gens
de guerre*, who did not even spare the inhabitants' work animals
needed for the ploughing of the soil, an act prohibited by the
contemporary norms of *jus gentium* including the Ordinances of
Henry V. He concluded that they committed worse cruelties than
the English enemy 'à l'exception du meurtre et de l'incendie'.[201]
It was to curb such excesses by the French soldiery and alleviate
the tremendous suffering of the inhabitants of the French towns
and villages, and especially of the peasantry, that Charles VII
promulgated his famous Ordinance (1439), 'Pour obvier aux pilleries & vexations des Gens de guerre' (see Chapter 8 below).

COMPELLING OBEDIENCE BY DESTRUCTION

The monk's condemnation of the English for burning requires
comment. We have seen that the real Henry's Harfleur proclamation of 1415 prohibited setting houses on fire. According to the
Gesta, the King issued two proclamations of rules of war in
Harfleur: the first in August, immediately after the landing; the
second in October, after the town's conquest. The first proclamation was clearly triggered by instances of unauthorized burning
of houses by English soldiery. Under pain of death, there 'should
be no more setting fire to places (as there had been to begin
with) and . . . churches and sacred buildings along with their
property should be preserved intact, and . . . no one should lay
hands upon a woman or on a priest or servant of a church,
unless he happened to be armed, offered violence, or attacked
anyone.'[202] The second proclamation provided, 'under pain of
death, [that] no man should burn and lay waste, or take anything
save only food and what was necessary for the march, or capture
any rebels save only those he might happen to find offering resistance'.[203]

However, these proclamations simply meant that *unauthorized*
acts were prohibited. Henry's Ordinances of War issued at
Mantes (1419), which confirmed earlier rules, made it clear that

---

[200] Ibid. 547.   [201] Ibid.   [202] *Gesta*, 27.
[203] Ibid. 61; Nicolas, *supra* note 6, at 219-20.

the burning of buildings was prohibited and was to be punished by death, *unless* carried out in pursuance of the King's orders. The evidence offered by the author of the *Gesta*, who was sympathetic to the King, confirms that the complaint of the Religieux de Saint-Denys was justified: the *Gesta* indicates that Henry routinely used the threat of burning to force the inhabitants to allow peaceful passage of his troops to Calais, and to provide them with food and wine. The inhabitants of Arques, for example, 'granted the king free passage and a fixed amount of bread and wine with which to refresh the army, in order to ransom their town and neighbourhood from being burnt'.[204] The inhabitants of Eu ransomed Eu and the neighbouring towns by providing the King with food and wine,[205] as did the inhabitants of Boves.[206] Kingsford describes the Eu incident as involving 'purchas[ing] protection for the neighbouring villages by a supply of food'.[207] But where the inhabitants refused to furnish supplies, the King did not hesitate to resort to large-scale destruction, and that was true even where the party that did not submit to Henry's demands was different from, but lived in proximity to, the inhabitants of the area subjected to the threat. Thus, when the inhabitants of the walled town of Nesle refused to ransom the neighbouring hamlets from burning, the King 'ordered these places . . . to be set on fire and utterly destroyed'.[208]

Although the burning of towns which refused to provide the King with the necessary supplies was harsh, the King's practice can be justified on grounds of both necessity and contemporary norms. In the late Middle Ages it was quite normal for armies to live off the countryside, even in time of peace. 'Appati', writes Keen, was 'only one of a number of names used to describe agreements between local inhabitants and soldiers living off the countryside.'[209] *Appatis* belonged to the spoils of war as indicated by the term 'raencons du pays'.[210] 'From the point of view of those paying *appatis*, they implied the purchase of immunity from war—hence the name *abstinences* or *souffrances de guerre*.'[211] The refusal of the inhabitants to agree to the provision

---

[204] *Gesta*, 63.   [205] Ibid.   [206] Ibid. 69.

[207] Charles Lethbridge Kingsford, *Henry V*, (1901), 137. Nicolas similarly speaks of 'buy[ing] off the burning' of their towns, or of 'redeem[ing] the villages . . . from burning'. Nicolas, *supra* note 6, at 221.

[208] Kingsford, *supra* note 207, at 71; see also Nicolas, *supra* note 6, at 231.

[209] *LW* 251 (App. I).   [210] Ibid.   [211] Ibid. 252.

of supplies would expose them to all the harsh measures allowed by contemporary laws of war, including killing and burning. Compelling compliance with the rights of belligerents by setting villages on fire would certainly not have been regarded as unlawful and perhaps not even as inhumane by Henry's contemporaries.

Viewing these practices through the prism of the modern law of war, it may be noted that Article 52 of the Hague Regulations allows the requisitioning in kind and services—and certainly of food—for the needs of the army of occupation.[212] Of course, the burning of whole towns to ensure compliance would violate modern international law,[213] which, by emphasizing the principle of proportionality and by limiting coercive measures to enforce requisitions 'to the amount and kind necessary to secure the articles requisitioned',[214] still leaves considerable discretion to the army of occupation.

A scorched-earth policy justified by legitimate military reasons was not considered to be a war crime in post-Second World War trials, but wanton, excessive devastation not justified by military necessity was so viewed.[215] Thus, the commander of German forces in the Finnmark province of Norway, who as a precautionary measure ordered the complete destruction of entire villages, communications, and transport facilities to prevent their use as aid and comfort to the advancing Russian troops, may have been justified by the military necessity exception stated in Article 23 (g) of the Hague Regulations. Although the defendant erred in his judgement, because the expected Russian advance did not take place, he was found not guilty of a criminal act.[216]

---

[212] US Department of the Army, *The Law of Land Warfare*, 153 (para. 412 *b*) (Field Manual No. 27–10, 1956).

[213] Art. 33 of the fourth Geneva Convention, *supra* note 3, prohibits reprisals against protected persons and their property and Art. 53 prohibits the destruction of real or personal property, whether public or private, except in cases where such destruction is rendered absolutely necessary by military operations.

[214] Field Manual No. 27–10, *supra* note 212, at 154.

[215] Commentary on the fourth Geneva Convention, *supra* note 29, at 302. Art. 54 of Protocol I, *supra* note 2, introduces far-reaching protection of objects indispensable to the survival of the civilian population. Dinstein concludes that '[t]he Protocol permits recourse to "scorched earth" measures only when the area affected belongs to the belligerent Party and is under its control (in contradistinction to enemy territory or even part of the national territory which is under the enemy's control)' and thus not in occupied territory. Dinstein, *supra* note 35, at 149–50.

[216] The *Hostages* case, *United States of America* v. *Wilhelm List et al.*, 8 Law

The Nuernberg Charter defined as war crimes the wanton destruction of cities, towns, or villages, or devastation not justified by military necessity. Although the occupant is 'vested with an almost absolute power'[217] 'as regards the safety of his army and the purpose of war',[218] and may therefore compel compliance with Article 52 of the Hague Regulations, the destruction of enemy property, and even more the general devastation of a locality in occupied territory not 'imperatively demanded by the necessities of war' is absolutely prohibited by Article 23(g) of the Hague Regulations.[219] Germans responsible for setting fire to houses in occupied France, either as a measure of intimidation intended to suppress the activities of the resistance movement in the area or as a measure of reprisal, were convicted of the war crime of violating the Hague Regulations, particularly Article 23(g) and Article 46 (providing for respect of private property), and of resort to unlawful or arbitrary reprisals.[220] It is none the less far from certain that setting a small number of houses on fire in order to compel the inhabitants to provide supplies to an occupying army (Article 52 of the Hague Regulations) would have been unlawful during the Second World War.

Article 33 of the fourth Geneva Convention prohibits '[c]ollective penalties and . . . all measures of intimidation' as well as 'reprisals against protected persons and their property'. Article 147 of that Convention defines as grave breaches 'extensive destruction and appropriation of property, not justified by military necessity and carried out unlawfully and wantonly'. Compelling requisitions through the destruction of towns in occupied territory would no longer be considered a lawful method of enforcement, notwithstanding any claims of military necessity.

Reports of Trials of War Criminals 34, 68–9 (The United Nations War Crimes Commission 1949).

[217] Lassa Francis Lawrence Oppenheim, *International Law*, (Hersh Lauterpacht 7th edn., 1952), ii. 437.

[218] Ibid.   [219] Ibid. 412–17.

[220] 8 Law Reports of Trials of War Criminals 29–30 (The United Nations War Crimes Commission 1949). 'Private homes and churches even may be destroyed if necessary for military operations. It [military necessity] does not admit the wanton devastation of a district or the willful infliction of suffering upon its inhabitants for the sake of suffering alone.' 11 Trials of War Criminals before the Nuernberg Military Tribunals under Control Council Law No. 10 at 1254 (1950).

In reality, invading or occupying powers still resort to practically unlimited, and frequently illegal, measures, such as the destruction of houses, to secure the compliance of the inhabitants with their orders, or as punishment for violations. In occupied Kuwait, for example, Iraqi authorities resorted to measures of destruction, dismantling, and pillaging of public and private property, many of which were 'deliberate, premeditated, systematic and large scale. They violated the guarantees of the fourth Geneva Convention because they were not necessitated by military considerations nor were they otherwise admissible under international law.'[221]

HENRY'S PROSCRIPTIONS AND THE MEDIEVAL ARMY

Henry's prohibition of plunder may seem surprising, as medieval rules of war liberally allowed the taking of spoils. In certain circumstances, real estate could be appropriated by the victorious prince;[222] but moveables, including those not taken on the battlefield, could become the property of the captor himself (depending on certain qualifications and the hazy entitlements of the prince and the captor, respectively).[223] Normally, moveables would be distributed among the various parties, including the captor, his captain and the prince.[224]

Vitoria maintained that '[a]ll movables vest in the seizor by the law of nations, even if in amount they exceed what will compensate for damages sustained.'[225] Although Vitoria advocated the protection of innocent civilians ('agricultural population and other innocent folk . . . ought not to be despoiled' if the war can be carried out effectively without their spoliation), he gave

---

[221] Report on the situation of human rights in Kuwait under Iraqi occupation, prepared by Mr Walter Kälin, Special Rapporteur of the Commission on Human Rights, UN Doc. E/CN.4/1992/26 at 58. Consider also the destruction of houses by the Israeli authorities on the West Bank and in the Gaza Strip, which was repeatedly censured by the United Nations and by the International Committee of the Red Cross as a violation of the fourth Geneva Convention.

[222] See Vitoria, 185–6 (56); Grotius, bk. III, ch. vi, pt. xi.

[223] *LW* 137, 139–40; Bouvet, 150.

[224] Giovanni da Legnano wrote that moveables 'become the property of the captor; but he is bound to assign them to the general of the war, who will distribute them according to deserts.' Legnano ch. 61, p. 270.

[225] Vitoria, 184 (51).

priority to the requirements of war by emphasizing that in a just war it is lawful to despoil even innocent enemy subjects so as to sap the enemy's strength.[226] Vitoria was less concerned about protecting enemy subjects' property than about ensuring that soldiers not loot without the authority of the prince or general.[227] Suárez similarly wrote that soldiers may take from their 'hosts' only what the king has authorized.[228]

The harshness of the punishment meted out to the soldier who stole the pyx can be explained in part by the unauthorized nature of the taking, the King's desire to maintain law and order and, most importantly, the violation of protected religious objects (that is, the church and pyx). The principal reason for the severity of the punishment of the man who stole the pyx was the specially sacrilegious nature of the offence—laying hands on the box where the Holy Sacrament was kept (and that Sacrament was no less holy by one whit if it was consecrated by a French priest). That surely is why the sanctity of the pyx is stressed in Henry's Ordinances of War as well as in those promulgated by Richard II (Ch. 8).

In contrast to some other medieval rulers, Henry did his best to enforce his ordinances of war. The soldier Bardolph's case was not the only one. A foreign soldier who stole a pyx from St Faro's abbey in 1421 was also hanged.[229] Moreover, Henry felt that he was reclaiming his own duchy: he had no interest in pillaging or destroying what he regarded as rightfully his own. His political and propagandistic purpose was to befriend, not antagonize, the population.

Because under Henry V the English were more interested in permanent conquest and occupation than they had been under Edward III, Henry had a stronger motivation to control his troops. Nevertheless, the gap between Henry's ordinances and the excesses of undisciplined soldiery who frequently plundered the countryside and lived off the land was great. It continued to be so even after his death, prompting Henry VI's regent in France to issue in 1424 yet another proclamation threatening severe pun-

---

[226] Ibid. 180 (39)–(40). Gentili, ii. 270, wrote that 'booty is commonly reckoned as a part of the fruits of victory.'

[227] Soldiers who loot without a prince's permission are bound to make restitution. Vitoria, 185 (53).

[228] Suárez, 837.   [229] Jacob, *supra* note 37, at 102.

ishment on all 'men-at-arms who have come from England [and are] living off the land or practising theft or extortion upon the poor people'.[230]

Despite their partially self-serving purpose and less than perfect enforcement, Henry's proscriptions, as described by Shakespeare, against molesting the inhabitants and taking any goods from them without proper payment were quite advanced for their era and are comparable to nineteenth- and twentieth-century texts such as the Lieber's Code,[231] the Oxford *Manual*,[232] and the Hague Regulations.[233] These texts are based on the distinction between private and public property, which was not central for writers on *jus gentium* in Shakespeare's era, and they grant far greater protection to the former. In contrast to the period of the Hundred Years War, today the right to appropriate property in occupied territory has become a monopoly of the state, and individual pillage is outlawed by both customary rules (of which Henry's ordinances are an important antecedent) and conventional rules. The taking of private property is strictly regulated and, in principle, is allowed only when required by the army. Requisitioned goods must be paid for, as ordered by Henry. The distinction between moveable and immoveable property has survived, but it has acquired a new meaning. Moveables belonging to the state (public property) may still be appropriated by the occupying state, but not those belonging to individuals (private property) unless particularly suited to a military purpose. The latter may be requisitioned, but they must be restored and compensation paid when peace is concluded. Immoveable property, even that belonging to the state, is protected from expropriation by the occupying power, whose rights may not exceed those of an administrator and usufructuary. Enforcement continues to be a serious problem, however. In recent conflicts, such as during the Iraqi occupation of Kuwait, both public (by the state and for the state) and private pillage were rampant.

Allmand has explored the reasons non-combatants were the true victims of the Hundred Years War, even more than in some

---

[230] Allmand, 'The War and Non-Combatant', *supra* note 50, at 163, 167.

[231] *Supra* note 181, sec. II.

[232] *The Laws of War on Land (Oxford Manual)*, pt. ii and Art. 32 (adopted by the Institute of International Law at Oxford, 1880), repr. in Dietrich Schindler and Jiří Toman (eds.), *The Laws of Armed Conflicts* (3rd edn. 1988), 35.

[233] *Supra* note 1, Arts. 23 (g), 28, 46, 47, 52, 53, 55, 56.

other wars.[234] Although following the reign of Edward III, the English wars were fought chiefly by paid professionals,[235] their pay was neither adequate nor regular. The ordinances of war did not take this reality into account. Although the troops were ordered to pay for what they took from the inhabitants for their subsistence, they did not always have the necessary funds to do so,[236] even in cases where proper discipline and supervision existed.

Naturally, soldiers saw in the war a unique opportunity to get rich. The needs of French soldiers were even more neglected than those of the English troops. The crown, writes Peter Lewis, would recruit ' "free" companies, whose livelihood depended most clearly upon making war pay'.[237] The excesses of the *compagnies* and the *écorcheurs* were worse than those of the English troops until the Ordinances of Charles VII of 1439 abolished the independent companies and led to the formation of *compagnies d'ordonnance*, the core of the French regular army.

Christine de Pisan was one of the contemporary writers on *jus armorum* who fully understood that a system of regular and adequate wages for the army was essential if excesses of the soldiery were to be curbed. She supported use of mercenaries in war, provided that they were paid by their superiors even in cases where they were not actively utilized.[238] Where a man fighting in a just war was paid his wages, plunder of the countryside should be avoided: 'spoyllynges nor robberye be not made vpon the countrey where frendes be | nor other dyverse grevaunces and dommages of whyche men of werre comynly usen wikkedly in whiche dooynge they mysdoo gretly.'[239]

Another factor responsible for the suffering of the French inhabitants was that while, notwithstanding Henry's sincere efforts, the English ordinances of war were not effectively enforced, the mass of the English soldiery was quite unfamiliar with the chivalric rules that guided the knights and the nobility and provided a modicum of protection for the weak, the sick, the women, and (in theory at least) all innocent civilians. The war

---

[234] 'The War and Non-Combatant', *supra* note 50.
[235] Lewis, *supra* note 161, at 47.   [236] Allmand, *supra* note 50, at 169–70.
[237] Lewis, *supra* note 161, at 47.   [238] Pisan, 199–201.
[239] Ibid. 200.

was 'a dirty and underhand [game for the army's] disreputable elements'.[240]

One of the major problems, as Maurice Keen perceptively observes, was that although the Hundred Years War was becoming a war of nations, the laws were still aimed at limited individual conflicts, largely based on the chivalrous soldier who, alas, 'was a heritage of this earlier, more individualist order of things'.[241] It was not surprising, therefore, that the French population 'suffered physical violence, arson, theft, destruction of home, animals and crops, in addition to having to pay either protection money (*pâtis*) or ransom to a less then merciful soldiery'.[242]

The composition of the English forces merits brief consideration. One component consisted of adventurers, who went to war for profit from pillage and ransom. Profit was, of course, also a motive of the nobility in going to war. Then there was the element of glory, or Maurice Keen's 'tinsel glint of chivalry' which clung to the calling of the men-at-arms.[243] What Peter Lewis wrote of the composition of the English forces during the French campaigns of Edward III was largely true of Henry V's forces as well:

The war was fought by paid professionals. The alien adventurers who joined his army with their companies clearly deserved this title; but it belonged no less to the English captains who made their fortunes abroad, to the English nobility who maintained their fortunes in land with the profits of a career in arms, and even to the rank and file raised in England in the fourteenth century.[244]

Of course, in contrast to Edward III, who sent expeditionary forces for relatively short campaigns, Henry's object was the permanent occcupation of the French territories. This aim required a permanent army and, as far as possible, the support or at least the acquiescence of the population, and therefore good military discipline and humane treatment of the inhabitants.

To capture lands still held by the Dauphin and his supporters,

---

[240] Allmand, *supra* note 50, at 168. [241] *LW* 217.
[242] Allmand, *supra* note 50, at 166.
[243] M. Keen, 'Chivalry, Nobility, and the Man-at-Arms', in Christopher T. Allmand (ed.), *War, Literature, and Politics in the Late Middle Ages* (1976), 32, 44.
[244] Lewis, *supra* note 161, at 47.

and to resist pressure from the French inhabitants, Henry needed not only garrisons, but also a large field army.[245] The failure of the newly established English settlements in France to provide adequate troops,[246] and the erosion, through scutage and other financial substitutes for personal service, of feudal obligations to serve, all led to an increase in paid voluntary service.[247] During the lifetime of Henry V and the early Bedford regency, captains indentured to serve on an annual basis; later they served for longer and longer periods.[248] That Henry's army was still largely a collection of personal retinues, cohesive among themselves and fairly independent of central control, was demonstrated by the content of indentures entered into by the captains and the King, or by the captains and their retinues.[249] The indenture was a formal contract between the King and the captain, or the captain and his subordinate subcontractor, establishing the conditions of service, the size, composition, and equipment of the retinue, the duration of service (typically a year), wages, and the division of the spoils of war, including ransoms and the disposition of prisoners.[250]

[245] Curry, *supra* note 52, at 199.   [246] Ibid. 199.
[247] Christopher T. Allmand, *The Hundred Years War* (1988), 93–4.
[248] Curry, *supra* note 52, at 201.   [249] Ibid. 195–6.
[250] Allmand, *supra* note 247, at 94. The following agreement of indenture was concluded in 1415 between Henry V and Thomas Tunstall:

'THIS Indenture, made between the King our Sovereign Lord of the one part, and Monsieur Thomas Tunstall of the other part; Witnesseth, that the said Thomas is bound to our said Lord the King, to serve him for a whole year in a voyage which the same our Lord the King in his own person will make, if it pleaseth God, in his Dutchy of Guienne, or in his kingdom of France: commencing the said year, on the day of the muster of the people of his retinue, at the place which shall be appointed by our said Lord the King, within the month of May next coming, if he shall be then ready to make the said muster.

'And that the said Thomas shall have with him, in the said voyage, for the whole year, six men at arms, himself counted, and eighteen horse archers; the said Thomas taking for wages for himself two shillings a day. And if in the company of our said Lord the King, the said Thomas shall go to the said Dutchy of Guienne, he shall take for the wages of each of the said men at arms forty marks, and for each of the said archers twenty marks, for the said whole year. And in case that the aforesaid Thomas goes to the aforesaid kingdom of France, in company with our Lord the King, he shall take for the wages of each of the said men at arms twelve-pence, and for each of the said archers six-pence, a day, during the year above said.

'And in case of the said voyage to France, the said Thomas shall take reward usual for him and his said men at arms, that is to say, wages, at the rate of one hundred marks for thirty men at arms the quarter. Of the which wages for the said parts of Guienne, half the first quarter shall be paid to the said Thomas at the making of this Indenture; and the other half when he shall have made the said muster ready to go to the said parts of Guienne, if our said Lord the King shall go there, or shall send him there. And in case it happens that after the said muster, our said Lord the King shall not go to his said Dutchy of Guienne, but shall go to the parts of France, then the said Thomas shall be paid so much as shall be owing to him for the said first quarter, besides the sum received by him as above, for the wages and reward, as well for himself as for the men at arms and archers above said, so passing to the said parts of France.

'And for surety of payment for the second quarter, our said Lord the King will cause to be delivered to the said Thomas, in pledge, on the first day of June next coming, Jewels, which by agreement with the said Thomas, shall be fully worth the sum to which the said wages, or wages with reward, for that quarter shall amount. The which jewels the said Thomas shall be bound to return to our said Lord the King, the hour that he can redeem them within a year and half and one month next after the receipt of the same jewels.

'And also that it shall be lawful for the said Thomas and for all others whatsoever, to whom the said jewels shall be delivered by the said Thomas, after the end of the said month, to dispose of the said jewels at their pleasure, without impeachment of the King or of his heirs, according to the contents of the Letters Patent, under the Great Seal of the King, granted to the aforesaid Thomas in this case. And for the third quarter, the said Thomas shall be paid for him and his said retinue, within six weeks after the commencement of the same third quarter, according to the quantity of wages, or wages with reward, for the country to which they may have gone, or shall be, during the said quarter.

'And respecting the payment of the wages, or wages with reward, as the case may be, for the last quarter of the year above said, if for the moiety of the said third quarter, the King, our said Lord, shall not give such security for the payment to the said Thomas as he shall reasonably demand, then, at the expiration of the third quarter, the said Thomas shall be acquitted and discharged towards our said Lord the King of the covenants specified in this present Indenture. And the said Thomas shall be bound to be ready at the sea, with his said people well mounted, armed, and equipped, suitably to their condition, for his muster on the first day of July next coming: and from the time of their arrival at the place above said, the said Thomas is bound to muster the people of his retinue before such person or persons as it may please our said Lord the King to assign, as often as he shall reasonably require.

'And the said Thomas shall have as usual at the charge of our said Lord, shipping for him and his retinue, their horses, harness, and provisions, and also re-shipping, as others of his condition in the said voyage. And if it shall happen, that our said Lord the King shall countermand the said Thomas before his passage of the sea, he shall be bound for the said sum to serve the same our Lord the King, in such parts as shall please him with the aforesaid men at arms and archers, according to the rate of wages accustomed in the parts where they shall be ordered by our said Lord the King, except those that may die, if any shall die, in the mean time.

'And if it shall happen that the Adversary of France, or any of his sons, nephews, uncles, or cousin-germans, or any King of any kingdom, or his Lieutenant, or other chieftains having command from the said Adversary of France, shall be taken in the said voyage by the said Thomas, or any of his said retinue, our said Lord the King shall have the said Adversary, or other person of the rank above said, who may be so taken, and shall make reasonable agreement with the said Thomas, or to those by whom he may be taken. And respecting other profits of

During earlier stages of the Hundred Years War, 'royal expeditions were often just as disorganised as the ravages of the free companies; indeed they were bound to be so for as long as plunder continued to offer infinitely greater rewards than pay.'[251] The most egregious examples of the cruel treatment of the civilian population were provided not by the armies but by the free companies and the *écorcheurs* that roamed the French countryside.[252]

Although Henry tried to the best of his ability to enforce the rules protecting the common people, this frequently was not true of his captains.[253] During later regency years, the failure of the peaceful occupation and the increasingly military nature of the regime made it necessary to centralize the control over the English army in France in the hands of the regent, and to improve discipline. Such developments were beneficial for the treatment of the French population. But other factors were exerting pressure in the opposite direction. Inevitably, then as now, occupation spawned resistance, and resistance met repression, culminating after the death of Henry V in the doctrine treating French resisters as rebels, rather than combatants entitled to combatant privileges (see below Chapter 11).

In considering the fate and the treatment of the French civilian population, the role of the French armies must be taken into account. Indeed, that population suffered from the excesses of French soldiery no less than from those of the English. While in England paid voluntary service of professional soldiers arranged through indentures became the rule well before the French campaigns of Henry V, the French feudal service system proved more resilient.[254] A 'relic of the feudal army' was available in France

"Gaignes de Guerre", our said Lord the King shall have as well the third part of the "gaignes" of the said Thomas, as the third of the third part of the 'gaignes' of the people of his retinue in the said voyage taken, as the "gaignes" of the prisoners, booty, money, and all gold, silver and jewels, exceeding the value of ten marks.

'In Witness of which things on the part of this Indenture relating to our said Lord the King, the aforesaid Thomas has put his Seal. Given at Westminster, the xxix day of April, the year of the reign of our said Lord the King, the third'.

Text (translation from Latin) reprinted in H. Nicolas, *History of the Battle of Agincourt*, (1832), App. II, 8. See also indenture between the Earl of Salisbury and William Bedyk, one of his retinue, ibid. 10. For another example of an indenture concluded by Henry V, see Grose, i. 72 and n. (e).

[251] *LW* 117.   [252] *LW* 192.   [253] *LW* 243.
[254] Lewis, *supra* note 161, at 47.

through the *arrière-ban*, a call to those between the ages of 18 and 60 to report for service in cases of necessity.[255] Because of the ineffectiveness of this system, Charles V already increasingly resorted to recruiting a paid, volunteer-based army, raised through *lettres de retenue*, contracts somewhat similar to, though less detailed, than English indentures.[256]

The free companies and the *écorcheurs* were a major scourge for the non-combatant population. The free companies had already been banned by Edward III in 1361,[257] and later by Charles VII in his famous Orléans *Ordonnance* of 1439. Nevertheless, both the French and the English frequently found it helpful to use the free companies as an instrument of warfare. These companies, which lived off the countryside and often became quite wealthy from ransoms and *appatis*, could usually be dislodged from a particular locality only by being paid to leave. Their loyalty shifted between the French and the English, but most of the time they simply worked for their own account, terrorizing the countryside and inflicting untold cruelties on the peasantry. Charles VII's Orléans *Ordonnance* of 1439, which was designed to suppress abuses of the free companies, effectively outlawed all private armies and laid the basis for the formation in 1445 of the *compagnies d'ordonnance*, which in fact formed the first French permanent army.[258] The *Ordonnance* of 1439 promulgated an extraordinarily detailed and enlightened set of rules for protecting the population from the excesses of soldiery. Alas, this was not the law during Henry V's French campaigns. In its preamble, the *Ordonnance* clearly described the intolerable situation to which it was designed to put an end:

In order to prevent and put an end to the great abuses and pillage committed by soldiers, who have long been, and still are, living at the expense of the people, without law and justice . . . considering the poverty, oppression, and destruction suffered by his people as a result of the said acts of pillage, which he strongly resents and has no intention of tolerating any longer in any way, but wishes instead to bring to an end with God's help, [the King] has ordered to be made and issued by way of an everlasting and irrevocable law, the following writs, acts, statutes and ordinances.[259]

---

[255] Allmand, *supra* note 247. at 93.   [256] Ibid. 94–5.
[257] *LW* 93, n. 1.   [258] Lewis, *supra* note 161, at 101–2.
[259] *Ordonnances des rois de France de la troisième race*, ed. L. G. de Vilevault

and L. G. O. F. de Bréquigny (1782), xiii. 306 (my own translation from French). The editors' Preface explains: 'Most of the companies of soldiers of that time, which were not so much concerned with the defence of France as with its devastation, had been raised by their captains without the permission of the King. The King abolishes all of them and decides from now on to appoint captains who alone would be able to raise a certain number of men-at-arms and archers, for whom they would be accountable. He forbids anyone to raise or lead any men-at-arms or to be in arms in the Kingdom without his written authorization. He states that the lords who have soldiers in their castles shall be accountable for them and obliged to pay for their upkeep without using that pretext to commit exaction on their land or to appropriate a part of the taxes levied by him on his subjects, with the consent of the three estates to finance the war. Ibid., p. xxvii (my own translation from French).

7

Henry's Challenge to the Dauphin:
The Duel that Never Was and
Games of Chivalry

Shakespeare's close reliance on Holinshed and Hall gave his
Henry V a certain historical basis (see Chapter 1), but also meant
that he probably was unaware of some events the chroniclers did
not mention. Consequently, certain events of great dramatic
potential were overlooked. Two such events, to be discussed in
this chapter, reflect chivalric norms to which lip-service was often
given, but which were not generally followed in practice: Henry's
duelling challenge to the Dauphin after conquering Harfleur, and
the French proposal that both parties jointly choose the place
and the time for the battle. In each case, one party to the conflict
offered, and the other party refused, to apply those norms.

Chivalry, as Huizinga observed, blended 'formulation of principles of international law . . . with the casuistical and often puerile
regulations of passages of arms and combats in the lists.'[1]
Although sentiments of honour had a real impact on affairs of
state and strategic interests might, on occasion, be sacrificed 'to
keep up the appearances of the heroic life',[2] rulers increasingly
realized that, for example, it was senseless to expose the interests
of a kingdom to the outcome of a single combat between leaders
or their champions.

In most cases, theoretical norms of chivalry yielded to interests
of state. Thus, during the initial stages of the Hundred Years
War, when Philip VI of France offered to fight Henry's
great-grandfather Edward III in a single battle (1347) in order
to relieve the besieged Calais, Edward III refused—at least

---

[1] J. Huizinga, *The Waning of the Middle Ages* (1924), 101.
[2] Ibid. 95.

according to Froissart[3]—because Calais's capture was his priority. In rejecting the offer of battle, Edward paid no lip-service to chivalric principles and had no qualms about acknowledging that accepting Philip's challenge would be contrary to his interest in quickly conquering Calais. As Holinshed put it, Edward 'meant not to accomplish [Philip's] desire, nor to depart from that, which to his great cost he had brought now at length to that point, that he might easily win it.'[4]

Soon after conquering Harfleur, Henry made an offer to the Dauphin 'to . . . end th[e] controversy respecting the right and dominion over the kingdom . . . without any other shedding of fraternal blood . . . by a duel between them, man to man'.[5] Because of Charles's 'mental disorder'[6]—madness—Henry challenged the French king's first-born son rather than his father. The quarrel would thus be placed in the hands of God.

Other sources recognize that this challenge was made and no sources question it, but the date indicated in its original Latin text (September 16 1415) is inaccurate;[7] the challenge was most

---

[3] See *Les Chroniques de Jean Froissart*, ed. J. A. Buchon, Collection des Chroniques Nationales Françaises, 2 (1824), Bk. 1 ch. 318, ed. n. 4. For Froissart's version of Edward's reply, see ibid. ch. 318. Edward claimed to have accepted the challenge. William Longman, *The History of the Life and Times of Edward the Third* (1869), i. 284–5.

[4] R. Holinshed, *Chronicles* (1807), ii. 647.

[5] *Gesta*, 57–9. Phyllis Rackin suggested that Shakespeare's Henry used Agincourt as an enormous trial by combat to establish the legitimacy of his rule and earn his place in providential history, thus removing the taint resulting from his father's usurping Richard II's crown. *Stages of History* (1990), 79.

[6] *Gesta*, 57.

[7] The text of the challenge to the Dauphin ('Rex Delphinum ad Duellum provocat') is reprinted in Thomas Rymer, *Foedera* (London, 1729), ix. 313. The following translation into English is by Harris Nicolas, *History of the Battle of Agincourt* (1832), App. VII:

'Henry by the grace of God King of England and of France, and Lord of Ireland, to the high and puissant Prince, the Dauphin of Vienne, our Cousin, eldest son of the most puissant Prince, our Cousin and Adversary of France. From the reverence of God, and to avoid the effusion of human blood, We have many times, and in many ways, sought peace, and notwithstanding that We have not been able to obtain it, our desire to possess it increases more and more. And well considering that the effect of our wars are the deaths of men, destruction of countries, lamentations of women and children, and so many general evils that every good christian must lament it and have pity, and We especially, whom this matter more concerns, We are induced to seek diligently for all possible means to avoid the above-mentioned evils, and to acquire the approbation of God, and the praise of the world.

'Whereas We have considered and reflected, that as it hath pleased God to visit

probably made on 26 September.[8] It articulated, for the first time, the blueprint which coalesced into a settlement in the Treaty of Troyes: should Henry be the victor, the Kingdom of France would belong to him upon Charles's death (see Chapter 10 below).

Harris Nicolas opined that because Henry was in full vigour of manhood while the Dauphin had not yet reached his twentieth year and died the following December, there was little bravery in the challenge, and even less 'justice' in expecting that such an important conflict should be 'hazarded on the result of such a meeting'.[9] However, in chivalric theory a political duel had much in common with a judicial duel. 'The notion of two princes fighting a duel in order to decide a conflict between their countries had nothing impossible about it in an epoch when the judicial duel was still as firmly rooted in practice and in ideas.'[10] A single

our said Cousin your Father, with infirmity, with Us and You lie the remedy, and to the end that every one may know that We do not prevent it, We offer to place our quarrel, at the will of God, between Our person and Your's. And if it should appear to you that you cannot accept this offer on account of the interest which you think our said Cousin your Father has in it, We declare to you that if you are willing to accept it and to do what we propose, it pleases us to permit that our said Cousin, from the reverence of God and that he is a sacred person, shall enjoy that which he at present has for the term of his life, whatever it may please God shall happen between Us and You, as it shall be agreed between his council, our's, and your's. Thus, if God shall give us the victory, the crown of France with its appurtenances as our right, shall be immediately rendered to us without difficulty, after his decease, and that to this all the lords and estates of the kingdom of France shall be bound in manner as shall be agreed between us. For it is better for us, Cousin, to decide this war for ever between our two persons, than to suffer the unbelievers by means of our quarrels to destroy Christianity, our mother the Holy Church to remain in division, and the people of God to destroy one another. We pray that you may have such anxious desire to it, and to seek for peace, that you will neglect no means by which it can be obtained. Let us hope in God, that a better or shorter way of effecting it cannot be found; and therefore in discharge of our soul, and in charge of your's, if great evils follow, we propose to you what is above said. Protesting that we make this our offer to the honor and fear of God, and for the reasons above mentioned, of our own motion without our loyal relations, counsellors, and subjects now around us, having in so high a matter dared to advise us; nor can it at any time to come be urged to our prejudice, nor in prejudice of our good right and title which we have at present to the said crown with its appurtenances; nor to the good right and title which we now have to other our lands and heritages on this side the sea; nor to our heirs and successors, if this our offer does not take full effect between us and you, in the manner above said. Given under our Privy Seal, at our town of Harfleur, the XVI day of September'.

[8] Nicolas, *supra* note 7, at 72.
[9] Ibid. 73.   [10] Huizinga, *supra* note 1, at 94–5.

combat between two princes followed from the conception of political disputes as quarrels in the legal sense.[11] Henry's challenge involved the determination of rights through the will of God ('[w]e offer to place our quarrel, at the will of God').

Trial by battle, wrote Holdsworth, was 'judicium Dei par excellence'.[12] At times it was used by princes (who employed champions) to resolve international controversies, and was regarded as a more natural solution than the submission of international disputes to arbitration.[13] In theory, trial by battle, like ordeal, rested on the belief that God would determine the outcome. But there were limits to this belief, as demonstrated by the fact that in many circumstances adversaries could employ champions (as in some international disputes). Holdsworth thus wrote that '[a] duellist in fact seems to have been reckoned a necessary adjunct to diplomacy.'[14] Although, as Holdsworth noted, in early law only such persons as infants, women, or those over 60 years of age could decline the battle and employ champions, the power to appoint champions was later extended to able-bodied litigants involved in writs of right,[15] although generally not to those involved in appeals of felony.

The use of champions, especially professional ones, was difficult to reconcile with the concept of the trial by battle as *judicium dei*. For those who believed that God decided the outcome of trial by battle, the weak and the old would have as good a chance as the professional gladiator, and the disparity in the strength of both parties should matter no more than it did in the combat between David and Goliath. There would have been no reason to resort to champions. If Henry believed in the role of Providence in such duels, Nicolas's comment, rational though it was, was perhaps not quite responsive.

It should be noted that some medieval writers on *jus armorum* questioned the very rationale of duels intended to prove a right.

[11] Huizinga, *supra* note 1, at 93.

[12] William Holdsworth, *A History of English Law*, ed. A. L. Goodhart and H. G. Hanbury (1956), i. 308.

[13] Ibid. 308–11. See generally Yoram Dinstein, 'International Law as a Primitive Legal System', 19 N.Y.U. J. Int'l L. & Pol. 1, 19–20 (1986).

[14] Holdsworth, *supra* note 12, at i. 309. On trials by battle, see also William Blackstone, *Commentaries on the Laws of England* (1978 edn.), iv. 346–8; ibid. iii. 337–41. On trials by battle before the court of chivalry, see G. D. Squibb, *The High Court of Chivalry* (1959), 22–4, and Holdsworth, *supra* note 12, at 310 n. 1.

[15] Holdsworth, *supra* note 12, at 309.

Acknowledging that 'royal custom and temporal lordship'[16] permitted the practice of proving one's right by combat, Bouvet emphasized that the law of the Church condemned it. He advanced three reasons against such duels. The first, empirical, was 'that it has often been experienced that the man who had right on his side has, notwithstanding this, lost the battle'.[17] The second, theological, was that when a man wished to prove his right by combat, he was 'testing whether [God] will render justice in such a contest; and . . . to tempt God is not lawful or permitted'.[18] The third, utilitarian, was that 'if such methods of proof are used, then are judges made and ordained to administer justice, in vain.'[19] Elsewhere, Bouvet suggested that trials by battle were condemned by the law of nations, civil law, and canon law.[20] He argued that duels should only be fought to settle disputes and accusations of major significance[21] and where no other forms of legal proof were available. Bouvet would probably contend that Henry's challenge for the title to the throne of France and the Hereford–Norfolk duel (see below) were matters which God alone could decide justly.

The conflict between the belief that a duel's outcome was determined by a judgment of God and the use of a hired champion was initially lessened by treating a champion as a witness, who had to assert that he knew the truth of the cause he was espousing. A statute promulgated in 1275, however, provided that champions need not swear as to their knowledge of the cause for which they were fighting,[22] in recognition of their free use.

Of course, from Henry's perspective, there may have been several good reasons for issuing the challenge, which strengthened his heroic image and furthered his propaganda purposes. Henry could thus appear both to his troops and to foreign powers to be concerned for human lives and willing to sacrifice his own to spare others. Like other princes who offered to determine the outcome of a controversy by single combat, Henry could stand 'before all the world as the champion of right who does not hesitate to sacrifice himself for his people'.[23] Of course, Henry's chances of winning the combat were excellent.

---

[16] Bouvet, 117.   [17] Ibid.   [18] Ibid.   [19] Ibid.   [20] Ibid. 196.
[21] Bouvet cited examples of cases where the Lombard law permitted wager of battle, ibid. 196–8.
[22] Holdsworth, *supra* note 12, at 309.   [23] Huizinga, *supra* note 1, at 93.

From the perspective of the French, the picture was wholly different, which may explain why Henry's offer was not even answered. Not only were the Dauphin's chances of winning poor, but the French were confident in the victory of their troops, which greatly outnumbered the English and which were less fatigued and had better supplies, as well as the support of the population. The French, therefore, had no interest in hazarding what they considered an almost certain victory on a most dangerous single combat.

Henry probably did not expect his offer to be taken up by the Dauphin. Rather, he was indulging in a chivalric game or rite, which was advantageous to him and nearly risk-free. Challenges between princes almost never led to combats. As Huizinga noted, '[t]he chivalrous fiction was also at the back of a peculiar form of political advertisement . . . to wit, the duel between two princes, always being announced, but never carried out.'[24]

Henry's challenge to the Dauphin was consistent with the continuing popularity of duels over points of honour, that is, outside the area of judicial duels. Indeed, that popularity was on the increase by the fifteenth century, but especially in sixteenth-century France and Italy. It was a reaction to 'the impersonality and mechanisation of war, above all to the gun'.[25] With the introduction of large groups of infantry and guns, the nobility feared losing their knightly role in warfare and developed 'a compensatory interest in the procedures of single combat'.[26]

A stronger analogy could be drawn between Henry's challenge and writs of right at common law. After all, it was a 'quarrel' as to Henry's claim of a 'good right and title', *jus proprietaris*, a hereditary right, that he offered to submit to single combat. Even this analogy is not entirely apposite, however. In common law, the battle was a means of testing an oath as to the right or truth, a principle not easily transferred to political disputes. But whatever the legal technicalities, the idea of a single combat was central to the mystique and mores of the chivalric era, and, therefore, to Henry's thinking.

[24] Huizinga, *supra* note 1, at 93.
[25] Malcolm Vale, *War and Chivalry* (1981), 166.
[26] Ibid. 165. For an excellent study of the growing popularity of duelling in the 16th c. and the reasons for it, see Sydney Anglo, 'How to Kill a Man at your Ease: Fencing Books and the Duelling Ethic', in Anglo (ed.), *Chivalry in the Renaissance* (1990), 1.

Both judicial duels and duels over points of honour[27] are mentioned in Shakespeare's plays. He distinguished true chivalric honour, which he respected, from duels over trivial points of honour, which he mercilessly ridiculed. In *1 Henry VI*, when Vernon and Basset asked the King to 'grant [them] combat' because of a quarrel of no significance, Shakespeare's King Henry angrily responds:

> Good Lord, what madness rules in brainsick men
> When for so slight and frivolous a cause
> Such factious emulations shall arise?
>
> .   .   .   .
>
> Beside, what infamy will there arise
> When foreign princes shall be certified
> That for a toy, a thing of no regard,
> King Henry's peers and chief nobility
> Destroyed themselves and lost the realm of France!
>
> .   .   .   .
>
> Go cheerfully together and digest
> Your angry choler on your enemies.
>
> > (*1 Henry VI*, iv. i. 111–13, 143–7, 167–8)

Pursuit of honour was central to the theory and practice of chivalry, and to the literature, especially the poetry, of chivalry.[28] As Vale observes, the chivalric sentiment of honour was grafted on the concept of service to the prince, especially in a just war, to produce a kind of national chivalry or chivalric patriotism.[29]

Shakespeare's work is replete with references to honour. In his plays chivalric honour took on added importance.[30] In creating

---

[27] See e.g., *1 Henry VI*, iv. i. Regarding combat resulting from an accusation of treason, see *2 Henry VI*, i. iii and ii. iv.

[28] See the excellent discussion of honour in chivalry by Vale, *supra* note 25, at 166–74. See also *LW* 20, 154.

[29] Vale, *supra* note 25, at 168.

[30] See particularly this speech by Thomas Mowbray in *Richard II*, i. i. 166–9, 177–85:
My life thou shalt command, but not my shame.
The one my duty owes, but my fair name,
Despite of death that lives upon my grave,
To dark dishonour's use thou shalt not have. . . . The purest treasure mortal times afford
Is spotless reputation; that away,
Men are but gilded loam, or painted clay.
A jewel in a ten-times barred-up chest
Is a bold spirit in a loyal breast.   *cont.*

Prince Edward a knight, Shakespeare's Henry VI declared: 'Edward Plantagenet, arise a knight— | And learn this lesson: draw thy sword in right' (*3 Henry VI*, II. ii. 61–2). In confronting Bagot, Aumerle claimed that Bagot's blood is 'all too base | To stain the temper of my knightly sword' (*Richard II*, IV. i. 27–8). Honour, chivalry, and knighthood were important elements in Shakespeare's plays. In medieval wars they were instrumental in enhancing compliance with chivalric rules and thus strengthening the protection of non-combatants.

From Holinshed, Shakespeare learned of the procedures, legal aspects, and terminology of duels, which were described in Holinshed's detailed accounts of, for example, the Katrington–Anneslie combat (1399).[31] In that combat, Anneslie, the 'appellant', accused Katrington, the 'defendant', of treason for having sold and delivered to the French a fortress (Saint-Sauveur-le-Vicomte) in France (Chapter 6 above). The combat was conducted in the presence of Richard II and the High Constable of England and fought out before the constable's court.[32] Other duels recounted by Holinshed included the combat betwen John Walsh and an esquire of Navarre which also involved an accusation of treason (1384),[33] and the famous dispute in 1398 between Henry V's father, Henry Bolingbroke, Duke of Hereford and Thomas Mowbray, Duke of Norfolk (the resulting duel was stopped by Richard II, who banished the contestants).[34] Such cases fell within the criminal jurisdiction of the court of chivalry (this court also had civil jurisdiction, for example over ransom) where the accuser (appellant) 'offered to support [his accusation] in single combat . . . which, in default of evidence, could result in a trial by battle . . . .[i]t was primarily used for the trial of treasons and homicides committed abroad.'[35] If the appeal was one of treason, the vanquished party would be executed.[36] Judicial duels

Mine honour is my life. Both grow in one.
Take honour from me, and my life is done.
Then, dear my liege, mine honour let me try.
In that I live, and for that will I die.

[31] R. Holinshed, *Chronicles* (1807), ii. 727–8. See comment by Keen, *LW* 127.

[32] Maurice H. Keen, 'The Jurisdiction and Origins of the Constable's Court', in John Gillingham and J. C. Holt (eds.), *War and Government in the Middle Ages* (1984), 159 n. 2.

[33] R. Holinshed, *Chronicles* (1807), ii. 764.

[34] Squibb, *supra* note 14, at 23–4.   [35] Ibid. 22. See also *LW* 205.

[36] Squibb, *supra* note 14, at 25.

under the law of arms were permitted only if it were shown 'that
the honour of at least one party was at stake, that both parties
were entitled by rank to fight one, and that there was not sufficient evidence to judge the case by ordinary process of law'.[37]

Because Norfolk was Earl Marshal, it is unclear whether the
the Bolingbroke–Mowbray dispute actually involved proceedings
in the court of chivalry (over which the Lord High Constable
and the Earl Marshal presided), but the law of chivalry was followed.[38] This dispute led to an abortive duel, triggered by
Bolingbroke's claim that Thomas committed treason by misusing
the King's funds placed at his disposal for paying the Calais garrison. Bolingbroke's charge against Mowbray was in fact more
serious than a matter of misusing funds intended for garrison
pay. He seems rather to have confided to Bolingbroke his fear
that they were 'the next for the chop' on account of their opposition to Richard in 1387, and suggested treasonable ideas about
how to protect themselves. At least, so Bolingbroke claimed.
Because there was no possibility of proof of the words of a private dialogue, a duel was to settle the dispute. That duel was
described in great detail by Holinshed,[39] and faithfully followed
in Shakespeare's dramatic rendering in *Richard II*:

> KING   Marshal, demand of yonder champion
> The cause of his arrival here in arms.
> Ask him his name, and orderly proceed
> To swear him in the justice of his cause.
> LORD MARSHAL [to Mowbray]
>
> .   .   .   .
>
> Speak truly on thy knighthood and thy oath,
> As so defend thee heaven and thy valour!
> MOWBRAY   My name is Thomas Mowbray, Duke of Norfolk,
> Who hither come engagèd by my oath—
> Which God defend a knight should violate—
> Both to defend my loyalty and truth
> To God, my king, and my succeeding issue,
> Against the Duke of Hereford that appeals me;
> And by the grace of God and this mine arm
> To prove him, in defending of myself,
> A traitor to my God, my king, and me.
> And as I truly fight, defend me heaven!

---

[37] *LW* 41.   [38] Squibb, *supra* note 14, at 23 n. 1.
[39] R. Holinshed, *Chronicles* (1807), ii. 844–8.

KING   Marshal, ask yonder knight in arms
Both who he is and why he cometh hither
Thus plated in habiliments of war;
And formally, according to our law,
Depose him in the justice of his cause.

.   .   .   .

BOLINGBROKE   Harry of Hereford, Lancaster, and Derby
Am I, who ready here do stand in arms
To prove by God's grace and my body's valour
In lists on Thomas Mowbray, Duke of Norfolk,
That he is a traitor foul and dangerous
To God of heaven, King Richard, and to me.
And as I truly fight, defend me heaven!

.   .   .   .

FIRST HERALD   Harry of Hereford, Lancaster, and Derby
Stands here for God, his sovereign, and himself,
On pain to be found false and recreant,
To prove the Duke of Norfolk, Thomas Mowbray,
A traitor to his God, his king, and him,
And dares him to set forward to the fight.
SECOND HERALD   Here standeth Thomas Mowbray, Duke of Norfolk,
On pain to be found false and recreant,
Both to defend himself and to approve
Henry of Hereford, Lancaster, and Derby
To God his sovereign and to him disloyal,
Courageously and with a free desire
Attending but the signal to begin.
LORD MARSHAL   Sound trumpets, and set forward combatants!
   [*but the King throws his warder down, stopping the duel*]
Stay, the King hath thrown his warder down.

(I. iii. 7–10, 14–30, 35–41, 104–18)

The play *Antony and Cleopatra* demonstrates that Shakespeare was aware that two rulers (Caesar and Antony) might opt to decide the outcome of a conflict by a single combat:

CLEOPATRA   He goes forth gallantly. That he and Caesar might
Determine this great war in single fight!

(Antony and Cleopatra, IV. iv. 36–7)[40]

What dramatic use Shakespeare would have made of Henry's challenge to the Dauphin had Holinshed mentioned it!

[40] See also *I Henry IV*, v. ii. 46.

The second event in which rules of chivalry were invoked by one belligerent occurred shortly before Agincourt when the French proposed to the English that both parties jointly choose the place and the time for the battle. The *Gesta* reported that on

the Sunday [20 October], the duke of Orleans and the duke of Bourbon, who are very closely related to the French king and were in command of the French army, sent a message to our king by three heralds that they would do battle with him before he reached Calais, although they did not assign a day or place. Whereupon our king, readily accepting this as an act of grace on God's part and relying entirely on divine help and the justice of his own cause, with great resolution and manly spirit gave encouragement to his army and made ready to do battle.[41]

According to other sources, Henry replied that he would neither seek nor avoid battle. When the French asked for deputies to decide a time and place for battle, Henry declared that he was not skulking in towns and fortresses, but was in the open fields, where they could find him.[42] The French proposal reflected the chivalric practice of stipulating a time and a place for combat,[43] based on the theory that honour required that both parties should enjoy equality in their battlefield positions. Even an agreement between the adversaries—such as that concluded between Edward III and Philip VI (1339)—to do battle on a certain date and place, did not always result in an actual battle.[44]

By rejecting the French offer Henry may have served his tactical needs. As the numerically weaker party, he probably had an interest in taking advantage of his mobility and in giving the French army as little time as possible to prepare for an orderly battle. Huizinga's comment is apt here:

the chivalrous point of honour continues to make itself felt, but when an important question arises for decision, strategic prudence carries the day in the majority of cases. Generals still propose to the enemy to come to an understanding as to the choice of the battlefield, but the invitation is generally declined by the party occupying the better position.[45]

---

[41] *Gesta*, 75.

[42] Note by the editors, ibid. n. 4. For a similar account, see James Hamilton Wylie, *The Reign of Henry the Fifth* (1919), ii. 125–6.

[43] Vale, *supra* note 25, at 165–6.   [44] Longman, *supra* note 3, at i. 152–3.

[45] Huizinga, *supra* note 1, at 97. For a case where Henry chose to expose himself and his troops to danger, rather than sacrifice a point of honour, see ibid. 95.

8

Medieval and Renaissance Ordinances of War: Codifying Discipline and Humanity

Medieval ordinances of war, as discussed above in Chapter 6, were issued either by kings for the campaigns in which they happened to be engaged, or by commanders-in-chief in accordance with the authority granted to them in their commissions from their kings. The ordinances were not promulgated in a void. On many questions they restated the customary *jus armorum*, as transmitted orally between heralds and other experts, as described by such writers as Honoré Bouvet, Giovanni da Legnano, and Christine de Pisan, and as applied by the courts. Several of the ordinances, as I shall show, mentioned customary law as a residuary source to be applied in cases for which explicit provision was not made.

Offenders were judged in the court of the Lord High Constable and the Lord Marshal, as mentioned above in Chapters 2 and 7, in lower courts of constables and marshals, and, in much later periods, in courts martial. In cases of great importance, prominent defenders were tried before the Parliament.[1]

This chapter explores in greater detail the development, from the beginning of the thirteenth century until the death of Hugo Grotius (1645), of those provisions of some ordinances of war which went beyond purely disciplinary or tactical matters, or such matters as the division of ransom and spoils of war. Of course, such disciplinary orders as were directly relevant to the protection of the population and the treatment of prisoners will be considered. I shall focus on the protective provisions of the ordinances, norms that articulated principles of humanity, and

---

[1] Grose, ii. 52–7.

other rules that shaped the evolving law of war, leaving aside jurisdictional provisions. Not surprisingly, in later ordinances the balance shifted in some measure from discipline to humanity.

Prior to the nineteenth century, law of war matters were governed by either national ordinances or bilateral treaties. Indeed, national ordinances were the principal means for developing and codifying the law of war. The first multilateral agreement was the (first) Geneva Convention for the Amelioration of the Condition of the Wounded in Armies in the Field of 22 August 1864.[2]

John's 'Constitutions to be Made in the Army of our Lord the King' (1214) ordered marshals to ensure that the army paid the full value of supplies found in churches and church yards, where in time of war peasants found shelter for themselves, their belongings, and cattle. Peasants and their families would thus benefit from the immunity of the Church: 'if it should be found necessary to take any thing from the churches or church yards, for the wants of the army, the superintendants of the churches shall remain there, in order that those things which the army may want, shall be exposed to sale, and that before they are removed they may be paid its value.'[3]

Of greater importance were the Ordinances of War made by Richard II at Durham (1385).[4] These ordinances prohibited robbery and pillage,[5] especially from the Church, as well as the killing or capture of unarmed persons belonging to the Church and of unarmed women. The touching of the pyx was prohibited and capital punishment imposed on the offender. The Ordinances proscribed the rape of women and stipulated that offenders were to be punished by hanging.[6]

---

[2] 22 Stat. 940, 1 Bevans 7, 22 Stat. 940, 55 BFSP 43 (1864–5). See generally Howard S. Levie, *Documents on Prisoners of War*, Naval War College, International Law Studies, 60 (1979), 5–44.

[3] Grose, ii. 57–8 n. u.

[4] The French text of these Ordinances is given in *The Black Book of Admiralty*, repr. in Travers Twiss (ed.), Monumenta Juridica, i (1871), 453. I shall cite the English translation (see ibid. Editor's n. 1) by Francis Grose: Grose, ii. 60.

[5] 'VII. Item, that no one be so hardy as to rob or pillage another of money, victuals, provisions, forage or any other thing, on pain of losing his head; nor shall any one take any victuals, merchandise, or any other thing whatsoever, brought for the refreshment of the army, under the same penalty ' Ibid. 61.

[6] 'III. Item, that none be so hardy as to rob and pillage the church, nor to destroy any man belonging to holy church, religious or otherwise, nor any woman, nor to take them prisoners, if not bearing arms; nor to force any woman, upon pain of being hanged.' Ibid. 60.

Henry V's Ordinances of War[7] (Mantes, July 1419) have been discussed in some detail in Chapter 6. Although issued four years after Harfleur and Agincourt, these were not the first ordinances that Henry promulgated after landing in France. Henry's Mantes Ordinances drew on those of Richard II, especially in the provisions protecting women from rape, and unarmed women and unarmed persons belonging to the Church from capture. The killing of persons belonging to the Church and pillage of churches were prohibited.[8]

Addressing the approaching execution of a soldier for having robbed a church, Shakespeare's Henry declared: 'We would have all such offenders so cut off, and we here give express charge that in our marches through the country there be nothing compelled from the villages, nothing taken but paid for, none of the French upbraided or abused in disdainful language' (*Henry V*, III. vi. 108–12). Consistent with Henry's reaction to the stealing of the pyx, an explicit provision prohibited the touching of the box in which the sacrament was kept.[9] Following Richard's example, Henry prohibited robbing merchants of their goods, and particularly to secure provisions for the army.[10]

In several respects, however, Henry's Mantes Ordinances were more protective of the population than Richard's Durham Ordinances. The ordinances prohibited entering a place where a woman was lying in, as well as robbing her.[11] Peasants involved in the cultivation of the soil and their work animals were protected from capture or harassment.[12] Importantly, burning or torching property—a practice extensively employed by Henry and other military commanders—without king's orders was prohibited.[13] The typical penalty for violation was death.

Another rule proscribed the capture of children below the age of 14, with the exception of the children of lords, captains or other persons of rank.[14] While the prohibitory portion of this provision had obvious humanitarian aspects, the exception was

---

[7] *Black Book of Admiralty*, *supra* note 4, at 459. See also Samuel Bentley (ed.), *Excerpta Historica* (1831), 30; Grose, ii. 66.

[8] *Black Book of Admiralty*, *supra* note 4, at Sec. 3.

[9] Ibid., sec. 2. See *supra* Ch. VI for discussion of Henry's reaction to the theft of the pyx.

[10] Ibid., sec. 8.   [11] Ibid., sec. 29.   [12] Ibid., sec. 33.

[13] Ibid., sec. 37.   [14] Ibid., sec. 28.

grounded in the expectation that handsome ransoms would be paid for the children's liberation.

That Henry was both sincere in attempting to enforce fully his ordinances and aware that his soldiers breached them is demonstrated by the orders he issued on 25 April 1421 to the captain of Rouen (similar orders were issued to other captains). Those orders stated or restated certain restrictions, and imposed severe punishments for violations.[15] In issuing these orders, it is likely that Henry was moved not only by the desire to maintain order and discipline, and to pacify the population of occupied Normandy, but also by the humanitarian consideration of protecting the peaceful population. The preamble explained the need for the measure:

Whereas many captains of town and fortresses, and their lieutenants in the dutchy [*sic*] of Normandy, usurp greater powers than the king has invested them with, or than is proper, oppressing and plundering his subjects, both of money and provisions, and committing divers enormities and excesses, and permitting the same to their soldiers.[16]

One of the new provisions prohibited the captains from exacting any grain or cattle from the inhabitants.[17] To address the possibility that the captains and soldiers 'in future plead ignorance of these matters [the king ordered that] certain inclosed articles . . . be publickly proclaimed [and that the captains and lieutenants] do not, by any means, usurp or encroach on the ordinary jurisdiction belonging to his bayliffs and other justices.'[18]

Henry did not take it for granted that his officers and soldiers would abide by these orders any more than those he had issued in the past. Determined to persevere in his attempts to enforce discipline and the protective rules which it encompassed, on 5 May 1421 Henry issued a commission of enquiry to Sir John Radcliff, instructing him to visit towns, castles, and fortresses to investigate 'the discipline and government [of Henry's officers] relative to . . . the safe keeping and wholesome government of the towns . . . assigned to them'.[19] Radcliff was instructed to learn, in particular, how the officers and soldiers 'behave . . . to the . . . people'.[20]

---

[15] Grose, ii. 79.   [16] Ibid. 79–80.   [17] Ibid. 80.   [18] Ibid. 81.
[19] Ibid.   [20] Ibid. 81–2.

Given the failure of his earlier attempts, Henry's scepticism about the prospects for compliance was mirrored in the language of his mandate to Radcliff

particularly to enquire respecting extortions, pillagings, robberies, impositions, appaticisements [money paid by the inhabitants to obtain the protection of their towns from the ravages of war], and other undue actions, by them as it is said, done, and perpetrated; and whether the said captains, *etc. etc.* have done, or attempted any thing, contrary to the king's admonitions, prohibitions, ordonnances, and mandates, so *repeatedly directed to them*; and also, many times proclaimed by the bailiffs.[21]

By the time Henry died on 31 August 1422 at the age of 35, a tired warrior, whose health suffered irreparable damage through the hardship of his campaigns (especially the siege of Meaux), his daunting task of establishing discipline and through it a modicum of protection for the inhabitants remained largely unaccomplished. His sincerity of purpose should not be questioned, however. Only Charles VII—among all contemporary princes—took steps to limit the excesses of soldiery comparable to Henry's efforts.

During the reign of Henry VI, John Talbot, Earl of Shrewsbury promulgated ordinances (*c.*1425) designed to govern the conduct of the army under his command.[22] The ordinances prohibited pillage and the taking of prisoners in pacified territories ('countre appatised'),[23] as well as destruction of fruit trees and vineyards.[24] They also extended particular protection to the Church.[25]

Perhaps the most comprehensive and impressive royal ordinance aimed at preventing the abuses of the soldiery and protecting the population was that issued by Charles VII at Orléans on 2 November 1439, to Prevent Pillage and Abuses by Soldiers ('Lettres de Charles VII, pour obvier aux pilleries & vexations des Gens de guerre').[26] Charles's goal, as discussed in Chapter 6, was to abolish the free companies and establish the core of a regular army. As the editors' preface emphasized, most of the

---

[21] Grose, ii. 82 (emphasis added).
[22] *Excerpta Historica*, *supra* note 7, at 28, 40.   [23] Ibid. 40.
[24] Ibid. 41.   [25] Ibid. 42.
[26] *Ordonnances des rois de France de la troisième race*, ed. Louis Guillaume de Vilevault and Louis G. O. F. de Bréquigny (1782), xiii. 306.

companies—raised by their captains without the permission of the king—'were not so much concerned with the defence of France as with its devastation'.[27] Charles ordered the abolition of the companies and directed that in the future only he would appoint captains and that only those captains would be able to raise a certain number of men-at-arms and archers, for whom they would be accountable. Both raising and leading of soldiers without Charles's written authorization were forbidden. Lords who had soldiers in their castles were to be accountable for them and obliged to pay for their upkeep. These lords were not, however, permitted to use this as a 'pretext'[28] to impose exactions on their lands or to appropriate a part of the taxes levied by Charles on his subjects with the consent of the three estates to finance the war.[29]

The goal of the ordinance, as defined in the preamble, was to prevent the 'great abuses and the pillage committed by soldiers [which Charles had no intention of tolerating any longer and which resulted] in poverty, oppression, and destruction suffered by his people'.[30] Invoking the threat of the supreme penalty of *lèse-majesté*, Charles prohibited plundering, imprisoning, or ransoming people in their homes or on the highways.[31] The seizure of merchants' and farmers' animals, carts, and tools was prohibited, as was molesting merchants and peasants.[32] Farmers, craftsmen, and others were to be allowed to work in peace; neither they nor their tools could be captured or ransomed.[33] Cattle were

---

[27] Ibid., Préface, p. xxvii (my own translation).   [28] Ibid.   [29] Ibid.

[30] Ibid., Preamble.

[31] '6. *Item*. The King orders captains, soldiers and all others, subject to the penalties attached to the crime of *lèse-majesté*—i.e. loss of all honours and public offices and of all rights, primarily those pertaining to nobility, for the offender himself and his descendants, and confiscation of his property—not to plunder or rob nor permit anyone to plunder or rob in any way churchmen, noblemen, merchants, farmers, or others on the highways or roads, in their dwellings or elsewhere, nor to take them away, imprison them, or ransom them, but instead, subject to the said penalty, to let them go and pass and stay in their houses and dwellings and elsewhere safely and securely.' Ibid.

[32] '7. *Item*. The King orders all captains and soldiers not to take nor stop any merchants, farmers, oxen or horses, or other animals used for drawing a plough or a carriage, or any carriage or cart drivers or their carriages or the goods they carry, nor to ransom them in any way, but to let them plough and drive and carry their goods peacefully and safely, without asking them anything and without stopping or disturbing them.' Ibid.

[33] '15. *Item*. The King orders all captains and soldiers to let farmers plough and craftsmen and other people work, whatever their trade, without disturbing

not to be seized or ransomed.[34] Destruction of corn, wine, and food supplies and the breaking of the vessels in which they were stored was prohibited.[35] The ordinance further barred cutting corn, destroying cornfields, vines, or fruit-trees, or extorting ransom for corn, grapes, and fruit, either before or after the harvest.[36] Burning tools, appliances, winepresses and other property was proscribed, as were burning or destroying of houses.[37] This provision was of obvious importance because burning and destruction of property was frequently used by soldiers to extort payments from a reluctant population.

Aware of the difficulties inevitably facing enforcement of such provisions, especially when the offenders were powerful and the King's justice weak, Charles included in the ordinance elaborate jurisdictional and penal provisions.[38] Not only were persons who robbed travellers or attacked people in their houses to be severely punished, but all law enforcement officers and all noblemen were ordered to fight the offenders as if they were enemies, capture

them in any way and without capturing and ransoming them or their tools or ordering or allowing anyone to do so.' Ibid.

[34] Ibid., Item 8.   [35] Ibid., Item 9.   [36] Ibid., Items 10–12.

[37] Ibid., Items 13–14.

[38] '20. *Item*. The King orders that the present and future members of his Parliament, his accountants, treasurers, bailiffs, *sénéchaux*, judges, provosts, lawyers, prosecutors, investigators, and all other law officers of his Kingdom, implement and enforce this Law and Ordinance and ensure its strict implementation by punishing the offenders without fail, according to this Law and Ordinance.

'21. Item. Furthermore, he orders that they investigate all abuses and offences committed by soldiers in . . . areas under their jurisdiction, in violation of this Law and Ordinance, and punish the offenders; if, however, they cannot carry out the punishment because the offenders are so powerful, owing to the lords' support or otherwise, they should proceed expeditiously with the adjournments, trials, sentences, judgments and statements against the offenders as reasonably required, and bring them immediately before the King or the Parliament Court to stand trial as reasonably required, and the King shall promptly ensure the enforcement of the said awards, judgments and statements, as required. . . .

'25. Moreover, since the above mentioned robberies, pillage, ransoming, and other misdeeds are often committed in places or on roads where it is impossible to get prompt judicial assistance or to call on captains for help, the King wishes and orders that the wounded be able to turn to justice and otherwise mobilize men-at-arms against the offenders in order to forcibly take them and bring them to justice; and if any such offender is killed, the King shall pardon the man who has done the killing and orders that no questions be asked from him, that the law officers of his kingdom do not allow any lawsuit to be initiated against him and that he should be deemed to have acted well.' Ibid.

them, and bring them to justice. The ordinance established incentives as well as punishments: the offenders' horses and any other belongings with them at the time of capture would thus become the property of the captor. The latter would not be held responsible for the death of any offenders killed during capture.[39]

The ordinance established the principle that a captain was responsible for offences committed by his subordinates. Offences were to be attributed to a captain if he did not bring the offender to justice.[40] Soldiers and others present during the commission of offences who did not prevent or resist abuses, such as robberies, or denounce them to the judicial authorities 'shall be held responsible for the offence as accessories to it and shall be punished in the same manner as the offenders'.[41]

The Statutes and Custom of the Marches (frontier) in Time of War (Statutis and Use of Merchis in Tym of Were),[42] adopted during the reign of James II of Scotland by Earl William of Douglas (1448) dealt primarily with tactical questions, with rights to prisoners and to ransom. More significantly, the statutes relied on custom as a source of law and as a rule of decision. The statutes were adopted after an assembly of lords and freeholders testified about the statutes, ordinances, and customs that had

---

[39] '16. . . . the King orders all *sénéchaux*, bailiffs, provosts and other law enforcement officers of his Kingdom and all noblemen and others, as soon as they know that such robbers, looters and highwaymen are in the country, to fight them with a group of men-at-arms or otherwise, as they would fight enemies, and capture them and bring them to justice; and the King shall give to those who capture them their horses, harnesses, and other things they may carry with them and all their spoils; the King wishes and orders that, if any of these offenders is killed during the fight or during his capture, the person who did the killing should not be blamed but instead praised for his action and should not be prosecuted in any way.' Ibid.

[40] '18. *Item.* The King orders that each captain or lieutenant be held responsible for the abuses, ills, and offences committed by members of his company, and that as soon as he receives any complaint concerning any such misdeed or abuse, he bring the offender to justice so that the said offender be punished in a manner commensurate with his offence, according to these Ordinances. If he fails to do so or covers up the misdeed or delays taking action, or if, because of his negligence or otherwise, the offender escapes and thus evades punishment, the captain shall be deemed responsible for the offence as if he had committed it himself and shall be punished in the same way as the offender would have been.' Ibid.

[41] Ibid., Item 19.

[42] 1 Acts of the Parliaments of Scotland 350 (App. IV) (1844). I am grateful to Mr C. C. Kidd of All Souls College for translating for me the text of these statutes from Scottish.

been used on the Marches in the days of Archibald the Grim, the third Earl of Douglas.[43] Not only did several articles of the statute explicitly mention the custom of the Marches as a basis of a particular rule, but the ultimate article recognized custom as a residuary source supplying the warden and his advisers with a rule of decision for cases not explicitly addressed:

Item. It is ordained that all other things that are not now put in writing which are matters of war used before in time of warfare shall be ruled by the warden and his council and by the eldest and most worthy borderers that best know of the old custom of the Marches, in all times to come.

The Statutes and Ordinances for the Warre issued by Henry VIII (1544)[44] were more detailed than those of Henry V, but drew heavily on Henry's Mantes text with regard to several matters important to the development of rules of war. The desecration of the sacrament or the pyx, and the seizure of provisions and other goods from any person having proper papers, without the agreement of senior officers, were both prohibited.[45] An important provision ordered officers to pay soldiers' wages regularly.[46] Because, as already observed, non-payment of wages often triggered pillage and other abuses, this order took on added significance.

Robbery of merchants bringing provisions for the troops was again proscribed.[47] The burning, without an order issued by the King or his 'head officer', of towns or houses was forbidden, 'except the king's ennemies be within it, and cannot be otherwise taken'.[48] Except when authorized by senior officers, the taking of horses or oxen from peasants was forbidden, and the death penalty was to be imposed on offenders.[49] In a territory which freely surrendered to the King's obedience or otherwise came under his authority, robbery, pillage and capture of prisoners was proscribed 'upon peyne of death'.[50] Following the Mantes text, special protection was extended to women lying in and their

---

[43] Ranald Nicholson, *Scotland: The Later Middle Ages* (1974), 346. See also the preamble to the Statute, *supra* note 42.

[44] Grose, ii. 85.   [45] Ibid. 86, art. II.   [46] Ibid. 88, art. VII.

[47] Ibid. 92, art. XVI.   [48] Ibid. 97, art. XXXI.

[49] Ibid. 98, art. XXXIV.   [50] Ibid. 98, art. XXXV.

[51] Ibid. 105, art. LII.

belongings,[51] and the capture of children below the age of 14 was prohibited (again with the exception of children of lords, captains, and rich men).[52]

The 1639 Lawes and Ordinances of Warre, for the Better Government of his Majesties Army Royall, in the Present Expedition for the Northern Parts, and Safety of the Kingdome, under the Conduct of . . . Thomas Earl of Arundel and Surrey[53] restated several of the provisions contained in earlier ordinances of war, such as the prohibition of rape, burning of houses,[54] or pillage of merchants and others.[55] A particularly clear and categorical provision was designed to protect the population of a territory under the King's obedience.[56] In the absence of explicit articles relevant to cases that might arise in the future, and until additional written orders were issued by the Lord General, this ordinance stipulated that resort should be made to the residuary source of 'ancient course of marshall discipline'.[57]

The laws and ordinances of war issued by the Earl of Northumberland for the army of Charles I in 1640, Lawes and Ordinances of Warre Established for the Better Conduct of the Service in the Northern Parts',[58] reiterated a number of provisions that appeared in earlier codes but, importantly, added several new rules. The first category included the prohibitions of desecrating churches and religious objects, of rape, robbery, and murder, and of injuring farmers or seizing their horses, cattle, or goods. Soldiers were forbidden to cut down trees, burn—without orders—houses and barns, or destroy ships, boats, and carriages which might be useful for the army, even 'in the enemies countrey'.[59] They were ordered to pay the normal value of requisitioned food.

The most important innovation was the explicit guarantee of the right to quarter: 'None shall kill an enemy who yeelds and throws down his arms, upon pain of death.'[60] Although, as I

---

[52] Ibid. 105, art. LIII.
[53] Charles M. Clode, *The Military Forces of the Crown* (1869), 429.
[54] Ibid. 431.   [55] Ibid. 436.
[56] Ibid. 434: 'No companies of souldiers, either of horse or foot, in their marching, retreating or enquartering in or thorow any townes or countries within the allegiance of the King, shall doe hurt, spoile, or injurie unto the persons or goods of the inhabitants, upon pain of death, or other such grievous punishment as the qualitie of the offence shall have demerited.'
[57] Ibid. 439.   [58] Grose, ii. 107.   [59] Ibid. 118.   [60] Ibid.

have shown, the right to be granted quarter was recognized by the customary *jus armorum*, and by some scholars, it was not stated in English ordinances of war at the time of Agincourt. Northumberland recognized and declared the principle in a written ordinance of war, and prescribed the death penalty for violations. Finally, the ordinance recognized the role of customary law as a residuary source for punishing matters not mentioned in the ordinances: '[a]ll other faults, disorders and offences, not mentioned in these articles, shall be punished according to the general customes and laws of warre.'[61]

In 1643, a very important ordinance was issued highlighting the rights of the population: Articles and Ordinances of War for the Present Expedition of the Army of the Kingdom of Scotland, by the Committee of Estates [and] the Lord General of the Army.[62] The ordinance provided for its wide publication, so '[t]hat no man pretend ignorance, and that every one may know the duty of his place, that he may do it.'[63] In addition to restating in categorical language the prohibitions of rape,[64] destruction, and pillage, and the obligation to pay the value of requisitioned food,[65] the ordinance contained a statement of the prohibition of murder in time of war as enlightened as those that can be found in the best Nuernberg judgments: '[m]urder is no less unlawful and intollerable in the time of war, than in time of peace, and is to be punished with death.'[66] Another significant provision was the order not to kill an enemy who has surrendered (right to quarter): '[i]f it shall come to pass, that the enemy shall force us to battle, and the lord shall give us victory, none shall kill a yielding enemy.'[67] The ordinance concluded with an eloquent provision establishing not only custom but also the law of nature as a residuary source, thus enhancing the principle of humanity which is inherent in the law of nature:

---

[61] Grose, ii. 126. Cf. ibid. 156, art. LXIV '[a]ll other faults, misdemeanours and disorders not mentioned in these articles, shall be punished according to the laws and customs of war, and discretion of the court-martial.' English Military Discipline: Of Councils of War or Courts Martial (issued 1686 during the reign of James II), ibid. 137.

[62] Grose, ii. 127.   [63] Ibid.   [64] Ibid. 132, art. VIII.

[65] Ibid. 134, art. X.   [66] Ibid. 132, art. VIII.

[67] Ibid. 136, art. XV. Also prohibited were 'ransoming of persons, spoiling [and] pillaging', ibid.

Matters, that are clear by the light and law of nature, are presupposed; things unnecessary are passed over in silence; and other things may be judged by the common customs and constitutions of war; or may upon new emergents, be expressed afterward.[68]

This provision is an important antecedent of the Martens clause, whose object was to substitute principles of humanity for the unlimited discretion of the military commander.[69]

---

[68] Ibid. 137.

[69] The Martens clause reads as follows: 'Until a more complete code of the laws of war has been issued, the High Contracting Parties deem it expedient to declare that, in cases not included in the Regulations adopted by them, the inhabitants and the belligerents remain under the protection and the rule of the principles of the law of nations, as they result from the usages established among civilized peoples, from the laws of humanity, and the dictates of the public conscience.' This clause appears in the preamble to (Hague) Convention (No. IV) Respecting the Laws and Customs of War on Land, with Annex of Regulations, 18 Oct. 1907, 36 Stat. 2277, TS 539, 1 Bevans 631 (a similar clause appears in the preamble to the parallel convention of 29 July 1899). See also Theodor Meron, *Human Rights and Humanitarian Norms as Customary Law* (1989), 46 and n. 127; Helmut Strebel, Martens' Clause, in [Instalment 3] Rudolf Bernhardt (ed.), *Encyclopedia of Public International Law* (1982), 252.

9

Agincourt: Prisoners of War, Reprisals, and Necessity

The events at Agincourt are comprehensible only if we consider how outnumbered the English forces were and how great their fear must have been. The tension which was felt in the English camp is palpable in the complaint attributed by Shakespeare to Warwick (in the Oxford edition by Wells and Taylor which I am using), or to Westmoreland (in other editions; Westmoreland was not on the Agincourt campaign at all), and in Henry's heroic reply:

> [WARWICK]   O that we now had here
> But one ten thousand of those men in England
> That do no work today.
> KING   What's he that wishes so?
> My cousin Warwick? No, my fair cousin.
> If we are marked to die, we are enough
> To do our country loss; and if to live,
> The fewer men, the greater share of honour.
> God's will, I pray thee wish not one man more.
> By Jove, I am not covetous for gold,
> Nor care I who doth feed upon my cost;
> It ernes me not if men my garments wear;
> Such outward things dwell not in my desires.
> But if it be a sin to covet honour
> I am the most offending soul alive.
> No, faith, my coz, wish not a man from England.
> God's peace, I would not lose so great an honour
> As one man more methinks would share from me
> For the best hope I have. O do not wish one more.
> Rather proclaim it presently through my host
> That he which hath no stomach to this fight,
> Let him depart.

(Henry V, IV. iii. 17–36)

Shakespeare drew heavily on Holinshed here (who attributed Warwick's statement to an unnamed 'one of the host'). The exchange itself is also reported in other sources, including the *Gesta*.[1]

As the Battle of Agincourt wore on, the outnumbered English appeared to have the upper hand. The fear that another French charge was about to begin, the presence on the battlefield of a large number of French prisoners who, though disarmed, could have risen against their English captors, and a French attack on the English baggage train possibly involving loss of life among the attendants—all combined to trigger an unexpected order by the King. Shakespeare's Henry, hearing a sudden call to arms, cries out:

> But hark, what new alarum is this same?
> The French have reinforced their scattered men.
> Then every soldier kill his prisoners.
> Give the word through.

> (IV. vi. 35–8)

The play reveals another reason for this order in the next scene:

FLUELLEN   Kill the poys and the luggage! 'Tis expressly against the law of arms. 'Tis as arrant a piece of knavery, mark you now, as can be offert. In your conscience now, is it not?

GOWER   'Tis certain there's not a boy left alive. And the cowardly rascals that ran from the battle ha' done this slaughter. Besides, they have burned and carried away all that was in the King's tent; wherefore the King most worthily hath caused every soldier to cut his prisoner's throat. O 'tis a gallant king.

> (IV. vii. 1–10)

After this disclosure, the King elaborates on his order regarding the prisoners:

---

[1] Holinshed thus describes the King's answer:
'I would not wish a man more here than I have, we are indeed in comparison to the enimies but a few, but, if God of his clemencie doo favour us, and our just cause (as I trust he will) we shall speed well inough . . . And if so be that . . . wee shall be delivered into the hands of our enimies, the lesse number we be, the lesse damage shall the realme of England susteine.' Holinshed, 35 (= R. Holinshed, *Chronicles* (1808), iii. 79–80.). *Gesta*, 79 attributes Warwick's comment to Sir Walter Hungerford.

KING   I was not angry since I came to France
Until this instant. Take a trumpet, herald;
Ride thou unto the horsemen on yon hill.
If they will fight with us, bid them come down,
Or void the field: they do offend our sight.
If they'll do neither, we will come to them,
And make them skirr away as swift as stones
Enforcèd from the old Assyrian slings.
Besides, we'll cut the throats of those we have,
And not a man of them that we shall take
Shall taste our mercy. Go and tell them so.

                                                        (ibid., 53–63)

Shakespeare thus explains Henry's cruel order to kill the French prisoners on two grounds: necessity, as the French appeared to be regrouping to attack; and reprisal for the unlawful attack on the servants[2] guarding the rear camp and for its plunder. In an effort to highlight Henry's humanity, Shakespeare focuses on the King's impetuous anger ('I was not angry since I came to France until this instant'). Bullough agrees that Shakespeare emphasizes and even explains Henry's command as an act of 'justifiable anger, needing no apology', characteristic of his impetuosity; Bullough adds, however, that 'Shakespeare's ambivalence is . . . suggested by Fluellen's disquisition.'[3] Holinshed offers a different version of the facts:

[C]erteine Frenchmen on horssebacke . . . to the number of six hundred horssemen, which were the first that fled, hearing that the English tents and pavillions were a good waie distant from the armie, without anie sufficient gard to defend the same . . . entred upon the kings campe, and there spoiled the hails, robbed the tents, brake up chests, and carried awaie caskets, and slue such servants as they found to make anie resistance. . . .

But when the outcrie of the lackies and boies, which ran awaie for feare of the Frenchmen thus spoiling the campe, came to the kings eares, he doubting least his enimies should gather togither againe, and begin a new field; and mistrusting further that the prisoners would be an aid to his enimies . . . contrarie to his accustomed gentlenes, commanded by

---

[2] Lackeys, boys, pages, sutlers, waggoners, and servants of the camp. James Hamilton Wylie, *The Reign of Henry the Fifth* (1919), ii. 148 n. 6.

[3] Geoffrey Bullough (ed.), *Narrative and Dramatic Sources of Shakespeare* (1962), iv. 367.

sound of trumpet, that everie man (upon paine of death) should incontinentlie slaie his prisoner.[4]

Thus the chronicler whom Shakespeare most closely followed recorded that the French killed only those servants who offered resistance.[5] Holinshed's version of the story formed a part of the mythology of Agincourt by his time. Shakespeare modified the story, apparently to cast Henry's order in the best possible light.

Although Holinshed telescoped the attack on the luggage train with the King's fear that the French forces were regrouping,[6] Shakespeare mentions the regrouping of the French troops together with the King's order to kill the prisoners. In the immediately following scene, the exchange between Fluellen and Gower rather sarcastically presents the killing of the 'poys and luggage' as triggering the King's retaliatory order.[7] However, the eyewitness account of the author of the *Gesta Henrici Quinti* describes the attack on the English baggage as preceding the principal engagement and thus occurring before the English had taken many prisoners. As Henry was preparing for battle, he ordered the baggage brought to the rear of his forces, where it would not fall into the hands of the enemy as booty:

And at that time French pillagers were watching it [the baggage train] from almost every side, intending to make an attack upon it immediately they saw both armies engage; in fact, directly battle was joined they fell upon the tail end of it where, owing to the negligence of the royal servants, the king's own baggage was, seizing on royal treasure of great value.[8]

---

[4] Holinshed, 38 (= R. Holinshed, *Chronicles* (1808), iii. 81).
[5] But E. Hall stated that the French killed the servants they could find. Hall, 69. Cf. Hague Convention (No. IV) Respecting the Laws and Customs of War on Land, Art. 13, 18 Oct. 1907, 36 Stat. 2277, TS No. 539, 1 Bevans 631. [Geneva] Convention Relative to the Treatment of Prisoners of War, Art. 81, 27 July 1929, 47 Stat. 2021 (pt. 2) TS No. 846, 2 Bevans 932; [Geneva] Convention Relative to the Treatment of Prisoners of War (Geneva Convention No. III), Art. 4 (A)(4), 12 Aug. 1949, 6 UST 3316, TIAS No. 3364, 75 UNTS 135. Under such provisions, service personnel accompanying the armed forces, without actually being members thereof, would be entitled to POW status but, as non-combatants, would not be a lawful object of attack unless they took a direct part in the hostilities. See also Protocol Additional to the Geneva Conventions of 12 August 1949, and Relating to the Protection of Victims of International Armed Conflicts (Protocol I), Art. 51 (3), opened for signature 12 Dec. 1977, 1125 UNTS 3.
[6] Holinshed, 38 (= R. Holinshed, *Chronicles* (1808), iii. 81).
[7] Cf. Bullough, *supra* note 3, at 366–7.　　　　　　　　　[8] *Gesta*, 85.

A large number of local peasants participated in this attack.[9] The
Gesta account made no mention of loss of life among the English
guarding the baggage and did not link the attack on the baggage
train with the killing of the prisoners, which took place near the
end of the battle in these wholly unrelated circumstances:

> But then, all at once, because of what wrathfulness on God's part no
> one knows, a shout went up that the enemy's mounted rearguard (in
> incomparable number and still fresh) were re-establishing their position
> and line of battle in order to launch an attack on us, few and weary as
> we were.[10]

The *Gesta* portrays the killing itself as wholly spontaneous, without the slightest mention of the King's orders: '[a]nd immediately
. . . the prisoners . . . were killed by the swords either of their
captors or of others following after, lest they should involve us in
utter disaster in the fighting that would ensue.'[11]

In the circumstances described in the *Gesta*, there would, of
course, be little cause for the historical Henry's anger, unless we
assume that it was triggered by the losses of royal treasure. Prior
to the deliberate killing of the prisoners, the battle was already
cruel and bloody. The *Gesta*, a source generous to the English,
speaks of the butchery of the French.[12] It recalls that there was
no time to take prisoners and 'almost all . . . were, as soon as
they were struck down, put to death without respite, either by
those who had laid them low or by others following after.'[13] This
butchery, which continued until the English were sure of their
victory, is vividly described by *The First English Life of King
Henry the Fifth*:

> no man approached the place of the battell, but either he must slay or
> else he was slayne . . . . no man was taken prisoner, but an innumerable
> were slayne . . . . And when it came to the middle of the fielde, the
> Englishmen were more encouraged to slaye there enemies then tofore.
> . . . there approached no man [of the French] to bataile, but only to
> death: of whom, after that an innumerable companie were slayne, and
> that the victorie surelie remayned to the Englishmen, they spared to
> slaye and tooke prisoners of the Frenchmen.[14]

---

[9] *Gesta*, 84 n. 1.   [10] Ibid. 91 (footnote omitted).
[11] Ibid. 92–3 (footnote omitted).   [12] Ibid. 91.   [13] Ibid.
[14] Charles Lethbridge Kingsford (ed.), *The First English Life of King Henry the
Fifth* (1911), 59–60.

Modern accounts by both Wylie[15] and Winston Churchill[16] speak of plunder but not killing. John Keegan refers to plunder by a body of armed peasants who were led by three mounted knights; they stole some objects and 'inflicted some loss of life'.[17] The anonymous early sixteenth-century biographer of Henry V explained that the King's order to kill the prisoners was triggered by his fear that he would have to fight them as well as the attacking French forces. This author did not even mention the assault on the baggage train.[18]

If Holinshed's version is correct, the French raid is unlikely to have violated any laws of war. The English rear camp constituted a lawful object of attack. In the absence of resistance, the immunity of persons serving the troops would have depended on whether they met the prevailing standards of innocence.[19] Assuming that the pages were not entitled to the immunity of children[20] and were to be treated as 'youths', their right to be spared would have turned on their surrender, either on 'fair terms' or unconditionally.[21] At least some medieval jurists regarded non-combatant servants of an army as a legitimate military target, even when they were not involved in any defensive or other fighting, and even when they were not armed. Thus the

---

[15] Wylie, *supra* note 2, at ii. 171. In his discussion of the attack on the King's baggage, Hibbert does not mention any loss of life. Charles Hibbert, *Agincourt* (1964), 127.

[16] Winston S. Churchill, *A History of the English-Speaking Peoples* (1956), i. 319. See also J. D. Griffith Davies, *Henry V*, (1935), 190.

[17] John Keegan, *The Face of Battle* (1978), 84.

[18] *First English Life*, *supra* note 14, at 60–1. Harris Nicolas, *A History of the Battle of Agincourt* (2nd edn. 1832), 124, writes that King Henry was advised that the French had attacked his rear and plundered his baggage, but he does not mention any loss of life among the baggage attendants. Many other historians also mention the attack on the baggage train, but not loss of life among the attendants. See E. F. Jacob, *Henry V and the Invasion of France* (1947), 105; George Makepeace Towle, *The History of Henry the Fifth* (1866), 340; Desmond Seward, *Henry V* (1988), 80; R. B. Mowat, *Henry V* (1920), 159. Allmand offers this rather lenient explanation for the King's order to kill the prisoners: it 'was an attempt to frighten them into submission, and to cause them to allow themselves to be herded off the field by the archers . . . If many were killed in the process, this was no deliberate wholesale massacre. It was, moreover, a "massacre" which was brought to an end immediately it was recognized that the threat from the French men-at-arms was not going to materialize.' Christopher Allmand, *Henry V* at 95 (1992).

[19] Vitoria, 180 (38)–(39).

[20] See Grotius, bk. iii, ch. xi, pt. ix.

[21] See Grotius, bk. iii, ch. xi, pts. xiii(2), xiv, xv; see also Gentili, ii. 216.

authoritative Giovanni da Legnano writes: 'Should those who attend in a war, but who cannot fight, enjoy the immunities [status] of combatants? Say that they should, provided that they are useful in counsel in other ways.'[22]

Perhaps Shakespeare himself was not quite persuaded that Fluellen's version of the law sufficiently justified the order to kill the prisoners. The sarcasm in Gower's response appears to be aimed both at the Welshman Fluellen and at the King. Indeed, the real Henry may later have been embarrassed by the order. In his eyewitness account of the Agincourt campaign, the anonymous English cleric attached to Henry's court clearly intended to justify Henry's foreign policy and to present him as a devout and humane Christian prince who was seeking peace with justice. Yet, in describing the killing of the prisoners ('by the swords either of their captors or of others following after, lest they should involve us in utter disaster in the fighting that would ensue'), he never mentioned the provocation of the French attack on the luggage train or even the existence of Henry's command.[23]

Although some of the French participants in the attack were subsequently punished by France for committing 'treason' and leaving their camp for private plunder,[24] those punitive measures were motivated not by the violation of the laws of war, but by the 'causing [of] the rumour [of a French counter-attack] which led to the hideous massacre of the prisoners on the battlefield'.[25] Under the circumstances, Fluellen's invocation of the law of arms may have reflected Shakespeare's desire to place the most favourable interpretation on the King's order. Legally, however, it was flawed.

Without a manifest breach of the law by the French, Henry could not claim the defence of reprisal, which was then generally permissible[26] and, according to some views, was even allowed against innocent private persons.[27] Indeed, it did not occur to

---

[22] Legnano, ch. 71, p. 274.

[23] *Gesta*, 93. See also Intro. by the Editors, ibid., pp. xviii, xxiii, xxviii.

[24] Holinshed, 38 (= R. Holinshed, *Chronicles* (1808), iii. 81).

[25] Wylie, *supra* note 2, at ii. 171 (footnotes omitted); see also Holinshed, 38 (= R. Holinshed, *Chronicles* (1808), iii. 81).

[26] See the discussion of the breadth of permissible reprisals by Giovanni da Legnano, chs. 124–65, pp. 308–30. Reprisals against prisoners of war are now outlawed. See e.g. Geneva Convention No. III, *supra* note 5, Art. 13.

[27] A rule protecting innocent private persons against reprisals was justified by Jacobus de Belvisio on the basis of the principle of individual responsibility:

Gentili, in his discussion of Agincourt (see below), that reprisals might be relevant. The usually humane Gentili, while pleading for compassion 'towards those who really suffer [retaliation] for the faults of others',[28] none the less accepted the principle of collective responsibility as manifested by reprisals, as a matter of law:

[I]t avails not in this case to say that those who were punished were not the ones who acted cruelly, and that hence they ought not to have been treated cruelly; for the enemy make up one body, just as an army is a single body. . . . [T]he individuals are responsible, even if a fault was committed by all in common.[29]

Writing soon after Gentili, Grotius challenged the legality of reprisals against prisoners, except in those cases of individual responsibility for a previously committed crime that 'a just judge would hold punishable by death'.[30] Grotius argued that collective responsibility was a fiction and should not be invoked to justify reprisals against innocent persons: 'nature does not sanction retaliation except against those who have done wrong. It is not sufficient that by a sort of fiction the enemy may be conceived as forming a single body.'[31]

If the massacre of the French prisoners, whose horror was vividly described by Holinshed,[32] was not excusable as a reprisal, could it have been justified on grounds of necessity? Alluding to the necessities of war, the eminent medieval jurist Giovanni da Legnano recognized the captor's right to kill prisoners where there was 'fear of a disturbance of the peace'.[33] Holinshed's

'a man ought not to be punished for another's offence.' Cited by Giovanni da Legnano, ch. 143, p. 321, who disagrees.

[28] Gentili, ii. 232. [29] Ibid. Cf. Genesis 18: 23–6:
'And Abraham drew near, and said, Wilt thou also destroy the righteous with the wicked? Peradventure there be fifty righteous within the city: wilt thou also destroy and not spare the place for the fifty righteous that are therein? That be far from thee to do after this manner, to slay the righteous with the wicked: and that the righteous should be as the wicked, that be far from thee: Shall not the Judge of all the earth do right? And the Lord said, If I find in Sodom fifty righteous within the city, then I will spare all the place for their sakes.'
[30] Grotius, bk. III, ch. xi, pt. xvi(1).
[31] Ibid., pt. xvi (2). '[R]etaliation that is lawful . . . must be inflicted upon the very person who has done wrong', ibid., ch. iv, pt. xiii (1).
[32] Holinshed, 38–9 (= R. Holinshed, *Chronicles* (1808), iii. 81–2).
[33] Legnano, ch. 69, p. 274. Many historians believe that necessity justified Henry's order to kill the prisoners. Thus, Harold F. Hutchison, *King Henry V*

account suggests that the King's fear of an impending attack, in which the French prisoners would join, was real.[34] The heavily outnumbered English would have had difficulty repelling another attack while guarding their numerous prisoners. In the same vein, Wylie, on the basis of the chroniclers, writes that the danger of a new assault triggered the King's order. But this explanation is undercut by the fact that the King made an exception for dukes, earls, and other high-placed leaders 'as fell [insofar as ransom was concerned] to the king's own share'.[35] Mindful of their expected ransoms, the captors were reluctant to carry out the order, 'but the king threatened to hang any man that disobeyed and told off 200 of his ever-handy archers to begin the bloody work.'[36]

In other wars as well, orders to execute captives clashed with the desire of captors to obtain ransom. The war of Burgundy against Ghent (1451–3) was regarded as a war against rebels, and therefore as a *guerre mortelle* in which rules of chivalry were not applicable and quarter was not given. In that war, the Duke of

(1967), 124, observes that '[b]y medieval standards Henry was obeying his soldier creed—military necessity justified any butchery.' See also Towle, *supra* note 18, at 339–40. Seward, *supra* note 18, at 81, strongly dissents: 'In reality, by fifteenth-century standards, to massacre captive, unarmed noblemen who, according to the universally recognized international laws of chivalry, had every reason to expect to be ransomed if they surrendered formally, was a peculiarly nasty crime.'

[34] *Supra* text at note 4. Nicolas, *supra* note 18, at 124, believes that '[i]mperative necessity' dictated the King's order.

[35] Wylie, *supra* note 2, at ii. 171. Hutchison, who supports the traditional justification of necessity, argues that the fact that Henry's own rich prisoners were exempted from being killed tallied with Henry's reputation for 'shrewd common sense—he simply could not afford to miss the chance of spectacular ransoms.' Hutchison, *supra* note 33, at 124.

[36] Wylie, *supra* note 2, at ii. 171–2. The archers, not being knights, may have had fewer scruples about killing members of the French nobility. Grose, i. 345, cynically observed that '[t]he hopes of ransom frequently acted in the place of humanity, avarice assuming the place of mercy.' Could archers enforce agreements to pay ransom? Although under the law of chivalry, which applied only to a particular class of persons, peasants could not enforce such agreements (*LW* 19), this was not necessarily true of archers. Many persons who were not knights but thought they were or aspired to be 'noble' (in the French sense) invoked 'knightly' or 'chivalrous honour'. In 15th-c. England swearing on 'my honour as a gentleman' (as opposed to knight) was beginning to come in. Esquires and gentlemen certainly promised on their honour to pay ransom, and took prisoners, and held them to ransom. In Henry V's time, even an archer might be a gentleman. Ransoms were certainly promised upon 'honour'; and captors—not only knights—were expected to behave 'honourably' to their prisoners (and *vice versa*). I am grateful to Dr Keen for his suggestions on this point.

Burgundy (Philip the Good) categorically ordered the execution of all prisoners. Malcolm Vale explained these ducal commands as 'suggest[ing] an unwillingness among some nobles to be deprived of potentially valuable captives'.[37]

Although the rank and the wealth of those members of the highest French nobility who were spared by the real Henry may have influenced his decision to exclude them from the mass of the prisoners to be killed, his primary motivation was probably the desire to secure generous ransoms for himself, rather than to accord them the privilege of rank. That great wealth and therefore the concomitant ability to pay lavish ransoms served as the criterion for separating the few that were to live from the many that were to die is morally unacceptable. Already Gentili complained that instead of punishing leaders who led their people to an unjust war, in

modern warfare . . . it is the common soldiers who are slain. The leaders, the rich, are saved, that they may ransom themselves. O unjust form of waging war and cruel traffic! . . . But our worthy leaders consult for their own interests in this new fashion; for if they should come into the hands of the enemy, they would no longer have to fear for their own lives, now that the lavish shedding of the blood of the common soldiers has become customary.[38]

Ransoms were usually huge. Grose reported that:

The usual price demanded for the ransome of a prisoner of war was . . . one year's rent of his estate, one third of which was by the royal ordonnances, the property of the chief captain under whom the captor served; out of which, one third of that third, equal to one ninth of the whole ransome, was to be paid by the captain to the king; stipendiary soldiers who had no estates, usually paid for their ransome one half of their year's pay.[39]

The collection of ransom was, therefore, of tremendous economic significance to the captor. Ransom and plunder were the medieval warrior's principal incentives for going to war. Ransom could also, and often did, bring economic ruin to the captive and his family.

Without the promise and the expectation of ransom, the rules of chivalry could not ensure the lives of prisoners. Francis Grose

[37] Malcolm G. A. Vale, *War and Chivalry* (1981), 160.
[38] Gentili, ii. 325.   [39] Grose, i. 344.

cynically observed that '[t]he hopes of ransom frequently acted in the place of humanity, avarice assuming the place of mercy.'[40] He thus explained the great slaughter of the Scots at the battle of Musselborough (1548): 'that their mean appearance gave little hopes [*sic*] of their ability to pay ransom'.[41]

Ransom could at least spare the lives of those able to pay it. Vale wrote that 'the incentive for the common soldier to conceal booty and to kill (rather than take prisoners) grew as the prospect of lucrative plunder diminished.'[42] Wars fought in the second part of the fifteenth century, when ransom ceased to be customarily granted, became even bloodier. The Swiss and German mercenaries did not take prisoners, because prisoners would make the search for booty more difficult. Moreover, in wars fought by larger groups kept apart by gunfire, the pursuit and the taking of prisoners became rare.[43] Vale notes, for example, that a Swiss battle order of 18 March 1476 required that all Burgundians and their allies be killed, and that, accordingly, no prisoners were taken at the Battle of Morat.[44] In the short term, at least, the decline of ransom resulted in more brutal wars.

Although ransom served as an incentive for sparing lives, it also had negative effects. It could trigger the taking as prisoners persons who would otherwise have been left in peace, and even of persons protected by the laws of war. For example, Henry's Ordinances of War prohibited the capture as prisoners of unarmed women and of unarmed men of the cloth, as well as of children under the age of 14, with the exception of the sons of lords or other persons of status. Captors of the sons of such wealthy persons were to deliver their prisoners to their superiors and eventually shared the ransom.

Chivalric rules were more protective of children. Invoking the principle of innocence, Christine de Pisan movingly though vainly argued against the taking as prisoners of little children, whether poor or rich:

I telle the certeynly that after right the litel child may nor ought not to be kept prysoner, for reason wil not accorde, that innocencye be a greued for it is veray trouthe that a childe in suche a cas is innocent & not coulpable of all werre in al manere of thingis, wherfore he ought not to bere the peyne of that wherof he is not in fawte nor of counseill nor

---

[40] Grose, i. 345 and n. i.   [41] Ibid.   [42] Vale, *supra* note 37, at 156.
[43] Ibid.   [44] Ibid.

of goodes he hathe nought holpen therto for he hathe as yet noon Ye maister, but supposed that the said child were ryche of hym self as of his fader & moders godes that be dede, mooste he paye, For it might be soo that his tutoures or they that haue the rule ouer his goodis shulde paye a subsydye of hys goodes to the kynge of Englande for to maynten his werre in Fraunce, Yet y telle the that nay, for what that his tutoures paied therof it were not of the childes wille whiche is not yet in age of discrecion, without faille maister thenne is not this daye this law wel kepte, thou saist to me trouthe fayre loue, nor yet be nomore kept nother the noble ryghtes of olde tyme that helde and truly dyde kepe the noble conquerours, Thus abusen with the right of armes they that now doo excersice them by the grete coueytyse that ouercometh them, soo ought to tourne them to a grete shame for to emprisone wymen or children & impotent & olde.[45]

Christine was following in the footsteps of Bouvet here, who had argued that children—being innocent of the war and unable to assist in its conduct—should not be made prisoners. He maintained that it was wrong to imprison old men who took no part in the war, as well as women and children 'for the former lack strength, the others knowledge'.[46] Emphasizing the obligations of chivalry, Bouvet insisted that 'all gentlemen should keep them from harm, and all knights and men-at-arms are bound to do so, and whoever does the contrary deserves the name of pillager.'[47]

Churchill, defending Henry, claims that the King ordered the killing of the prisoners in the belief that he was being attacked from the rear; although '[t]he alarm in the rear was soon relieved,' by then the massacre was almost over.[48] Less categorically, Keegan writes that the order to kill the prisoners was prompted by either the attack on the rear camp or the continued menace of the French.[49]

However genuine the King's fear of an attack on his outnumbered troops may have been, the order to kill the French prisoners, already *hors de combat*, could hardly be justified on the ground that they might have joined the ranks of the attackers. The captured French were still encumbered by their heavy armour, as their basinets (helmets) alone had been removed.[50]

---

[45] Pisan, 232–3. [46] Bouvet, 185. [47] Ibid.
[48] Churchill, *supra* note 16, at i. 319–20. [49] Keegan, *supra* note 17, at 84.
[50] Wylie, *supra* note 2, at ii. 171.

Dismounted, defenceless, and barely able to move, they were hardly a menace to the English troops. In the face of real necessity, a threat of execution would not have been required to enforce Henry's order. Burne argued, however, that because many prisoners had not yet been divested of their weapons, 'if [the archers] let go of their captives and moved off to repel the impending attack their captives would have been free to pick up weapons that sprinkled the ground and attack them in the rear, possibly in conjunction with their comrades who were still running amok in the English camp.'[51] This justification of the killings on grounds of necessity is unpersuasive.

Did the order violate the applicable laws of war? While maintaining that, 'speaking absolutely, there is nothing to prevent the killing of those who have surrendered or been captured in a just war so long as abstract equity is observed,'[52] Vitoria suggested that this harsh rule had been tempered by the law of nations and the customs of war; consequently, 'after victory has been won . . . and all danger is over, [they] are not to be killed.'[53] Because Henry believed that the victory had not been won and that the danger persisted, he would not have violated Vitoria's standards, and certainly not the earlier medieval norms described by Giovanni da Legnano. Even Crompton, Shakespeare's contemporary, and 'an apprentice of the common law', in a book published in the same year Shakespeare wrote his play, fully justified Henry's order to kill the prisoners:

the French as they are men of great courage and valour, so they assembled themselves againe in battell array, meaning to have giuen a new battell to king Henry, which king Henry perceiving, gave speciall commandment by proclamation, that every man should kill his prisoners: whereupon many were presently slaine, whereof the French king having intelligence, dispersed his army, and so departed: whereby you may see the miseries of warre, that though they [the prisoners] had yeelded and

---

[51] Alfred H. Burne, *The Agincourt War* (1956), 86. The editors of *Gesta* agree with Burne: 'The tendency among historians who have condemned Henry's slaughter of the prisoners . . . has been to forget that the English were not out of danger after their victory over the French vanguard; they must have been exhausted, and the captives in their ranks were very numerous. The arrival of enemy reinforcements was quite probable, as Anthony of Brabant's appearance had shown. Henry clearly thought that he must fight again . . . and had to make a quick decision to enable his men to face the danger with least disadvantage to themselves.' *Gesta*, 92–3 n. 1.

[52] Vitoria, 183 (49).   [53] Ibid.

thought themselves sure of their lives, paying their ransome, according to the lawes of armes, yet uppon such necessary occasion, to kill them was a thing by all reason allowed, for otherwise the king having lost diverse valiant Captaines and souldiers in this battell, and being also but a small number in comparison of the French kings army, and in a strang countrey, where he could not supply his neede upon the sudden, it might have bene much daungerous to have againe joyned with the enemy, and kept his prisoners alive, as in our Chronicles largely appeareth.[54]

But such medieval writers as Bouvet and Christine de Pisan argued that the killing of prisoners should be prohibited, though with some exceptions.[55] They advocated even more protective rules for prisoners subjected to inhumane treatment. A knight who escapes although he had given his word to remain in captivity offends God and man. This is

on the assumption, however, that his master does not use any extradordinary harshness towards him; for if he were kept in such close imprisonment that he was in danger of falling into languor, or mortal sickness, or any grievous ill of body, and for that reason took his opportunity to escape, he would commit no offence . . . . And if his master were so cruel as to be in the habit of killing or causing the death of his prisoners in his prisons, and if, on opportunity arising, he quitted such a host, I would blame him not at all.[56]

The right to escape in breach of a knight's promise applied not only in cases where the captor preferred to have his prisoners killed in prison, rather than to have them put to ransom, but also if the captor refused to accept a reasonable ransom and

---

[54] Richard Crompton, *The Mansion of Magnamitie* (1599; unpaginated), ch. 6 *in fine*.

[55] Bouvet, 134 argued that 'he who in battle has captured his enemy, especially if it be the duke or marshal of the battle . . . should have mercy on him, unless by his deliverance there is danger of having greater wars.' Elsewhere, Bouvet explains that 'to kill an enemy in battle is allowed by law and by the lord, but out of battle no man may kill another save in self-defence, except the lord, after trial.' Ibid. 152. Pisan, 222, would prohibit the killing of prisoners even in battle: 'Soo saye I to the well that it is ayenst all ryght and gentylnesse to slee hym that yeldeth hym.' Arguing against 'a thynge Inhumayne and to grete a cruelness' and answering critics who invoked the ancient right of the captor to kill his prisoners, sell them, or otherwise dispose of them, she asserted that 'amonge crysten folke where the lawe is altogyder grounded vpon myldefulnes and pyte [it] is not lycyte nor accordynge to vse of suche terannye whyche be acursed and reproued.' Ibid. Nevertheless, after the battle, she would allow the prince to kill a prisoner who would be dangerous to the prince if allowed to go free. Ibid.

[56] Bouvet, 159.

insisted on 'ransom beyond [the prisoner's] condition'.[57] Christine de Pisan argued that not only was the killing of prisoners prohibited, but there existed an obligation to accord them humane treatment. Although the law of arms proscribed the escape of a prisoner who gave his word to remain in captivity, that promise was contingent on his being humanely treated. It ceased to be binding if his treatment by his captors endangered his life or health:

That is to wyte that the sayde mayster doo not to hym noon other evyl nor hurt than to put hym in a couenable pryson, as ryght hath lymyted & wil,

But I accorde wyth the wel, yf he were kept soo straytly and soo euyll delt wyth all that hys lyff or helthe were putte in Jeopardye therby, and that Inhumayne or cruelle a thyng it were, I afferme unto the that yf he can fyn-de meanes for to escape awaye that a ryght grete wyt it were, nor for noo trespas it ought not to be taken.[58]

Rules such as those promoted by Bouvet and Christine de Pisan were in fact enforced by courts applying rules of chivalry. The case of an English knight, Simon Burley (see above Chapter 2), is illustrative.[59] In a decision rendered in 1371, the *Parlement de Paris* decided that an escaped prisoner must return to the captor's custody, but only because his claim of ill-treatment had not been proven.[60]

I shall now return to the question of grant of quarter. Gentili's humane position on the duty to give quarter has already been discussed. Faithful to the chivalric code of conduct,[61] Gentili suggested that an implied contract is formed between the captor and the captive, 'a bargain with the enemy for his life'. The 'rights of humanity and the laws of war . . . order the sparing of those who surrender.'[62] Gentili did not agree that danger justified the killing of captives and he praised those who 'did not slay their captives,

---

[57] Bouvet, 159.   [58] Pisan, 237.

[59] Pierre-Clement Timbal, *La Guerre de cent ans vue à travers les registres du Parlement (1337–1369)* (1969), 328.

[60] Ibid. 329.   [61] See *supra* Ch. 6, text at notes 157, 144–6, 174–5.

[62] Gentili, ii. 216. Cf. Grotius, bk. iii, ch. iv, pt. x (2) ('So far as the law of nations is concerned, the right of killing such slaves, that is, captives taken in war, is not precluded at any time, although it is restricted, now more, now less, by the laws of states.') Elsewhere, however, Grotius advocated sparing captives who have surrendered unconditionally. Ibid., ch. xi, pt. xv.

no matter how great danger threatened them'.[63] He had harsh words for Henry:

I cannot praise the English who, in that famous battle in which they overthrew the power of France, having taken more prisoners than the number of their victorious army and fearing danger from them by night, set aside those of high rank and slew the rest. 'A hateful and inhuman deed,' says the historian, 'and the battle was not so bloody as the victory.'[64]

Perhaps Gentili's stricture on Henry's action, had it been known to Shakespeare, would explain the playwright's sensitivity and his desire to depart from Holinshed's account. But Shakespeare's apparently deliberate departure from Holinshed can plausibly be explained, without reference to Gentili, as an attempt to put Henry's order in the best possible light.

Notwithstanding Gentili's condemnation, it cannot be concluded that Henry clearly violated contemporary standards. Wylie reports that, even though the writers of the time regarded the massacre as an inhumane deed, his French critics refrained from blaming Henry because 'in those days the French would have done the same themselves had they been in so perilous a case.'[65] Killing prisoners in an emergency was not unprecedented[66] and, while quarter was normally granted in Anglo-French wars, the virtual absence of 'contemporary criticism' of Henry's action[67] suggests that, cruel though it was, his order did not violate the accepted norms of behaviour. It is difficult to characterize the order as an act of wanton brutality, given the importance of the expectations of ransom to the English soldiery as a whole.

It is, however, impossible to excuse the King's threat, made when his victory had already been assured, after the massacre of

---

[63] Gentili, ii. 211–12.　　　　　　　　　　　　　　　　[64] Ibid.

[65] Wylie, *supra* note 2, at ii. 175. Hibbert, *supra* note 15, at 129, observes: 'Even the French chroniclers write of [Henry's] action as though it were dictated by painful necessity.'

[66] Maurice H. Keen, *Chivalry* (1984), 276 n. 7.

[67] Ibid. 221. Note the matter-of-fact, non-judgmental reference to the massacre by the French chronicler the Religieux de Saint-Denys: 'Le roi d'Angleterre, croyant qu'ils [the French] voulaient revenir à la charge, ordonna qu'on tuât tous les prisonniers.' *Chronique du Religieux de Saint-Denys*, trans. and ed. L. Bellaguet, Collection de documents inédits sur l'histoire de la France, ser. 1. (1844), v. 565.

the French prisoners, not to give quarter and to kill the remaining prisoners, if the French continued to fight:

> KING   Take a trumpet, herald;
> Ride thou unto the horsemen on yon hill.
> If they will fight with us, bid them come down,
> Or void the field: they do offend our sight.
> If they'll do neither, we will come to them,
> And make them skirr away as swift as stones
> Enforcèd from the old Assyrian slings.
> Besides, we'll cut the throats of those we have,
> And not a man of them that we shall take
> Shall taste our mercy. Go and tell them so.
>
> (*Henry V*, IV. vii. 54–63)

Shakespeare appears to follow Holinshed:

the king perceiving his enimies in one part to assemble togither, as though they meant to give a new battell for preservation of the prisoners, sent to them an herald, commanding them either to depart out of his sight, or else to come forward at once, and give battell: promising herewith, that if they did offer to fight againe, not onelie those prisoners which this people alreadie had taken; but also so manie of them as in this new conflict, which they thus attempted should fall into his hands, should die the death without redemption.[68]

Holinshed based his account on Titus Livius, whose influence is also apparent in the account which appears in *The First English Life of King Henry the Fifth* by the anonymous author known as Translator of Livius: 'if they come to battaile, both those of theires that then were prisoners, and also all they that should after be taken, without mercie or redemption shoulde be put to death.'[69]

Henry's threat to refuse quarter and to kill the prisoners still in his hands, should the French continue fighting, as they could lawfully do, was most likely in violation of the contemporary laws of war. It was, nevertheless, passed over in silence by most commentators, probably because the French took the threat seriously and further killing was avoided.

Agincourt was not the only setting, during the reign of Henry V, in which privileged categories of combatants were killed. In

---

[68] Holinshed, 39 (= R. Holinshed, *Chronicles* (1808), iii, 82).
[69] *First English Life, supra* note 14, at 61.

January 1420, for example, English forces slaughtered a large number of Armagnacs who were retreating under safe conduct.[70] That same month, a Castilian fleet defeated an English naval force before La Rochelle, taking many prisoners, 'some of whom were landed at the town and slaughtered by the Bastard of Alençon'.[71] In these and other cases, the protective rules were clear, but the practice, sadly, was different.

In modern law the killing of prisoners of war constitutes, of course, a 'grave breach' of the third Geneva Convention,[72] and the killing of civilians a grave breach of the fourth Geneva Convention.[73] Such acts can no longer be excused by either reprisal or necessity, and were condemned as war crimes violating the Hague Regulations,[74] the 1929 Geneva POW Convention[75] and international customary law by the Nuernberg tribunals, which in many cases imposed capital punishment on the perpetrators. Sadly, even now the killing of protected persons is not exceptional.

---

[70] James Hamilton Wylie and William Templeton Waugh, *The Reign of Henry the Fifth* (1929), iii. 196.

[71] Ibid. 197.   [72] *Supra* note 5, at Art. 130.

[73] Convention Relative to the Protection of Civilian Persons in Time of War (Geneva Convention No. IV), 12 Aug. 1949, 6 UST 3516, TIAS No. 3365, 75 UNTS 287 at Art. 147.

[74] *Supra* note 5, at Art.. 4

[75] (Geneva) Convention Relative to the Treatment of Prisoners of War, opened for signature 27 July 1929, 47 Stat. 2021, TS No. 846, at Art. 2.

10

Heralds, Ambassadors, and the Treaty of Troyes

The scene on the battlefield at Agincourt, when the English appeared to have won and the French herald Montjoy arrived on yet another mission to Shakespeare's Henry, is vividly described by the playwright:

> EXETER   Here comes the herald of the French, my liege.
> GLOUCESTER   His eyes are humbler than they used to be.
> KING How now, what means this, herald? Know'st thou not
> That I have fined these bones of mine for ransom? . . .[1]
> MONTJOY No, great King.
> I come to thee for charitable licence,
> That we may wander o'er this bloody field
> To book our dead and then to bury them,
> To sort our nobles from our common men—
> For many of our princes, woe the while,
> Lie drowned and soaked in mercenary blood.
> So do our vulgar drench their peasant limbs
> In blood of princes, and their wounded steeds
> Fret fetlock-deep in gore, and with wild rage
> Jerk out their armèd heels at their dead masters,
> Killing them twice. O give us leave, great King,
> To view the field in safety, and dispose
> Of their dead bodies.
> KING   I tell thee truly, herald,
> I know not if the day be ours or no,
> For yet a many of your horsemen peer

---

[1] See also the heroic answer by Shakespeare's Henry to the French herald Montjoy before the Battle of Agincourt, in which Henry ruled out the possibility of being ransomed in case of defeat: 'Herald, save thou thy labour. | Come thou no more for ransom, gentle herald. | They shall have none, I swear, but these my joints— | Which if they have as I will leave 'em them, | Shall yield them little. Tell the Constable.' (IV. iii. 122–6)

And gallop o'er the field.

MONTJOY   The day is yours.[2]

(*Henry V*, IV. vii. 64–84)

Heralds performed an important function in medieval warfare, as is seen in Shakespeare's *Henry V*.[3] Shakespeare also mentioned heralds[4] and ambassadors[5] in other plays. The herald's function derives from an ancient tradition. The institution of the herald's office was mythically attributed to as ancient a source as Julius Caesar.[6] Heralds were attired in distinctive habits designed to protect them from acts of violence ('MONTJOY   You know me by my habit', *Henry V*, III. vi. 115). Keen notes that heralds carried white wands as a sign of their personal immunity from war[7] and that their immunity was one of the few effective norms providing security against attack.[8] The high expectation that the immunity of heralds would be respected is demonstrated by the fact that one of the three heralds sent to Henry to advise him some time before he reached Calais that the French would fight him was Jacques de Heilly, who had been a captive in England but had escaped to France.[9] That de Heilly did not fear recapture by the English during his mission speaks for itself. De Heilly's good fortune did not last long, however, for he was killed at Agincourt.[10]

Heralds carried messages and defiances between the warring parties ('MONTJOY   Thus says my King: ". . . To this add defiance"', *Henry V*, III. vi. 119, 132–3); mediated and arranged the time and place of important battles (including Agincourt) in such a manner that, according to 'the etiquette of chivalry . . . [neither side would] take . . . unfair advantage of the other';[11] and arranged truces.[12] They were the recognized experts on the

---

[2] See also III. vi and IV. iii.

[3] George W. Keeton, *Shakespeare and his Legal Problems* (1930), 70–1; George W. Keeton, *Shakespeare's Legal and Political Background* (1967), 87–8. See also the The Othes of Heraudes, repr. in Travers Twiss (ed.), *The Black Book of Admiralty*, Monumenta Juridica, i. (1871), 297 and The Othe of the 'Kynges of Armes in their Creacion' ibid. 295.

[4] e.g. *King Lear*, v. iii. 107–20.   [5] e.g. *1 Henry VI*, v. iv. 144.

[6] *LW* 57.   [7] *LW* 109.   [8] *LW* 217.

[9] James Hamilton Wylie, *The Reign of Henry the Fifth* (1919), ii. 125 and n. 6.

[10] Ibid., n. 6.   [11] Ibid. 140.

[12] On the role of Montjoy at Agincourt, see Holinshed, 39–40 (= R. Holinshed, *Chronicles* (1808), iii. 82).

code of chivalry,[13] whose verdicts were decisive for members of the 'international order of knighthood',[14] including even princes. They 'refereed' tournaments and at battles recorded those who were present, those who had distinguished themselves, and those who had died. Heralds were also experts in the science of armoury, with jurisdiction over every aspect of the bearing of arms by the nobility.[15] Henry V and Charles VI used heralds extensively to carry messages both before and after the invasion.[16] After the conclusion of the Treaty of Troyes, Charles VI ordered that the conclusion of the treaty 'fut publié par la voix du héraut'.[17]

At Agincourt, before the beginning of the battle, the King ordered his heralds who were wearing their distinctive clothing to attend to their offices.[18] Later, Montjoy advised the winner of his victory.[19] Jacob regarded the Montjoy of Shakespeare's play as a 'fabrication derived from the Mountjoy King-at-arms mentioned by Hall'.[20] In fact, Montjoy is mentioned not only by Hall ('Mountioy')[21] but also by Holinshed ('Montjoie').[22] Whatever the historical facts may be, for Shakespeare, Montjoy certainly was not a fabrication, but a figure based on the dramatist's principal historical sources. However, the episode in which Montjoy advised the winner of his victory has few parallels in other engagements. Heralds carefully refrained from participating in hostilities,[23] and the law of arms required that they be protected. Accidents and violations were, of course, inevitable. During his invasion of Flanders, Bishop Spenser of Norwich sent a herald to

[13] *LW* 16, 50; see also Maurice H. Keen, *Chivalry* (1984), 137–40. See also the oath of the heralds, *supra* note 3.
[14] *LW* 50.   [15] Malcolm G. A. Vale, *War and Chivalry* (1981), 94.
[16] See *Gesta* 56–7, 93 n. 2, and Intro. by the editors, p. xxxiv; *Chronique du Religieux de Saint-Denys*, ed. and trans. L. Bellaguet, Collection de documents inédits sur l'histoire de France, ser. 1 (1844), v. 501, 507, 527.
[17] *Chronique du Religieux de Saint-Denys*, vi (1862), *supra* note 16, 433, 439.
[18] *The First English Life of King Henry the Fifth*, Charles Lethbridge Kingsford (ed.), (1911), 58. (This is a work of 1513 by an anonymous author known commonly as the Translator of Livius.)
[19] Holinshed, 39–40 (= R. Holinshed, *Chronicles* (1808), iii. 82); see also Charles Hibbert, *Agincourt* (1964), 134.
[20] E. F. Jacob, *Henry V and the Invasion of France* (1947), 98.
[21] Hall, 70.
[22] Holinshed, 39–40 (= R. Holinshed, *Chronicles* (1808), iii. 82).
[23] 'Throughout the battle of Agincourt the heralds of both sides stood together on a hill, away from the fighting in which their order had no part.' *LW* 195.

the troops of West Flanders to enquire whether they were supporting Pope Urban, as did Bishop Spenser, or Pope Clement,
whom the urbanists considered schismatic, 'but the rude people,
not understanding what apperteined to the law of armes, ran
upon the herald at his approching to them, and slue him before
he could begin to tell his tale'.[24] The herald's killing triggered a
major English attack. A French herald was slain at Agincourt.[25]

In some European countries, especially in France, heralds were
soon to disappear, together with the medieval social order and
the rules of chivalry. The rise of standing armies in the mid-
fifteenth century and the introduction of standard uniforms eliminated the need for experts who could recognize an individual by
his coat of arms. Vale points out that '[e]ven the ancient heraldic
duty of carrying messages, challenges and summonses was gradually taken' from the heralds,[26] who were replaced by drummers,
fifers, and trumpeters as envoys and messengers. There are still
heralds in England, however, serving as the sovereign's official
and salaried officers of arms.

Heralds were distinguished from envoys. Heralds regularly
acted as privileged messengers. Henry V himself sent a herald to
deliver a letter to Charles VI during the negotiations that preceded the campaign described in Shakespeare's play. Hence, they
played a role in diplomatic exchanges, by delivering ultimatums
and defiances, collecting safe conducts for embassies, and carrying messages between belligerents, but did not serve in a real
plenipotentiary capacity. Plenipotentiary functions were carried
out by envoys or ambassadors. Heralds lacked the status and
were not expected to have the expertise to qualify them to act as
ambassadors.

Ambassadors, who held significant roles in *Henry V* as special
envoys, or, in modern parlance, heads of special missions[27]
(rather than permanent diplomatic missions[28]), were to become a

---

[24] R. Holinshed, *Chronicles* (1807), ii. 758.
[25] See *supra* text accompanying note 10 and *Gesta*, 75, editors' n. 4.
[26] Malcolm G. A. Vale, *War and Chivalry* (1981), 151.
[27] Within the meaning of Art. 1 of the Convention on Special Missions,
opened for signature 16 Dec. 1969, Annex to GA Res. 2530 (XXIV), 24 UN
GAOR Supp. (No. 30) at 99, UN Doc. A/7630 (1970).
[28] See Vienna Convention on Diplomatic Relations, *done* 18 Apr. 1961, 23
UST 3227, TIAS No. 7502, 500 UNTS 95.

permanent institution.[29] Kenneth Fowler observes that in the fourteenth century governments employed special missions or *ad hoc* embassies rather than resident ambassadors, and that they often included, for the English, high nobility and, for the French, senior ecclesiastics. Much negotiating was done by legal experts. It was necessary to secure safe conducts for the ambassadors.[30] The extension of ambassadorial safe conducts was even used by Henry as a means of influencing the negotiations and quickening their pace.[31] Shakespeare's ambassadors deliver messages between the courts of France and England[32] that include territorial claims, an ultimatum, a declaration of war, and the corresponding replies. The real Henry V and Charles VI used ambassadors in the abortive negotiations that preceded the invasion of France,[33] in which negotiations the question of the adequacy of ambassadorial full powers was of considerable significance.[34]

Although only ad hoc embassies were used, the practice was to send the same persons repeatedly to negotiate treaties, truces, and breaches of truces.[35] This continuity in personnel ensured a considerable degree of expertise, especially regarding English diplomats. The role of legal experts, trained in civil and canon law, in negotiations was critical,[36] especially for both the English and the French in the negotiations leading to the Treaty of Troyes.[37]

Like heralds, ambassadors enjoyed immunity,[38] but the rules of immunity must still have been relatively 'soft' and unreliable for Henry's ambassador, Exeter, to feel impelled to threaten the King of France with Henry's might:

---

[29] See Harold Nicolson, *Diplomacy* (1963), 30–1.

[30] Kenneth Fowler, 'Truces', in Kenneth Fowler (ed.), *The Hundred Years War* (1971), 184, 186–7.

[31] *Chronique du Religieux de Saint-Denys, supra* note 16, at v. 509.

[32] See *Henry V*, I. ii, and II. iv.   [33] See e.g. *Gesta*, 14–15 and n. 1.

[34] See e.g. *Chronique du Religieux de Saint-Denys, supra* note 16, at v. 503, 509, 519; Jacob, *supra* note 20, at 71.

[35] Christopher T. Allmand, *The Hundred Years War* (1988), 116–17.

[36] Ibid.

[37] Maurice Keen, 'Diplomacy', in Gerald L. Harriss (ed.), *Henry V: The Practice of Kingship* (1985), 184–5, 190–1.

[38] Grotius, bk. II, ch. xviii, pt. vii, who agreed that retaliation against ambassadors was not allowed. For a 14th-c. statement of the immunity of ambassadors from reprisals, see Legnano, ch. 139, p. 319. For an example of early 15th-c. inviolability of ambassadors and their property, see Pisan, 234–5.

EXETER   Dispatch us with all speed, lest that our king
Come here himself to question our delay—
For he is footed in this land already.
KING CHARLES   You shall be soon dispatched with fair conditions.
A night is but small breath and little pause
To answer matters of this consequence.

(Henry V, II. iv. 141–6)

Similarly, French ambassadors were anxious not to remain in Henry's court, as he suggested (6 July 1415), to await Charles's reply to Henry's proposals, which he wanted to send to France by his own emissaries.[39] Nevertheless, although ambassadors were often regarded as 'legalised spies',[40] rulers usually recognized the privileges and immunities of diplomats, so that their work could be carried out 'without fear of harm being done to them on their travels, particularly in the lands of an enemy',[41] and even gave them (as they did to heralds) generous presents.

Well before Henry's invasion of France, the fourteenth-century exponent of rules of chivalry, Honoré Bouvet, described with considerable sophistication the rules governing the immunity of ambassadors (which even covered immunity from jurisdiction with regard to personal obligations):

In brief, I say that, according to written law, ambassadors and legates pass in security through a country, and while they are going to the King outside the realm, no man may hinder, disturb, or injure them. And they are still further privileged, for if any one of them was under obligation to a French merchant his goods could not be distrained on this occasion, for the law does not allow this; nor does it permit that the legate of a prince or of a notable place should be brought to judgment for the things done on his journey.[42]

The immunity of ambassadors from reprisals[43] was addressed by Ayala:

he [the prince who during a truce is provoked by another prince's wrongdoing] could offer no violence to the enemy's envoys, they being protected by the Law of Nations and declared inviolable and sacred, apart from any agreement for peace or a truce and even in the heat of

---

[39] *Chronique du Religieux de Saint-Denys, supra* note 16, at v. 521.
[40] Allmand, *supra* note 35, at 118.   [41] Ibid.
[42] Bouvet, 186.   [43] See *supra* note 38.

war. And it is immaterial that the enemy have already broken a truce and done violence to envoys sent from the other side to them.[44]

Ayala thus viewed the immunity of ambassadors as independent of agreements, and hence grounded in customary law. A prince was required to respect this immunity even in time of war and, more interestingly, even when violence had already been inflicted on his own envoys (violations *in pari materia*).

This remains true in modern international law. In 1980, the International Court of Justice confirmed that '[e]ven in the case of armed conflict or in the case of a breach in diplomatic relations those provisions [of the Vienna Convention on Diplomatic Relations, which reflects a long-established legal regime] require that both the inviolability of the members of a diplomatic mission and of the premises, property and archives of the mission must be respected by the receiving state.'[45] The court affirmed its belief that the rules of diplomatic law constitute a self-contained regime which imposes obligations on the receiving state with regard to diplomatic missions, and specifies the means to counter abuses by their members.[46] Irrespective of the truthfulness of various Iranian allegations against the United States, Iran's 'feeling of offence could not affect the imperative character of the legal obligations incumbent upon the Iranian Government which is not altered by a state of diplomatic tension between the two countries.'[47] Reprisals by the host country against diplomats for *any* violations the sending country may have committed are thus clearly prohibited.

Equally interesting was the role entrusted to ambassadors by Shakespeare's Henry V in negotiating the treaty of peace:

> KING HARRY   If, Duke of Burgundy, you would the peace
> Whose want gives growth to th'imperfections
> Which you have cited, you must buy that peace
> With full accord to all our just demands,
> Whose tenors and particular effects
> You have enscheduled briefly in your hands.

[44] Ayala, 71.

[45] *Case concerning United States Diplomatic and Consular Staff in Tehran (United States of America v. Iran)*, 1980 ICJ Rep. at 3, 40.

[46] Ibid. 40. For a recent critique of self-contained regimes, see Gaetano Arangio-Ruiz, Fourth Report on State Responsibility, UN Doc. A/CN.4/444/Add.2 (1992).

[47] 1980 ICJ Rep., *supra* note 45, at 41.

BURGUNDY   The King hath heard them, to the which as yet
There is no answer made.
KING HARRY   Well then, the peace,
Which you before so urged, lies in his answer.
KING CHARLES   I have but with a cursitory eye
O'erglanced the articles. Pleaseth your grace
To appoint some of your council presently
To sit with us once more, with better heed
To re-survey them, we will suddenly
Pass our accept and peremptory answer.
KING HARRY   Brother, we shall.—Go, Uncle Exeter
And brother Clarence, and you, brother Gloucester;
Warwick and Huntingdon, go with the King,
And take with you free power to ratify,
Augment, or alter, as your wisdoms best
Shall see advantageable for our dignity,
Anything in or out of our demands,
And we'll consign thereto.

(v. ii. 68–90)

The negotiation of the Treaty of Troyes (1420) lasted several months.[48] Although Henry himself took a leading role,[49] Shakespeare's Henry, echoing Holinshed,[50] provides here a prime example of ambassadors' full powers to negotiate and conclude a treaty of peace.[51] With the advent of modern technology, which

---

[48] 'Henry V', *Encyclopaedia Britannica* (11th edn. 1910), xiii. 285. For a detailed discussion of the negotiations, see Paul Bonenfant, *Du Meurtre de Montereau au traité de Troyes* (1956).

[49] Holinshed, 84–86 (= R. Holinshed, *Chronicles* (1808), iii. 107–8); see also J. D. Griffith Davies, *Henry V* (1935), 250.

[50] '[T]he king of England should send in the companie of the duke of Burgognie his ambassadours unto Trois in Champaigne sufficientlie authorised to treat and conclude of so great matter.' Holinshed, 94 (= R. Holinshed, *Chronicles* (1808), iii. 113). Henry V complained of the futility of the pre-invasion negotiations with Charles VI on the ground that the French ambassadors 'did not have full power to treat' (letter of 7 April 1415), and he demanded that the powers of the French ambassadors about to be sent should be 'sufficiently ample' (letter of 15 April 1415). Harris Nicolas, *A History of the Battle of Agincourt* (2d edn., 1832), App. 1, 3. See also Charles Lethbridge Kingsford, *Henry V* (1901), 113. On the English ambassadors' argument that they lacked power to conclude an agreement, see James Hamilton Wylie, *The Reign of Henry the Fifth* (1914), i. 442.

[51] See Ernest Mason Satow, in Paul Gore-Booth (ed.), *Guide to Diplomatic Practice* (1979), 58–9. An ancient chronicle notes:
'He [Henry] there found the King and Queen of France, their daughter . . . and the Duke of Burgundy, who then ratified and confirmed every article of the treaty which had been agreed upon by their ambassadors, according to the stipulations

permits rapid communication between capitals and negotiators, the practice of granting ambassadors such full powers has almost fallen into desuetude, particularly in negotiations of vital importance.

The Anglo-French bargaining, in which both parties were assisted by competent lawyers, involved delicate points of law. The treaty was, for the most part, negotiated not by Charles, who was mentally ill, but by Philip the Good, the Duke of Burgundy and, to an important extent, by Isabel, Charles's wife and the Queen of France. It was, of course, concluded in Charles's name.

As part of the terms of peace, Henry was to marry King Charles's daughter Catherine. He therefore sought to secure his right to the crown of France, for which he had gone to war, without the embarrassment of deposing his future father-in-law. In fact, Henry wanted the immediate right to govern France, as well as a guarantee that the title to France would be transferred to him upon the death of Charles. This blueprint must have been in Henry's mind for several years, for it already appeared in his challenge to the Dauphin of September 1415, (discussed above in Chapter 7). The solution was to recognize Henry as the heir of the King of France and France's regent, instead of Charles's legitimate son, the Dauphin.[52] In the concluding scene, Shakespeare portrays the negotiations that led to this resolution and the promise of peace that it held:

> [WARWICK]   The King hath granted every article:
> His daughter first, and so in sequel all,

made between the two kings and the Duke of Burgundy, with the consent of the citizens of Paris.'
'A Fragment of the Chronicle of Normandy from the Year 1414 to the Year 1422' (c.1581), repr. in Benjamin Williams (ed.), *Henrici Quinti Angliae Regis Gesta* (1850), 252. On the background of the Chronicle, see the editor's Preface, p. viii.

[52] Holinshed, 95, 102–3 (= R. Holinshed, *Chronicles* (1808), iii. 113, 117–18). Holinshed reports: 'It was also agreed, that king Henrie, during his father in lawes life, should in his steed have the whole governement of the realme of France, as regent thereof.' The grant to Henry of the right to govern France was justified on the ground that Charles 'is withholden with diverse sickenesse, in such manner as he maie not intend in his owne person for to dispose for the needs of the foresaid realme of France.' Ibid. 95, 99 (= R. Holinshed, *Chronicles* (1808), iii. 113, 115). It was provided that during his lifetime, Charles would possess the crown of France, 'and dignitie roiall of France, with rents and profits for the same.' Ibid. 98. See also Davies, *supra* note 49, at 250–1.

According to their firm proposèd natures.

EXETER Only he hath not yet subscribèd this:

where your majesty demands that the King of France, having any occasion to write for matter of grant, shall name your highness in this form and with this addition: . . . 'Notre très cher fils Henri, Roi d'Angleterre, Héritier de France' . . .

> KING CHARLES Nor this I have not, brother, so denied,
> But your request shall make me let it pass.
> KING HARRY I pray you then, in love and dear alliance,
> Let that one article rank with the rest,
> And thereupon give me your daughter.
> KING CHARLES Take her, fair son, and from her blood raise up
> Issue to me, that the contending kingdoms
> Of France and England, whose very shores look pale
> With envy of each other's happiness,
> May cease their hatred . . .

> > (*Henry V*, v. ii. 327–47)

Wylie and Waugh summarize the Treaty of Troyes as follows:

It was agreed that Henry should marry Catherine without imposing any burden on her parents or the French and that she should receive the usual dowry of an English queen—40,000 crowns a year. He would suffer Charles and Isabel to retain the state and dignity of king and queen of France; for the rest of Charles's life, he would never style himself king of France, and in places subject to the French crown all writs and grants of privileges, pardons, offices, or benefices should be drawn in Charles's name. Immediately after Charles's death, however, the crown of France should belong to Henry, to pass to his heirs for ever; and in the meanwhile, seeing that Charles's health was bad, the regency should be exercised by Henry, with the counsel of the nobles and wise men of France. He would strive to reduce to obedience all France then subject to the dauphin, especially those parts to the right of the Loire; all his conquests over the dauphinists outside Normandy should be to the advantage of the French crown, and on his becoming king, Normandy and all his other conquests in France should be subject to it. Persons in territory conquered by Henry, if obedient to Charles and willing to swear to the Treaty, should be restored to their possessions, unless Henry had already granted them to others [Burgundians whose property had already been given away by Henry would be compensated with lands to be conquered from the dauphinists]. Henry would appoint good and fit officers to govern the kingdom, rule it according to existing laws and customs, maintain the *Parlement* in its authority and all churches, colleges, and universities in their privileges.[53]

Rather than follow the model of the Treaty of Brétigny, which transferred various French territories to English sovereignty, Henry intended to use the Treaty of Troyes,[54] upon his marriage to Catherine, to change the French line of succession.[55] As Keen puts it, 'the crown of France was not to be dismembered and the bounds of the kingdom would remain much as they had traditionally been; but the Valois heir would be disinherited in favour of a Plantagenet who would marry a Valois princess and secure the inheritance to a Plantagenet–Valois line.'[56] By having himself described in the treaty as Charles's son and heir of France, Henry hoped to avoid a direct conflict with the Salic law prohibiting the passing of the French crown through females or the female line. Accordingly, the carefully drafted Treaty of Troyes made no reference to the Plantagenet claim to the crown of France. To avoid future challenges to its validity, on the ground either of Charles's madness (Kingsford observed that because of his sickness, Charles was ready to agree to whatever was proposed;[57] Wylie and Waugh noted that when Henry arrived at the palace of Troyes, Charles initially did not show any sign of recognition[58]) or of his lack of authority to alienate the crown or change the Valois succession, the treaty required that it be ratified by the estates of both kingdoms,[59] proclaimed in both coun-

[53] James Hamilton Wylie and William Templeton Waugh, *The Reign of Henry the Fifth*, (1929), iii. 198–9.

[54] For useful summaries of the Treaty of Troyes, see Jacob, *supra* note 20, at ch. 8; Charles Lethbridge Kingsford, *Henry V* (1901), 304–5; *Chronique du Religieux de Saint Denys*, *supra* note 17, at v. 411–31. The Latin and the French texts of the treaty are reprinted side by side in Thomas Rymer, *Foedera* (The Hague, 1740), iv. 171 (pt. 3); for the English text, which was published by Henry V in England, see ibid. 179. The articles are numbered in the French and Latin texts, but not in the English text. The articles which I shall cite are drawn from the English text, but their numbering from the French text.

[55] 'ALSO, that, after the Deth of our Sayd Fadir, and from thens forward, the Coroune and the Roialme of France, wyth all thare Ryghtes and Appurtenauntz, shull Remeindre, and Abyde, and be of Us, and of our Heires for evermore.' Article 6 of the French and the Latin texts.

[56] Keen, 'Diplomacy', *supra* note 37, at 181.

[57] Kingsford, *supra* note 54, at 303.

[58] Wylie and Waugh, *supra* note 53, at iii. 202–3.

[59] The above discussion draws on Keen's excellent analysis of the Treaty of Troyes, 'Diplomacy', *supra* note 37, at 181–99.

tries, and that the French lords, communities and subjects take an oath to observe the treaty and its provisions for the governance of France.[60] Indeed, the proclamation and the ratification processes were carried out in both countries.[61] Moreover, to deter violations through the supreme crime of *lèse-majesté*, Charles VI proclaimed by *lettres générales* that those who disobeyed the treaty would be considered 'comme rebelles et désobéissants à notre autorité et punis rigoureusement, comme criminels de lèse-majesté, les violateurs de la paix, les trangresseurs de nos ordres et commandements'.[62] A quite progressive provision allowed the allies of either party to accede ('adhérer' in the French text) to the treaty within a period of eight months,[63] and thus to enjoy benefits under the treaty.[64]

Charles and Isabel would maintain their titles, dignity, and

---

[60] 'Also, that We mowe the more commodiously, surely, and freely Doo, Excercise, and Fulfill thes thynges aforesayd, it is Accordid that the Worthey, Grete, Nobles, and Estates of the sayd Roialme of France, as well Spiritual as Temporall, and also Citees, Notables, Comunialtees, Citezenes, and Burgeys of Townes, of the same Roialme, that be Obeyssant at this tyme to our sayd Fadir, shall maak this Othes that folowe.

'FIRST, that to Us, beryng the Facultye and Excercise of Disposition and Governance of the forsayd Comune Profit, and to cure Hestes and Commaundementz, yeu shall mekely and obediently Obey and Entend, in all manere of thynges concernyng th'Exercice of Governance of the same Roialme.

'ALSO, that yoo Worthy Grete Nobles and y Estates of the sayd Roialme, as well Spirituell as Temporell, and also Citees, and Notables Comunialtees, and Citezins and Burgeis of the same Roialme, in all maner of thynges well and trewely shall kepe, and to here Pouer so shall Doo be keped of all other, as mych as to hem longeth, or to ony of hem, all the Thynges that be APPOYNTED or ACCORDED betwene our foresayd Fadir, and Modir and Us, withe the Counsaill of thame whome Us list for to call too.' Article 13 of the French and the Latin texts.

[61] William Stubbs, *The Constitutional History of England* (1880), iii. 97. Keen, 'Diplomacy', 194–5.

[62] *Chronique du Religieux de Saint-Denys*, *supra* note 17, at vi. 441.

[63] 'ALSO that all yo Confedered and Allied of our sayd Fadir, and of the Roialme of France aforesayd, and also our Confederates and of the Roialme of Engeland aforesayd (the whych in Eght Moneths from the tyme of this Accord of Peas y notified to thayme, woll declare by here Lettres that they woll drawe to this ACCORDE, and woll be comprehendid undir the TRETEE and ACCORD of this PEAS) be comprehendid undir the Bondes, Surtee, and th'ACCORD of this PEAS; savyng na the les ayther of the said CROUNES, and also all manere of Accions, Ryghtes, and Remedies that longeth to oure sayd Fadir, and to his Subgettes, and to Us, and to oure Soubgettes, ageynes such manere of Allyes and Confederattes.' Article 26 of the French and the Latin texts.

[64] Wylie and Waugh, *supra* note 53 , at iii. 203.

income.[65] Henry was designated regent of France, in order to govern France as of the date of the treaty and while Charles was still alive, using only the title conferred upon him by the treaty and refraining from using the title of King of France until Charles's death.[66]

The Treaty of Troyes is of extraordinary interest to international lawyers. Although the treaty deals with the personal union of two kingdoms,[67] while the Hague Regulations of 1907[68] and

---

[65] 'ALSO, that we shall not Distourbe, Disase, nor lett oure Sayd *Fadir*, bot that he holde and possede, as long as he lyveth, as he holdeth and possedith at this tyme, the Croune and the Dignitee Roialle of France, and Rentes, Fruytes, Proffitz of the same, to the Sustinance of his Estate and Charges of the Roiaulme; and our *forsayd Modir* also hold, as long as she Liveth, the Estate and the Dignitie of Quene, after the maner of the sayd Roiaulme, with covenable and convenient part of the sayd Rentes and Profitz.' Article 2 of the French and the Latin texts.

[66] 'ALSO, that, duryng the *Lyve of oure Sayd Fadir*, yn all Places nowe, or in tyme commyng, Suget to hym, Lettres of Comune Justice, and also of Grauntes, Offices, Benefices, and Yiftes, Pardonnes, or Remissions, and Privileges, shall be Write and Procede under the Name and Seal of our *Sayd Fadir*:

'And, for as muche as some singular Cases mywe falle that mowe not be forseyne be Mannes wit, in the whiche it mygt be necessaire and behoveful that we doo write oure Lettres, in syche manere of Cases, if ony hape, for the Good and Suretee of our sayd Fadir, and for the Governance longyng to Us, as it is before sayd, and for to eschewe Perilles and Disseases that otherwyse likly myght swe in place suget to our sayd Fadir, to write oure Letters, be the whiche we shall Commande, Charge and Defende, after Nature and Qualitee of the Nede, in our Fadres behalf and oures, as Regent of France.

'ALSO, that, *duryng our Fadres Lyve*, we shall not Nempe or Wryte Us Kyng of France; but utterly we shull abstayne Us from that Name as long as our sayd Fader Lyveth.

'ALSO, that, our *Sayd Fadir*, duryng his Lyf, shall Nempne, Call, and Wryte Us in France in this manere,

Notre Treschier Fitz Henry Roy d'Engleterre, Heriter de France;

And in Latyn, in this manere, *Praecarissimus Filius noster Henricus Rex Angliae, Haeres Franciae, &c.*' Articles 20–2 of the French and the Latin texts.

[67] See Jacob, *Henry V, supra* note 20, at 149. Both realms would be 'under the same person[,] . . . keeping nevertheless in all maner of other things to either of the same realmes, their rights, liberties, customes, usages, and lawes, not making subject in any maner of wise one of the same realmes, to the rights, lawes, or usages of that other.' Holinshed, 103 (= R. Holinshed, *Chronicles* (1808), iii. 118).

[68] Regulations Annexed to Hague Convention (No. IV) Respecting the Laws and Customs of War on Land (particularly Arts. 43, 46, 48), 18 Oct. 1907, 36 Stat. 2277, TS No. 539, 1 Bevans 631. See also Jacob, *Henry V, supra* note 20, at 155. Cf. Art. 48 of the Hague Regulations to the 'taxation' provision of the Treaty of Troyes, text at note 87 *infra*. Although a comparison between a personal union established by a treaty of peace and occupation can be misleading, several important segments of the French population refused to accept the

the fourth Geneva Convention of 1949[69] concern occupied territories, the former anticipates the latter in providing for the maintenance of French laws, courts, and other institutions.[70]

Perhaps the most interesting feature of the treaty was its central theme that France would not be Anglicized.[71] Its institutions would remain French, administered by Frenchmen according to French laws and customs.[72] Although there would be, after Charles's death, only one dynasty, each country would be governed through its own national institutions and procedures,[73] and English control would be exercised only at the highest level.[74] Even as regent, Henry would govern with the advice of French nobles.[75] The court of the *Parlement* would maintain its

validity of the treaty and the legitimacy of the personal union, and viewed the post-Troyes situation as a foreign occupation.

[69] Geneva Convention (No. IV) Relative to the Protection of Civilian Persons in Time of War, 12 Aug. 1949, 6 UST 3516, TIAS No. 3365, 75 UNTS 287 (particularly Arts. 54, 64).

[70] Consider these excerpts from Holinshed's version: 'Also that we of our owne power shall doo the court of parlement in France to be kept and observed in his authoritie and sovereignetie. . . .

'Also we to our power shall defend and helpe all and everie of the peers, nobles, cities, townes, communalties, and singular persons, now or in time comming, subjects to our father in their rights, customes, privileges, freedomes, and franchises, longing or due to them in all manner of places now or in time comming subject to our father.

'Also we diligentlie and truelie shall travell to our power, and doo that justice be administred and doone in the same realme of France after the lawes, customes, and rights of the same realme. . . .

'Also we to our power shall provide, and doo to our power, that able persons and profitable beene taken to the offices as well of justices and other offices belonging to the governance of the demaines, and of other offices of the said realme of France, for the good right and peaceable justice of the same, and for the administration that shall be committed unto them.' Holinshed, 99–100 (= R. Holinshed, *Chronicles* (1808), iii. 115–16). On the Treaty of Troyes, see also Harold F. Hutchison, *King Henry V*, at (1967), 186–9; Jacob, *Henry V, supra* note 20, at 148–55; George Makepeace Towle, *The History of Henry the Fifth* (1866), 410–13; R. B. Mowat, *Henry V* (1920), 229–37; Desmond Seward, *Henry V* (1988), 145–6; Wylie and Waugh, *supra* note 53, at iii. 198–204.

[71] Keen, 'Diplomacy', *supra* note 37, at 195.

[72] Cf. Art. 27 of the Geneva Convention No. IV, *supra* note 69 ('Protected persons are entitled . . . [to] their manners and customs.').

[73] Jacob, *Henry V, supra* note 20, at 147.   [74] Ibid. 155.

[75] The regency clause of the treaty reads as follows: 'Also, for alsmych as our *sayd Fader* is holden wyth divers Sekenes, in sych maner as he may not entend in his owne Persone for to dispose for the nedes of the forsayd Roialme of France, therefore, duryng the Lyve of our sayd' Fader, the Faculte and Excercise of the Governance and Disposission of the Good publique and commune Proffit of the sayd Roialme of France, with the Consaille of Nobles and Wise Men of the same

authority,[76] as the single, supreme, lay court of France.[77] Justice would be administered according to French laws and customs,[78] a provision reflected in the spirit of Article 43 of the Hague Regulations of 1907[79] and Article 54 of the fourth Geneva Convention.[80] Henry would respect the customs, privileges, and franchises of peers, communities and towns.[81] Able persons would be appointed to administrative positions, in accordance with the laws and customs of France.[82] The Church and clergy loyal to Charles and accepting the treaty would maintain their

Roialme, that be obeyssant to our sayd Fader, and that lovyth the Proffit and the Worship of the same Roialme, shall be and abide to Us; so that, frome hens forwarde, we moue Governe the same Roialme by Us, and also by other, whiche, wyth the Counsaill of the sayd Nobles, we list for to Depute: the which Faculte and Excercise of Governance, thus beyng toward Us, we shall labour and purpose us spedefully, diligently, and trewely to that, that may be and ought for to be to the Worship of God, and of our sayd Fadir and Modir and also to the commone Good of the sayd Roialme; and to that Roialme, wyth the Counsaill and Helpe of Worthy, Grete, and Noble of the same Roialme, for to be Defendid, Pesid, and Governed after that Ryght and Equite wolle.' Article 7 of the French and Latin texts.

[76] 'Also, that, we, to our Pouer, shall doo that the Court of the Parlement of France be keped and observed in his Auctoritee and Superioritee, and in all that is dewe to hyme, in all manner of Places that now, or in tyme to come, is, or shall be, suget to our sayd Fader.' Article 8 of the French and the Latin texts.

[77] Christopher T. Allmand and C. A. J. Armstrong, *English Suits before the Parliament of Paris 1420–1436* (1982), 1–2.

[78] 'Also, that we diligently and trewely, to our Pouer, shall Travaille, an do that, that Justice be administred and doon in the Roialme of France, after the Lawes, Custumes, and Ryghtes of the same Roialme, wyth outen personell acception; and that we shall kepe and holde the Sugettes of the same Roialme in Tranquillitee and Peas; and, to our Pouer, we shall Defende thaime ayaynes all maner of Violence and Oppression.' Article 10 of the French and the Latin texts.

[79] *Supra* note 68.

[80] *Supra* note 69. See Art. 54: 'The Occupying Power may not alter the status of public officials or judges in the occupied territories.'

[81] 'Also, that We, to our pouer shall defende and kepe all and everith Peres, Nobles, Citees, Tounes, Comunaltees, and Singulers, nowe, or in tyme commyng, suget to our *Sayd Fadir*, in hir Ryghtes, Custumes, Priviles, Fredoms, and Franchises, longyng or dewe to thaime, in all manere of places nowe, or in tyme commyng, suget to our sayd Fadir.' Article 9 of the French and the Latin texts.

[82] Also, that, to our Pouer, we shall Purvoye and do that Able Persones and Profitable be taken to th'Offices, as well of Justice of Parlement, as of Baillages, Seneschalfies, Provostries, and other Offices, longyng to the Governance o the Demayne, and all other Offices in the sayd Roialme of France, for the good ryght, and paisible Governance of the same Roialme, and for the Administracions that shall be committed unto thaime; and that they be sych Persones that, after the Lawes and the Ryghtes of the same Roialme, and for the Utilitie and Profite of our sayd Fadir, and that forsayd Royalme, oght for to be taken and deputed to the same Offices.' Article 11 of the French and the Latin texts.

rights and privileges.[83] It followed that English clergy would not be foisted upon the Church in France.[84]

Universities and other educational institutions would also retain their rights and privileges.[85] The treaty, very much like Articles 48 and 49 of the Hague Regulations of 1907,[86] provided that taxes would not be imposed except in case of necessity, and according to French laws and customs approved by the Kingdom of France.[87] In fact, Henry did not 'attempt to lay taxes on his French subjects without their assent, though he maintained the ordinary indirect taxation of the French kings, notably the *gabelle*'.[88] A signally important provision established (subject to the consent of the three estates of the two kingdoms) a permanent personal union between England and France, with each subject to the sovereignty of one and the same king, but governed under its own laws and customs, and not subject to the laws and customs of the other.[89] The significance of the union was so great

[83] 'ALSO, that all maner of Persones of Holy Chirche, Beneficed in the Duchie of Normandie, or any other places in the Roialme of France, suget to Us, obedient to *our sayd Fadir*, and faveryng the Partye of the *Dukes of Bourgoyn*, the whyche shall Swere for to kepe this present Accord, shall Rejoise peisible here Benefice of Holy Chirche in the Duchie of Normandie, or in the places aforesayd.'

'ALSO, that lykewise all manere of Persones of Holy Chirche, Obedient to Us, and beneficed in the Roialme of France, in places suget to our *Sayd Fadir*, that shall swere for to kepe this present Accord, shall Rejoise peisible here Benefices of Holy Chirche and Places next above sayd.' Articles 15–16 of the French and the Latin texts.

[84] Jacob, *Henry V, supra* note 20, at 155.

[85] 'ALSO, that all maner of Chirches, Universitees, and Studies Generalles, and also Colliges of Studiers, and other Collegges of Holy Chirche, beyng in places nowe, or in tyme commyng, Suget to our *Sayd Fadir*, or in the Duchie of Normandie, or other Places of the Roialme of France Suget to Us, shall Rejoise here Ryghtes, Possessions, Rentes, prerogatives, Libertees, and Franchises, longyng or dewe to thaime, in ony maner of wise, in the sayd Roialme of France; savyng the Ryght of the Croune of France, and of every other Persone.' Article 17 of the French and the Latin texts.

[86] Hague Regulations, *supra* note 68.

[87] 'ALSO, that we shall not putt noon Imposicions or Exaccions, or doo to be putte, to the Sugetes of our says Fadir, withouten cause reasonable and necessarre, nor otherwise than for the comune Good of the says Roialme of France, and after the Seyng and Askyng the Laws and Custumes resonable and approved of the says Roialme.' Article 23 of the French and Latin texts.

[88] Jacob, *supra* note 20, at 155.

[89] 'ALSO, that, we shall Travaill, for our Pouer, to th'effecte that, be th'Advis and Assent of Three Estates of ayther of the Roialmes of France and of Ingland, all manere of Obstacles doon awey in this partye, ther be Ordined and Provided

that Jacob compares it to the Act of Union proposed by Britain to France on 16 June 1940,[90] and Allmand and Armstrong observe that under the Treaty of Troyes 'England undertook her most serious external obligation prior to entry to the European Economic Community five hundred and fifty years later.'[91]

The creation of the union which would transform the subjects of Charles, upon his death, into the subjects of Henry, may have had important implications in *jus gentium*. Normally a treaty of peace, though 'perpetual', would be destroyed by a party's breach.[92] However, since the Treaty of Troyes, in addition to establishing peace, created a union, and vested sovereignty in Henry, it can perhaps be argued that Henry could insist on the continuing validity of the treaty and on his right to treat his French opponents as rebels even in the case of the most serious breaches.

Despite all the precautionary steps taken to ensure its continued validity, the Treaty of Troyes would not long survive the nationalistic opposition that it provoked in France, and which led to its eventual abrogation by the Burgundian French in 1435. The Religieux de Saint-Denys reported that after the treaty's conclusion, many complained that it deprived the Dauphin of royal authority, which was granted to the King of England, in favour of Princess Catherine,[93] and that others argued that the peace made between the French and the English, whose languages, laws, and customs were so different, would not last long.[94]

The Salic law (see Chapter 3 above) returned to haunt the

that, frome the tyme that We or ony of oure Heires kome to the CROUNE of France, both the CROUNES, that is to sey of France and of England, perpetuelly be togedyr, and be in Oone and in the same Persone, that is to say, Oure from thens Terme of our Lyf, and thens foreward in the Persones of oure Heires, that shall be oone after and other, and that both Roialme shall be Governed from that tyme, that We or ony of oure Heires come to the same not severally, under divers Kynges in oone tyme, bot undir oone and the same Persone, the whiche for the tyme shall be Kyng of either Roialme and Soverayn Lord, as it is before sayd: Kepyng ne the les, in all maner other thynges, to ayther of the same Roialmes here Ryghtees, or Custumes, Usages, and Lawes; not makyng subget in oony manere of wise oone of the same Roialmes to th'oder, nor puttyng under, or submittyng the Ryghtes, Laws, Custumes, or Usages of that oone of the sayd Roialmes, to the Ryghtes, Lawes, Custumes, or Usages of that other of the same.' Article 24 of the French and the Latin texts.

[90] Jacob, *Henry V, supra* note 20, at 154.
[91] Allmand and Armstrong, *supra* note 77, at 1.   [92] Ayala, 70.
[93] *Chronique du Religieux de Saint-Denys, supra* note 17, at vi. 437.
[94] Ibid. 439.

English monarchs: the French jurists opposed to the treaty invoked the law in a new and expanded interpretation as a fundamental constitutional principle prohibiting the alienation of the French crown to a foreigner.[95]

Apart from Salic law, whether Charles could alienate French sovereignty presents a complex question under *jus gentium*. Gentili argued that '[a] king may not alienate his subjects, nor give them another king; for a people is free even though it be under a king. . . . Moreover, there is no such thing as the alienation of free men, because there is no commerce in them. . . . These things . . . are a matter of natural right.'[96] Gentili believed this was true even of emperors or pontiffs, who had 'the freest possible power . . . [which power] is not for purposes of tyranny, but of administration',[97] and did not include the right to transfer administrative power to others. In contrast, Grotius distinguished between 'patrimonial kingdoms', a term clearly applicable to Charles's France on the one hand, and aristocratic or democratic governments on the other.[98] In the latter case, kings 'are not able to alienate by treaty either the whole sovereignty or a part of it, since they hold their royal authority not as a patrimony, but as if in usufruct'.[99] The consent of the whole people would therefore be required for a valid transfer of the 'undivided sovereignty'. Following the Treaty of Troyes, a segment of the French people, including its principal institutions and authorities, but excluding the Dauphin and the Armagnacs, did, indeed, ratify the treaty. In patrimonial kingdoms, Grotius added, a king may alienate his crown, and transfer a part of his sovereignty, unless he received the kingdom 'on the condition of not dividing it'.[100] Addressing rebellions ('War of subjects against superiors') Grotius supported the right of the people to resist the kingdom's alienation by the king or its being placed in subjection; a people can even 'oppose a change in the manner of holding the sovereign power'.[101]

Did the Salic law not impose limitations on partial, and certainly complete transfer of sovereignty by the King of France?

---

[95] See John Milton Potter, 'The Development and Significance of the Salic Law of the French', in 52 English Historical Review 249–53 (1937). See also Ch. 3, *supra*.

[96] Gentili, ii. 373.

[97] Ibid. 372.

[98] Grotius, bk. III, ch. xx, pts. iv–v.

[99] Ibid. pt. v.

[100] Ibid.

[101] Ibid. bk. I, ch. iv, pt. x.

But if the Salic law did create such a condition, could it not be circumscribed by the approval of the treaty by the three estates of France?[102]

---

[102] Maurice Keen observed that in medieval legal theory 'the most secure manner in which the fundamental laws of a country could be changed was by the incorporated authority of the whole people and their sovereign (personal or collective).' Keen, 'Diplomacy', *supra* note 37, at 194–5.

11
Rebels

Although it remains difficult to characterize a conflict as international or internal, the principal criteria for distinguishing between them have been established.[1] In medieval *jus gentium*, however, the difference between international and internal strife was at best blurred. In areas over which rulers asserted sovereignty, they claimed the right to treat as rebels those who dared oppose them. In the tangled web of feudal relationships which was characterized by hierarchy rather than equality, such assertions, often arbitrary, were common.

This was particularly true in the case of sieges. The decision as to how to treat an adversary was indirectly informed by a geographical and tactical factor: quarter was normally given to those considered equals who were defeated in the field. Quarter was granted because 'the law of arms protected the life of the Christian captive who had given his faith to an enemy.'[2] As Keen suggests, accepting a challenge to battle entailed acceptance of God's judgment, but '[t]o refuse the summons of a prince who claimed a town as of right was . . . an insult to his majesty and punishable as such.'[3] Life, honour and property were at the mercy of the conqueror.

Apart from the Lollard discontent and the abortive Scrope and Cambridge conspiracy discussed in the play, the historical Henry did not encounter major domestic challenges to his rule and had no qualms about treating as rebels people who dared resist him in that part of France which he claimed as his own. In Henry's era, such a position was virtually unchallenged. Only much later did Renaissance writers question, at first timidly, the morality of treating foreign subjects as rebels. Of course, for Henry, residents of Normandy were *his*, not Charles's, subjects. Some two

[1] Theodor Meron, 'On the Inadequate Reach of Humanitarian and Human Rights Law and the Need for a New Instrument', 77 AJIL 589, 598–600 (1983); id., *Human Rights in Internal Strife* (1987), 43–50.
[2] *LW* 124.
[3] *LW* 123–4.

hundred years after Henry's campaigns, Suárez complained that aggressive war was frequently waged against foreign nationals ('non-subjects'), who deserved neither punishment nor subjection to foreign jurisdiction unless they 'have committed some wrong on account of which they render themselves subjects'.[4] He appeared thus to suggest a distinction between foreigners, who did not owe loyalty to the prince, and subjects of the prince, who did owe him allegiance. The latter therefore deserved severe punishment for the breach of the oath.

The common-law doctrine distinguished between subjects who levied war against the sovereign, who were therefore considered 'traitors', and aliens involved in similar acts, who were considered 'enemies'. The distinction turned on allegiance. In the case of the *Marshalsea* (1455), Prisot, CJ stated: 'If they were the king's lieges, they would not be called the king's enemies, but traitors, for enemies are those who are outside the allegiance.'[5] In a Note (1571) by Sir James Dyer on the *Perkin Warbeck* case (1499), Sir James observed that 'Perkin Warbeck [an alien] who feigned himself to be one of the sons of king Edward IV, could not be judged as a traitor but as the king's enemy.'[6] Enemy aliens were not shielded from trial. Perkin Warbeck was tried and convicted not by a common-law court but by the military court

---

[4] Suárez, ii. 816. See also Peter Haggenmacher, *Grotius et la doctrine de la guerre juste* (1983), 409–26.

[5] Year Book Hil. 33 Hen VI, f. 1, pl. 3. Also cited by J. Dyer, *infra* note 6. In 1323, Andrew de Harclay, Earl of Carlisle was convicted for treason and executed for having adhered to Robert Bruce, the King's enemy, and accepting him as King of Scotland. J. G. Bellamy, *The Law of Treason in England in the Later Middle Ages* (1970), 52. On the trial as a traitor (1318) of Gilbert de Middleton, a knight within the king's allegiance who raised an army of Scots who were the king's enemies (Gilbert also, to the great embarrassment of the king, robbed two visiting cardinals), see ibid. 47.

[6] Cited by John H. Baker in an edition of the Reports of Sir James Dyer to be published by the Selden Society. The circumstances of the Perkin Warbeck case are well explained by the indictment of his supporters: 'Remember that in the year 10 Hen. VII, Sir William Stanley and Sir Robert Clifford, knights, were indicted of *high treason* at Westminster for that they had communication together at St Martin's in the Fields near Charing Cross concerning Perkin Warbeck, born at Tournai in Burgundy, being an *enemy* to the king, they falsely naming him second son of King Edward IV, Warbeck then being beyond the sea, and they conspired, imagined and compassed the death and destruction of the king and subversion of the realm, and by levying of war in the realm to deprive and depose the king of his crown and regality.' *R. v. Stanley* (1495), *English Historical Records*, xiv. 530–1. Emphasis added.

(the marshal's court) and hanged.[7] As an enemy he was spared the stigma of treason, but did not have the privilege of a jury trial either.

The *Gesta* reports that standing before the walls of Harfleur, Henry 'offered, in accordance with the twentieth chapter of the Deuteronomic law, peace to the besieged if, freely and without coercion, they would open their gates to him and, as was their duty, restore that town, which was a noble and hereditary portion of his crown of England and of his duchy of Normandy'.[8] He warned the defenders of Harfleur—the 'rebels'—'of the penal edicts contained in the aforesaid law which it would be necessary to execute upon them as a *rebellious people* should they thus persist in their obstinacy to the end'.[9]

Henry's purposes were, however, not only to conquer Normandy but to befriend its population and thus to obtain peaceable possession and good title that would be recognized both by France and foreign powers, including Emperor Sigismund. These practical and imperative goals necessarily tempered the severity of the theory whereby the French, or at least those resisting Henry in besieged cities, were deemed rebels liable to severe punishment. Henry's compromise drew on the medieval dichotomy between the guilty and the innocent and had much in common with the active distinction between combatant and

[7] See the contemporaneous note on the case by Sir John Port: 'Memorandum. Perkin Warbeck, who was born a Picard and called himself the second son of King Edward IV, namely the duke of York, and levied war against our lord the king, being the king's enemy and not a subject was arraigned before Sir John Digby, knight-marshal, and was found guilty by proofs and hanged at Tyburn.' John H. Baker (ed.), *The Notebook of Sir John Port*, Publications of the Selden Society 102 (1986), 125. The trial of Roger Damory for treason (1322) by what appeared to be a court of chivalry 'for having been in arms against his liege lord King Edward II' shows that courts of chivalry and constables also understood that treason could only be committed by a person owing allegiance to the sovereign. Maurice H. Keen, 'The Jurisdiction and Origins of the Constable's Court', in John Gillingham and J. C. Holt (eds.), *War and Government in the Middle Ages* (1984), 159, 165. Later constables also 'summarily sentenced to death traitors taken in arms in the field.' Ibid.

[8] *Gesta*, 35. See also Deuteronomy 20: 10–14.

[9] *Gesta*, 37 (emphasis added). Shakespeare's Henry's speech before the walls of Harfleur (see Ch. 6 *supra*) did not explicitly mention Deuteronomy 20, but resembled it in the terms of surrender. Naseeb Shaheen, *Biblical References in Shakespeare* (1989), 183. It may be noted that in the English law of the later Middle Ages rebellion was not a synonym for treason, but was a lesser and somewhat ill-defined crime. Bellamy, *supra* note 5, at 72–3, 75. Levying war against the king constituted common-law treason. Ibid. 73.

innocent civilians characteristic of modern law of war.[10] The application of this categorization is illustrated in two episodes.

First, after the surrender of Loviers which had resisted him, Henry ordered that 'the gunners that had discharged anie peece against the Englishmen should suffer death'.[11] One is reminded of Vitoria's argument on the authority of Deuteronomy more than a century later that, in an enemy city that has been taken by force, the killing of 'all who have borne arms against us' was justified.[12] Vitoria appeared thus to be advocating particularly severe sanctions against rebels, or persons who had breached an oath and joined the prince's adversaries, in contrast to foreign combatants.

Second, after the capture of Falaise, Henry ordered that those inhabitants who had agreed to surrender the town would not be deprived of their goods. However, the goods of those that had opposed surrender would be at the King's pleasure and they themselves would have to leave Falaise:

[The King] commaunded that all the goods of the inhabitants, only of them that consented to the deliveraunce of the Towne, shoulde remaine wholie to there former possessors and owners without any diminution. And the goods of them that were obstinate and contrarious to this deliveraunce of the Towne were used at the Kings pleasure, and persons commaunded to avoyde the Towne.[13]

French resistance in occupied Normandy, both before and after the Treaty of Troyes, stemmed to a large extent from abuses by the English soldiery, who pillaged the countryside despite all efforts by the King to enforce discipline and to pacify the population. For the King, Normandy was English territory, but his soldiers exploited and mistreated it as if it were an occupied territory. Resistance was thus directed more against the English soldiery than it was in defence of France's sovereignty.[14]

[10] See e.g. Protocol Additional to the Geneva Conventions of 12 August 1949, and Relating to the Protection of Victims of International Armed Conflicts (Protocol I), opened for signature 12 Dec. 1977, 1125 UNTS 3, 16 ILM 1391 (1977), at art. 51 (3) ('Civilians shall enjoy . . . protection . . . unless and for such time as they take a direct part in hostilities').

[11] Holinshed, 69 (= R. Holinshed, *Chronicles* (1808), iii. 99).

[12] Vitoria, 182 (45).

[13] Charles Kingsford (ed.), *The First English Life of King Henry the Fifth* (1513) (1911), 103; see also *LW* 123.

[14] Roger Jouet, 'La Résistance à l'occupation anglaise en Basse-Normandie (1418–1450)', *Cahier des Annales de Normandie*, 5 (1969), 33–7.

It was not always clear when a resistant's true motivation was patriotic or political.

For Henry, it was imperative that rebels be considered common-law criminals and denied the customary *jus armorum* right of captured combatants to freedom for ransom exchange. Hence the significance of calling them 'brigands', 'larrons', or 'aggresseurs de chemin'. Criteria were developed to distinguish resistants or brigands from 'regular' soldiers of the King of France, who would be entitled to privileges of recognized combatants.[15]

The penalties for resistance were harsh. Rebels who had sworn an oath of loyalty to Henry were treated as traitors, first beheaded and then the body hanged. Rebels ('brigands') who had not breached an oath to Henry were hanged like common-law criminals.[16] The possessions of all convicted rebels were confiscated for the King's pleasure, and not, as in the case of common law-criminals, for their Lord's pleasure.[17] Sentences of imprisonment were rare: capital punishment was typically imposed.[18] Although common-law criminals could find refuge in a church, such asylum was apparently refused to fugitive rebels.[19]

The English soldier faced great temptation to agree to ransom captured rebels rather than to deliver them up to the King's justice. To encourage compliance with his orders and to provide compensation for a ransom's loss, a system of bonuses was introduced for delivery of 'brigands' up to the King's justice where delivery led to a conviction and execution resulted.[20]

After Henry's death, and during the regency in France of John Duke of Bedford, the French resistance expanded and intensified. England's difficulties were aggravated by the peasant revolts of 1434–5 and by the unravelling of the Treaty of Troyes, exemplified by the expected defection of the principal English ally Philip the Good of Burgundy to the French side. Such defections

---

[15] Thus Roger Jouet suggests that '[a]ppartenir à une garnison française, même d'une manière assez vague, semble avoir été suffisant pour être considéré comme prisonnier de guerre. Un homme capturé en Normandie, s'il pouvait faire la preuve qu'il venait d'un territoire non soumis au roi d'Angleterre et qu'il appartenait à une troupe française, était relâché contre rançon; si, au contraire, il n'avait jamais quitté la Normandie et s'y était livré à des actes contre les Anglais sans avoir de lien avec une garnison française, c'était un "brigand" et il était puni comme tel.' Ibid. 42 (footnote omitted).

[16] Ibid. 25–6.   [17] Ibid 24.   [18] Ibid. 50.   [19] Ibid. 52.
[20] Ibid. 43–4.

involved repudiation of the treaty's oath of allegiance and thus constituted crimes of treason.

In this context Sir John Fastolf submitted a report to Henry VI' Great Council in France (1435),[21] containing advice as to how to conduct the war in France. This report was remarkable for the harshness of the total war, or in Vale's perceptive analysis, *guerre mortelle*, that it advocated against the French rebels.[22] Fastolf proposed to terminate what he considered the wasteful policy of laying siege to localities that resisted England and to resort instead to destruction of the countryside. He advocated a virtual scorched-earth policy designed to produce famine[23] (with the object of compelling obedience), and proposed to prohibit the

---

[21] Joseph Stevenson (ed.), *Letters and Papers Illustrative of the Wars of the English in France during the Reign of Henry the Sixth*, Rolls Series 1861-4, ii (pt. 2). 575–85.

[22] Malcolm G. A. Vale, *Sir John Fastolf's 'Report' of 1435: A New Interpretation Reconsidered*, Nottingham Mediaeval Studies, 17 (1973), 78. Vale observes: 'We are dealing, not with enemies, but with rebels, for whom the civil lawyers had laid down certain severe penalties. Fastolf appears to be advocating a harsher form of war, to be waged against those who had recently defected from English allegiance . . . Fastolf may have spoken for many of those who had a vested interest in the war when he expressed the wish that "frome hensforthe al manere of traitours attaint of treson be ponysshed regereuslie", especially members of the clergy. His answer to the problem was as punitive as it was strategic and tactical . . . The wasting campaigns which he recommended were to be both punitive and exemplary. Ransoming and the taking of appatis were to be forbidden to the commanders. The population was not to be spared, because the war, owing to alleged French refusal, was no longer "betwixt men of werre and men of werre". Fastolf seems to be arguing for the prosecution of something approaching *guerre mortelle*, in which the giving of no quarter and taking of no prisoners was added to the burning and pillaging of open or public war. Fastolf's memorandum reads very much as recommending a judicial reprisal to be taken against rebels who had broken their solemn oaths.' Ibid. 80–1 (fnn. ommited).

[23] Such measures were proscribed by Art. 54 (2) of Protocol I, *supra* note 10 (for international conflicts) and art. 14 of Protocol Additional to the Geneva Conventions of 12 August 1949, and Relating to the Protection of Victims of Non-International Armed Conflicts (Protocol II), opened for signature 12 Dec. 1977, 1125 UNTS 609, 16 ILM 1442 (1977) (for non-international conflicts). Article 54 (2) of Protocol I reads as follows: 'It is prohibited to attack, destroy, remove or render useless objects indispensable to the survival of the civilian population, such as foodstuffs, agricultural areas for the production of foodstuffs, crops, livestock, drinking water installations and supplies and irrigation works, for the specific purpose of denying them for their sustenance value to the civilian population or to the adverse Party, whatever the motive, whether in order to starve out civilians, to cause them to move away, or for any other motive.' Article 14 of Protocol II provides: 'Starvation of civilians as a method of combat is prohibited. It is therefore prohibited to attack, destroy, remove or render useless, for that purpose, objects indispensable to the survival of the civilian

ransoming and the taking of *appatis*, to refuse quarter, and to undertake vigorous prosecutions for treason of those—including clergy—who broke their oath of allegiance to the King.[24]

population, such as foodstuffs, agricultrural areas for the production of food-stuffs, crops, livestock, drinking water installations and supplies and irrigation works.'

[24] 'First, it semythe, undere the noble correccion above-said, that the king shuld doo ley no sieges nor make no conquest oute of Normandie, or to conquest be way of siege as yet; for the sieges hathe gretely hindred his conquest in tyme passed, and distruyd his peple, as welle lordis, capetaines, and chieftaines, as his othere peple, and wasted and consumed innumerable good of his finaunces, bothe in England, and in Fraunce, and of Normandie. . . .

'. . . brennyng and distruynge alle the lande as thei pas, bothe hous, corne, veignes, and alle treis that beren fruyte for mannys sustenaunce, and alle bestaile that may not be dryven, to be distroiede; and that that may be welle dryven and spared over the sustenaunce and advictailing of the ostis, to be dryven into Normandie, to Paris, and to othere placis of the kingis obeissaunce, and if good-ely them think it to be done. For it is thoughte that the traitours and rebellis must nedis have anothere manere of werre, and more sharpe and more cruelle werre than a naturelle and anoien ennemye; or els be liklines in proces of tyme no manere of man, ner tounes, ner countries shalle rekenene shame to be traitours nere to rebelle causeles ayens theire souvereyn lorde and ligeaunce at alle tymes aftere theire owne wilfulle [disob]ediens. . . .

'. . . none of the chieftains shuld in no wise raunsone, appatise, ner favour no contre nor place that thei passe thoroughe for no singuler lucre nor profite of them silfe; but that thei doo and execute duely that that thei come fore. And it semethe veraly that be these weies and governaunce the king shalle conquere his reaume of Fraunce, and greve and distruye his ennemyes and save his peple and his soldiours, and yeve theme grete courage to the werre; and shalle cause the cities, tounes, and contreis that be rebellid causeles fayne to seche unto his grace; and shalle yeve also grete exsample to alle thayme that bithe this day in his obeis-saunce to kepe alleweies of theire trouthis.

'. . . he hathe offered unto his adversaries, as a goode Cristen prince, that alle menne of Holy Chirche, and also the comyns and labourers of the reaume of Fraunce, duelling or being oute of forteresse, shuld duelle in seuerte pesible, with-out werre or prince, but that the werre in eithere partie shuld be [and] rest alonly betwixt men of werre and men of werre, the whiche offre the said adversarie have utterly refused, and be concluded to make theire werre cruelle and sharpe, with-out sparing of any parsone. . . .

'. . . this werre shulde be continuede fourthe still puissantly iij. yere day at the leste, to thentent to drive thennemies therbie to an extreyme famyn, and to begyn yerelie at the sesons in the manere abovesaide to be emploied in soche contreis as shalbe thoughte most expedient; and speciallie, where as there [is] most suste-naunce both of theire vitaile and of theire finaunces, and as shalbe advised be the king and his counseile. . . .

'. . . yt is thoughte expedient that the king ordeyne that frome hensforthe al manere of traitours attaint of treson be ponysshed regereuslie, and that no prive-lage of clergie save thayme as hathe be used here before; but that the baillies doo unto thayme uppon justice after there cas and demeritis and liche as ys used in Englonde.' *Letters and Papers, supra* note 21, at 579–83.

Obviously, the principal victims of many of such policies were the civilian non-combatants.

The legal justifications advanced by Fastolf for the ruthless policies he advocated are noteworthy. First, combat against traitors and rebels required a different, and necessarily a crueller, type of war than that conducted against a natural and ancient enemy.[25] Second, the proposal made by the King of England to his adversaries suggesting that the war on both sides be conducted exclusively by regular soldiers ('that the werre in eithere partie shuld be [and] rest alonly betwixt men of werre and men of werre'[26]) had been refused. Christopher Allmand observes that '[s]ince this relatively humanitarian approach had been spurned, Fastolf was prepared to support the harshest methods.'[27]

Vale notes that Fastolf's proposals were not put into practice because both raids and sieges continued through the war (the sieges contrary to Fastolf's advice), and the policy of negotiating '"particular" truces with Burgundy meant that the campaigns of wasting and burning could not take place'.[28] For historians of the law of nations, however, Fastolf's report continues to be of interest as an extreme, unashamedly candid presentation of the thesis that all measures of repression against internal rebels, including the most brutal, were tolerated, and that constraints accepted for external wars were irrelevant. In a case of international conflict, a modern counterpart would be the Nazi Barbarossa Jurisdiction Order, issued for the Soviet Union by General Wilhelm Keitel on 13 May 1941.[29] Unlike Fastolf's

---

[25] Ibid. 580.   [26] Ibid. 581.

[27] Christopher T. Allmand, 'The War and Non-combatant', in Kenneth Fowler (ed.), *The Hundred Years War* (1971), 163, 180.

[28] Vale, *supra* note 22, at 82 (footnote omitted).

[29] '*I. Treatment of crimes committed by enemy civilians*
1. Until further order the military courts and the courts martial will not be competent for crimes *committed by enemy civilians.*
2. *Francs-tireurs* will be liquidated ruthlessly by the troops in combat or while fleeing.
3. *Also all other attacks by enemy civilians against the armed forces*, its members, and auxiliaries will be suppressed on the spot by the troops with the most rigorous methods until the assailants are finished . . . .
4. . . . Against *localities* from which troops have been attacked in a deceitful or treacherous manner, *collective coercive measures* will be applied upon the order of an officer of the rank of at least battalion etc., commander. . . .
5. It is *strictly forbidden to keep* suspects in *custody* in order to put them at the disposal of the courts after the reinstatement of jurisdiction over indigeneous inhabitants.'

report which, according to the English view, concerned an internal conflict, this counterpart was, unfortunately, put into practice. Despite the tremendous normative progress achieved by the modern law of war, cruelty and barbarism continue to characterize internal wars, with the most elementary humanitarian principles often observed only in the breach.[30]

Henry's invocation of Deuteronomy and the harsh treatment he reserved for rebels could lead a modern observer to assume that medieval jurists would have proscribed rebellion as the gravest heresy. This was, however, not true for all jurists. Giovanni da Legnano, perhaps the most important fourteenth-century writer on *jus armorum*, argued that a man might declare a war against his own superior when it was clear that the

Cited in Judgment, *United States of America* v. *von Leeb* (1948), 11 Trials of War Criminals before the Nuernberg Military Tribunals under Control Council Law No. 10 at 462, 521–22 (1950).

Of course, modern law too permits the punishment, even executions, of guerrillas whose status as belligerents has either not been recognized or who have otherwise not obtained privileged status under international law. But the law, which General Keitel violated, requires strict application of judicial guarantees in both international and internal conflicts; regarding the latter, see e.g. common Article 3(1)(d) of the Geneva Conventions. Convention for the Amelioration of the Condition of the Wounded and Sick in Armed Forces in the Field (Geneva Convention No. I), Aug. 12, 1949, 6 UST 3114, TIAS No. 3362, 75 UNTS 31; Convention for the Amelioration of the Condition of Wounded, Sick, and Shipwrecked Members of Armed Forces at Sea (Geneva Convention No. II), Aug. 12, 1949, 6 UST 3217, TIAS No. 3363, 75 UNTS 85; Convention Relative to the Treatment of Prisoners of War (Geneva Convention No. III), Aug. 12, 1949, 6 UST 3316, TIAS No. 3364, 75 UNTS 135; Convention Relative to the Protection of Civilian Persons in Time of War (Geneva Convention No. IV), Aug. 12, 1949, 6 UST 3516, TIAS No. 3365, 75 UNTS 287.

[30] Note e.g. that the International Committee of the Red Cross (ICRC) found it necessary to remind those involved in the fighting in Bosnia-Herzegovina 'not to direct any attack against the civilian population, not to attack, destroy, remove or render useless objects indispensable to the survival of the civilian population [and] to spare the lives of those who surrender and treat all captured combatants humanely.' ICRC Press Release No. 1705 (10 Apr. 1992). More recently the ICRC reported that: 'Following the visits its delegates have conducted during the last few days to places of detention in Bosnia-Herzegovina, it is evident to the International Committee of the Red Cross (ICRC) that innocent civilians are being arrested and subjected to inhumane treatment. Moreover, the detention of such persons is part of a policy of forced population transfers carried out on a massive scale and marked by the systematic use of brutality. Among the long list of methods used are harassment, murder, confiscation of property, deportation and the taking of hostages . . . all in violation of international humanitarian law.'

superior was acting unlawfully, and especially outside his authority.[31] In this case 'resistance should be offered.'[32]

Similarly, a vassal could declare war against his lord, and a
soldier against his officer, if the master's act went beyond the
bounds of the law.[33] Of course, because the lord would be most
unlikely to concede that he had acted *ultra vires* and because he
could enforce obedience and impose punishment through his
superior power, Giovanni's recognition that natural law included
a right of rebellion would have little practical importance.

In keeping with the spirit of his times, Alberico Gentili,
Shakespeare's contemporary in Elizabethan England and an
adviser to the crown, categorically rejected any right to rebel, as
did Shakespeare and Crompton:

> One who is a subject does not by rebellion free himself from subjection
> to the law. . . . There is also another reason why such men do not come
> under the law of war; namely, because that law is derived from the law
> of nations, and malefactors do not enjoy the privileges of a law to which
> they are foes.[34]

Gentili's position would better serve Elizabeth's position than
Henry's, however, for Gentili qualified his broad statement by
the following caveat, which might support the French rebels'
claim to combatant rights:

ICRC Press Release No. 1725 (13 Aug. 1992). Outside of the former Yugoslavia,
however, the international community regards the conflict as international.

[31] Legnano, 289, ch. 89. Cf. the following: 'whenever any form of government
becomes destructive of these ends, it is the right of the people to alter or to abolish it, and to institute a new government'. Declaration of Independence of the
United States (4 July 1776), repr. in Thomas A. Ladanyi, *The 1987 Constitution
with Comparative Text of the 1787 Constitution* (1987), 102; 'All Germans shall
have the right to resist any person or persons seeking to abolish that constitutional order, should no other remedy be possible.' The Constitution of Germany,
Art. 20 (4), repr. in Albert P. Blaustein and Gisbert H. Flanz (eds.), *Constitutions
of the Countries of the World* (1991), vi. 90; *Dennis* v. *United States*, 341 U.S. 494,
501 (1951): 'Whatever theoretical merit there may be to the argument that there is
a "right" to rebellion against dictatorial governments is without force where the
existing structure of the government provides for peaceful and orderly change.'
See also Tony Honoré, 'The Right to Rebel', 8 Oxford J. Legal Stud. 34 (1988)
and Jordan Paust, 'The Human Right to Participate in Armed Revolution and
Related Forms of Social Violence: Testing the Limits of Permissibility', 32 Emory
L. J. 545 (1983).

[32] Legnano, 289, ch. 89.   [33] Ibid. 291, ch. 93.

[34] Gentili, ii. 22 On Shakespeare's treatment of traitors, see Christopher Pye,
The Regal Phantasm (1990), 117–31.

One thing I say by way of warning, namely, that no one should understand me as speaking of other rebels than those who were subject to authority. For those who have proved false to friendship, to a treaty, or even to voluntary dependence, retain the rights of war and the other privileges of the law of nations, as all history bears witness.[35]

How did Shakespeare, writing nearly two hundred years after the Agincourt campaign, regard rebels? As a loyal Elizabethan, Shakespeare made his heroes distinctly unsympathetic and even hostile to rebels and to rebellions. Typically, they used strong pejorative and derogatory terms when addressing rebels. '[R]ebels' arms triumph in massacres' (*1 Henry IV*, v. iv. 13). Rebels attracted suspicion ('[t]rust not the Kentish rebels', *2 Henry VI*, IV. iv. 56) and deserved punishment:

> WORCESTER He [the King] will suspect us still and find a time
> To punish this offence in other faults.
> Supposition all our lives shall be stuck full of eyes,
> For treason is but trusted like the fox
>
> .   .   .   .
>
> He calls us 'rebels', 'traitors', and will scourge
> With haughty arms this hateful name in us.
>
> (*1 Henry IV*, v. ii. 6–9, 39–40)

A 'condition of the worst degree' was that of 'gross rebellion and detested treason' (*Richard II*, II. iii. 107–8). Rebellions were 'foul' (ibid. III. ii. 26); '[t]he cockle of rebellion, insolence, sedition' (*Coriolanus*, III. i. 74). Those involved in them were '[r]ebellious subjects, enemies to peace' (*Romeo and Juliet*, I. i. 78), 'barbarous villains' (*2 Henry VI*, IV. iv. 14), '[r]ebellious hinds, the filth and scum of Kent' (ibid. IV. ii. 121). They harmed the country. 'Rebels wound [the kingdom] with their horses' hoofs' (*Richard II*, III. ii. 7). They were a cause of despair. The tragedy of civil strife was epitomized by Shakespeare's Henry VI:

---

[35] Ibid. 24. In Ch. 10 I discussed Grotius's position on the right to rebel in the context of the Salic law and the Treaty of Troyes. I should like to add one observation, which could be remotely helpful to the French rebels' claims. Grotius argued that a kingdom 'is forfeited if a king sets out with a truly hostile intent to destroy a whole people.' Grotius, bk. I, ch. iv, pt. xi. Such could be the case where 'a king rules over several peoples, [and] may wish to have one people destroyed for the sake of another, in order that he may colonize the territory thus made vacant.' Ibid.

O piteous spectacle! O bloody times!
.   .   .   .
Weep, wretched man, I'll aid thee tear for tear;
And let our hearts and eyes, like civil war,
Be blind with tears and break, o'ercharged with grief.

(*3 Henry VI*, ii. v. 73, 76–8)

Rebels were also destined to lose '[r]ebellion in this land shall lose his sway' (*1 Henry IV*, v. v. 42); '[q]uenching the flame of bold rebellion | Even with the rebels' blood' (*2 Henry IV*, Ind. 26–7); '[t]hus ever did rebellion find rebuke' (*1 Henry IV*, v. v. 1).

Although for the most part harsh toward rebels, including Jack Cade, Shakespeare was on occasion ambivalent, and perhaps even sympathetic to them, allowing Cade to ridicule such pillars of the medieval society as knighthood:

CADE   To equal him I will make myself a knight presently. [*Kneels*] Rise up, Sir John Mortimer. [*Rises*]

(*2 Henry VI*, iv. ii. 118–19)

Tudor audiences must have cheered Cade when, in berating the 'base peasants' who were about to abandon him, he voiced a claim of freedom and dignity for their class:

I thought ye would never have given out these arms till you had recovered your ancient freedom. But you are all recreants and dastards and delight to live in slavery to the nobility. Let them break your backs with burdens, take your houses over your heads, ravish your wives and daughters before your faces.

(ibid. iv. viii. 179–85)[36]

Perhaps owing to a degree of sympathy for Wales, Shakespeare was respectful of the Welsh leader Owen Glendower (Owain Glyndŵr), who with Henry Percy (Hotspur), Percy's father, the

---

[36] Cf. Albert Colby Sprague, *Shakespeare and the Audience* (1966), 263–4. For an explanation of Shakespeare's treatment of Cade's rebellion as rooted in the 'Peasants' Revolt', in the collation of several popular protests, and in a theory of ancient rights of the peasantry, see Annabel Patterson, *Shakespeare and the Popular Voice* (1989), 38–41. Phyllis Rackin's interesting discussion of Shakespeare's use of Jack Cade's rebellion merits attention. She believed that '[d]espite the present reality of the grievances that Cade's rebellion expresses, Shakespeare's London audience is not very likely to have sympathized with his plans . . . to destroy their city's famous monuments. . . .' *Stages of History* (1990), 214. See generally, I. M. W. Harvey, *Jack Cade's Rebellion of 1450* (1991).

Earl of Northumberland, and Mortimer joined forces in a rebellion against Henry designed to divide the country among themselves. Despite Hotspur's efforts to ridicule him, Glendower cut a dignified and even a heroic figure when he described his three victories (1400, 1401, and 1402) over Henry IV's futile attempts to invade Wales and put an end to the Welsh revolt (finally repressed in 1408):

> GLYNDŴR   Three times hath Henry Bolingbroke made head
> Against my power; thrice from the banks of Wye
> And sandy-bottomed Severn have I sent him
> Bootless home, and weather-beaten back.

(1 Henry IV, III. i. 61–4)

Glendower was equally dignified in responding to Hotspur's ironic remarks about his command of the English language:

> GLYNDŴR   I can speak English, lord, as well as you;
> For I was traind up in the English court,
> Where, being but young, I framèd to the harp
> Many an English ditty lovely well,
> And gave the tongue a helpful ornament—
> A virtue that was never seen in you.

(ibid. 118–23)

Shakespeare's generally hard line on rebels should be seen in the context of the Elizabethan era. In 1570, the Pope excommunicated the Queen and absolved her subjects from allegiance. His efforts to bring about counter-reformation in England prompted Elizabeth to resort to harsh measures against Jesuit missionaries, some of whom were hanged as traitors to England, and other Catholics.[37] The implicit, and perhaps explicit, object of the counter-reformation was the deposition of the Queen. Maurois writes that in 1580 the Papal Secretary of State stated that 'whoever may dispatch [Elizabeth] from this world with the pious intention of serving God, not only will not sin, but will acquire merit'.[38] The siege mentality and the consequent persecution of Catholics in England were rooted in several causes, including the Pope's Bull, the Jesuit activity in England against Elizabeth and her Church, the Pope's-King's military campaign in Ireland, and

---

[37] George Macaulay Trevelyan, *History of England* (1953), ii. 130–1.
[38] André Maurois, *The Miracle of England* (1940), 227.

the Massacre of St Bartholomew—the infamous slaughter of Huguenots in Paris.

A large number of Catholic clergy and lay persons were executed in England in the late sixteenth century, and many others were persecuted. Maurois writes that those persecuted included John Shakespeare, the poet's father.[39] It has been suggested that John Shakespeare's withdrawal from public (borough) activities reflected his decision to become a 'recusant' and neither to take an oath of supremacy nor attend Anglican services.[40] He was listed in the Stratford Recusancy Reports to the Privy Council returned by the Warwickshire commission (1592).[41] Like many other Catholics, John Shakespeare was bound over on a misdemeanour charge of a breaching of 'the Queen's peace' and was fined for failing to appear in court to answer the charges against him.[42] Despite considerable danger, he wrote a confession of faith, 'a spiritual will, a signed confession of his unswerving adherence to the Roman Catholic faith'.[43] In the course of the persecution of Catholics, Edward Arden (a relative of John's wife Mary (Arden) Shakespeare) was convicted of high treason and executed. His head was displayed at London Bridge (1583).[44]

The difficulties faced by the Catholic father must have left a mark on the Protestant son. The persecution of Catholics and the harassment of his father could suggest that in adopting a harsh line towards rebels, William Shakespeare set out to prove that his loyalty was beyond reproach, as he perhaps did also in his *King John*, which is strongly anti-Catholic and anti-papal (see particularly III. i and V. ii). Such an explanation is unnecessary, however, for Shakespeare was not alone among loyal Elizabethan writers censuring rebellions and civil wars in the strongest possible terms.[45]

---

[39] André Maurois, *The Miracle of England* (1940), 227.

[40] Heinrich Mutschman and Karl Wentersdorf, *Shakespeare and Catholicism* (1969), 44.

[41] Ibid. 60 and App. 2.   [42] Ibid. 49–50.

[43] Ibid. 55. For the text, see ibid., App. 1.

[44] Ibid. 53. See also Anthony Burgess, *Shakespeare* (1970), 22.

[45] In a book published in 1599, the year *Henry V* was written, a senior member of the Bar ('apprentice of the common law') Richard Crompton, for example, wrote: 'Sedition is perillous, although it thew to have never so good a countenance of honest cause: and it were better for the authour of such sedition, to suffer anie losse or iniurie, then to be the cause of so great an evill.

As diseases, wounds, and the griefes and troubles of the mind, both to the

In contrast to the historical Henry, Shakespeare appeared to confine the term 'rebels' to English subjects[46] in his treatment of Henry V and, with some exceptions[47] in his other 'kings'.[48] For Shakespeare the French were—correctly—an 'enemy'; Cambridge, Scrope and Grey were just traitors, guilty of 'high treason' (*Henry V*, II. II. 163–4, 142–6). The speech by Shakespeare's Henry before the walls of Harfleur mentioned neither rebels nor rebellion, but only 'war' (*Henry V*, III. iii. 98). Only once did Shakespeare speak of 'rebellion' in *Henry V*—in contrasting suppression of the Irish rebellion[49] to victory over France—and only once of 'civil war' ('Now beshrew my father's ambition! He was thinking of civil wars when he got me' (v. ii. 223–4). Yet in this play the dramatist referred to 'war' about thirty times, often in its modern state-to-state connotation ('that never war advance | His bleeding sword 'twixt England and fair France' (v. ii. 349–50).[50]

Knowing or unknowing, Shakespeare's distinction between rebels and enemies corresponded to that already made in the common law. In shifting toward a differentiation between internal rebellion and external war, Shakespeare distanced himself

bodie and mind are hurtfull, so likewise civill warres to the common wealth are pestiferous and daungerous. For civill warres bring forth and nourish want of reverence towards God, contimneth authoritie, lawes and government, without which . . . Sedition causeth change of lawes, contempt of . . . , base estimation of sciences, it procureth horrible revenge, forgetfulnesse of paretage, consanguinitie and friendship, it causeth extortions, violence, robberies, wastings of countries, lacking of townes, burning of buildings, . . . banishments, savage murthers, alterations and overthrow of pollicies, with other infinite and intollerable miseries, pitiful to behold, sorowfull to expresse, and lamentable to thinke of.' Richard Crompton, *The Mansion of Magnanimitie*, (unpaginated) (1599, repr. 1975), ch. 7.

[46] See *supra* at 201–2.

[47] See e.g. '[i]f they [the 'fickle wavering nation' of France] perceive dissension' in English ranks they might 'be provoked [t]o willful disobedience, and rebel!' (*1 Henry VI*, IV. i. 138–42); and ibid. v. vi. 169–72: 'YORK Then swear allegiance to his majesty, | As thou art knight, never to disobey | Nor be rebellious to the crown of England, | Thou nor thy nobles, to the crown of England. *[Charles and the rest give tokens of fealty]*

[48] One may wonder whether Shakespeare's regard for Owen Glendower in *1 Henry IV* may have been related to the unclear status of Wales prior to the Act of Union.

[49] '[F]rom Ireland coming, [b]ringing rebellion broachèd on his sword' (*Henry V*, v. Prol. 31–2).

[50] Shakespeare's Henry VI told Vernon and Basset to desist from insisting on their duel over trivial points of honour and to 'digest [their] angry choler [on the French] enemies' (*1 Henry VI*, IV. i. 167–8).

from the medieval law of war and moved towards the modern law of war, with its distinction between international and internal wars and acceptance of more humane treatment for those involved in the former.

Modern international lawyers would consider Henry's invasion of France, were it to occur today, an international armed conflict governed by the Hague Convention (No. IV),[51] the Geneva Conventions for the Protection of Victims of War of 12 August 1949,[52] and Additional Protocol I.[53] From this perspective, French combatants would enjoy the right of quarter and, upon capture, POW privileges. Civilians would benefit from protection from massacres and such measures as collective punishment, reprisals, and hostage-taking. Those resisting, if they met the requirements of applicable international treaties, would be entitled to POW privileges and could not be tried by the occupying power for lawful acts of war carried out against it.

Modern humanitarian law recognizes that persons who are not nationals of an occupying power are 'not bound to it by any duty of allegiance'.[54] Nevertheless, even in the context of occupations by foreign powers, confusing and confused concepts such as 'war rebellion' and 'war treason' (*kriegsverrat*, a notion deriving from medieval concepts of fidelity toward the lord), were used until the Geneva Conventions. Richard Baxter's seminal work[55] contributed to their abandonment. Both war treason and war rebellion were based on the belief that the population of an occupied country owed allegiance, albeit temporary, to the occupying power and that rebellion constituted a moral breach or a violation of international law. Originating in a period 'of transition from the rigorous law of conquest to the more modern and more enlightened view of belligerent occupation',[56] these concepts transferred from municipal law inappropriate connotations of treason or rebellion against the sovereign and served to justify harsh punitive measures. Baxter demonstrated that modern inter-

---

[51] Convention Respecting the Laws and Customs of War on Land, with Annex of Regulations (Hague Convention No. IV), signed 18 Oct. 1907, 36 Stat. 2277; TS 539; 1 Bevans 631.

[52] See *supra* note 29.   [53] Protocol I, *supra* note 10.

[54] Fourth Geneva Convention, *supra* note 29, at Art. 68.

[55] Richard R. Baxter, 'The Duty of Obedience to the Belligerent Occupant', 27 Brit. Y.B. Int'l L. 235 (1950).

[56] Ibid. 258.

national law denied that the population of an occupied territory owed the occupying power any duty of obedience founded on any legal or moral obligation,[57] and that the only source of such a duty of obedience was 'the power of the occupant to demand it'.[58]

Even in the modern era it happens that a state defends its invasion of foreign territory by arguing that it is merely reclaiming its own lost territory, as did Iraq in invading Kuwait.[59] Therefore, such a state argues that it is not an occupier bound to respect the Hague and the Geneva Conventions, but a state exercising sovereign authority over its territory and subjects and, thus, entitled to apply its own criminal laws to rebels.[60] Such claims are seldom taken seriously, however.

The applicability of international law to internal conflicts is less than half a century old. Prior to the Geneva Conventions for the Protection of Victims of War of 12 August 1949,[61] of which only one article (Common Article 3) concerns non-international armed conflicts, there were no treaties imposing constraints on the conduct of the adversaries in civil wars. Common Article 3 has since been supplemented by Additional Protocol II (1977).[62] Although that Protocol has expanded and improved the content of protective norms stated in Common Article 3, it raised the threshold of applicability to an exceedingly high level,[63] and is, therefore, rarely implemented. Even these treaties permit, however, the application to domestic rebels of the criminal law of the land, including those defining and punishing acts of treason.

---

[57] Ibid. 243.

[58] Ibid. 261. Baxter argued that resistance and guerrilla activities in occupied areas did not violate international law. Hostilities conducted by such persons merely deprived them of protections due under international law to POWs or peaceful civilians. Richard Baxter, 'So-Called "Unprivileged Belligerency": Spies, Guerrillas, and Saboteurs', in 28 Brit. Y.B. Int'l L. 323, 342–43 (1951). Recent humanitarian law adopts a more protective attitude towards people fighting against colonial domination and alien occupation. Protocol I, *supra* note 10, at Arts. 1(4), 43–4.

[59] Oscar Schachter, 'United Nations Law in the Gulf Conflict', 85 AJIL 452, 453 (1991).

[60] Protocol II, *supra* note 23, grants rebels judicial guarantees and protections against inhuman treatment, but does not shield them from the criminal law of the land, and, in many countries, from capital punishment. See generally Rosemary Abi-Saab, *Droit humanitaire et conflits internes* (1986).

[61] *Supra* note 29.　　　[62] *Supra* note 23.

[63] Theodor Meron, *Human Rights in Internal Strife*, *supra* note 1, at 45–6.

12
Conclusions

By its very nature medieval society was not an ideal environment for the development of clear, logical, and humane laws of war. There were, for example, few independent states and even fewer states that could be seen as equal. Government depended on a tangled web of hierarchical relations between princes, and between princes and knights. Class allegiance to the order of knights was more important than national loyalty. Unclear notions of statehood made it difficult to gauge which princes enjoyed sufficient sovereignty to wage a lawful war. The unclear notion of sovereignty blurred the distinction between international wars and civil wars. There was no clear differentiation between subjects and aliens and therefore between enemies and rebels. Vague and misused concepts of guilt and innocence often served as yardsticks for treatment of adversaries. The adequate distinction between *jus ad bellum* and *jus in bello* was still embryonic and often ignored, and not infrequently led to refusal to grant combatant privileges to the other party's soldiers when the justness of the war was challenged. Moreover, complicated distinctions separated privileged from unprivileged civilians, reserving protection only for the privileged classes. The difference between normative, disciplinary, and tactical rules was often blurred. Various rules and rituals protected the knightly class in their contests and combats, especially in the field; however, no comparable rules governed behaviour of the combatant towards the civilian population. The development of the law lagged behind the transition from contests between individual knights to battles between armies of warring nations,[1] which was already taking place. Finally, medieval society accepted an artificial distinction between combat in the field and assaults (sieges) of towns and fortresses which often resulted in the cruel treatment of townspeople.

---

[1] *LW* 245.

Given these circumstances it would have been natural to expect that few laws of war would have been spawned in the Middle Ages. To the contrary, however, the Middle Ages left us a rich tradition of laws of war. This may, perhaps, be attributed to the fact that war was the norm rather than the exception, a way of life and an opportunity for material enrichment, glory, and fulfilment. War sustained an entire class of chivalric élite, whose honour and feudal and knightly relationships thrived on rites and rules.

Some of the laws of war originating in the Middle Ages constituted broad principles, such as those defining necessity, proportionality, and humanity, and broad tenets of *jus ad bellum*. Others formed narrower and more defined rules laying down specific proscriptions and requirements of a medieval code. Medieval law, for instance, defined and regulated permissible reprisals, and division of spoils of war and ransom. It prescribed rules for the siege and the sacking of captured towns, and for the treatment of hostages and prisoners of war. Medieval law set out the duties of vassals, and, for example, the parameters of the obligation to grant quarter, the privileges of certain categories of civilians and the special treatment of heralds and ambassadors, and the rights of persons furnished with safe conducts. Rules prohibited the use of poisonous and certain other weapons, addressed perfidy and ruses of war, and covered the conclusion of hostilities, including supervision and breaches of a truce, and the making of treaties of peace.

Not only did these norms of law of war exist, but they were far more than abstract ideals. Although then, as still today, ensuring compliance was a major difficulty, medieval laws of war were often enforced through military discipline, courts of the constable and the marshal, and the courts of chivalry. Most importantly, laws were observed because chivalric honour required deference to the rules. A breach of the code brought about dishonour and shame. The threat of dishonour was obviously a more compelling deterrent for the knight—especially for the higher ranks of nobility—than for the common soldier. The soldier's predilection for pillage and profit combined with the absence or irregularity of adequate wages made the enforcement of rules of war difficult,[2] even for those few princes, Henry V and

---

[2] Ignorance of chivalric rules and erosion of chivalric honour's role as catalyst for humane and civilized behaviour frequently contributed to violations, especially

Charles VII being the most notable examples, who were determined to protect the population from the excesses of the soldiery.

Some of the medieval rules reflected considerable ambiguity and arbitrariness. The rules regarding the treatment of hostages, for example, were imprecise and unclear. Could captors kill a hostage delivered up as a pledge to keep an agreement even though the agreement itself was scrupulously kept? Did the agreement imply that the captors had unlimited discretion over the hostages' fate? It was not clear whether hostages were intended to serve as sacrificial lambs, good ransom material, or innocent pawns to ensure observance of treaties over which they had no influence. Further, the rules which allowed knights, but not peasants, the option of quarter in exchange for ransom were neither humane nor chivalrous.

The role of ransom was both beneficial and harmful, saving lives and thus advancing the principles of humanity on the one hand, while promoting the capture of persons who would otherwise be let free on the other. As the practice of ransom declined, fewer soldiers were taken prisoner—many more were simply killed. Other rules, such as those instituting sophisticated, sometimes even third-party procedures for the supervision of the observance of truces and settlement of truce-related claims, were remarkably advanced for their era, as was the art of negotiating and concluding peace agreements.

Medieval laws of war were largely customary. Evidence of these laws was provided by heralds, courts of chivalry, military courts and, most importantly, the writings of such authors and compilers as Giovanni da Legnano, Honoré Bouvet, and Christine de Pisan. While purporting to describe existing customs, the writers shaped the content and in the process influenced the development of norms. Another source of the law of war was statutory. Indeed, in medieval times interest in *jus gentium* was not limited to scholars and tribunals. Medieval kings such as Richard II and Henry V of England and Charles VII of France promulgated detailed proclamations and ordinances on war. Henry's proclamations, which attracted the attention of Holinshed and Shakespeare, were informed by pragmatic concerns of good order and military discipline as well as considera-

in so far as the non-knightly soldiers, and even the lowest ranks of nobility, were concerned.

tions of humanity. These proclamations and ordinances were addressed to such matters as the right to ransom and other spoils of war, the prohibition of pillage, the protection of women, ecclesiastics, and churches, and the obligation to pay the full value of food requisitioned. Considerations of humanity, frequently compelled by religious principles, blended with the imperatives of military order and resulted in raising the standard of protection for the civilian population.

Progressing from the early to late Middle Ages and on to the Renaissance, these ordinances, which initially addressed almost only disciplinary and tactical matters, gave increasingly greater weight to protective norms and principles of humanity. Some ordinances contained eloquent articulation of these principles. A 1643 ordinance, for example, proclaimed that '[m]urder is no less unlawful and intollerable in the time of war, than in time of peace.' Other significant provisions proclaimed that ignorance of the law did not excuse violations, and mentioned custom—and more rarely the law of nature—as residuary normative sources. Allusion to custom served to limit the arbitrary discretion of the military commander with respect to matters not explicitly stated in the ordinances. Endorsement of law of nature enhanced the principle of humanity which is inherent in that law. Taken together, the references to custom and the law of nature were a modern precursor of the 1907 Martens clause. The laws of war stated in these ordinances served to expedite the formation of customary law.

I have examined clusters of medieval norms that underlie Shakespeare's account in *Henry V* of a phase of the Hundred Years War. These clusters concern the just war doctrine, declarations of war, the responsibility of princes, the treatment of the population of occupied territory—including the case of siege— and prisoners of war, the conduct of diplomacy, and the making of peace treaties. I have used *Henry V* as a vehicle to analyse the issues of law that governed, or should have governed, that historic conflict, and to develop an intertemporal, historical perspective on the law of war and its evolution.

An analysis of the detailed rules pertaining to necessity, reprisals, and the protection of prisoners of war and civilians, especially women, reveals that resort to humane principles, while advocated by some Renaissance scholars—particularly Gentili—

was frequently rejected by other Renaissance writers on *jus gentium*. These authors gave preference to harsher, *Staatsraison* rules. A more humane approach, however, was not alien to some medieval writers, especially Christine de Pisan, who insisted that religious and chivalric principles demanded a high degree of respect and mercy for the human person.

Like their twentieth-century counterparts, both medieval and Renaissance works on the law of war reflected the tension between principles of humanity and military necessity, broadly construed. Their authors defined some of the issues still central to the law of war and enunciated policies and principles that have shaped norms of modern international law on matters such as combatant privileges and the protection of civilians. The ancestry of these protective rules was recently acknowledged by the US Department of Defense in a report to Congress on the conduct of the Gulf War.[3] The long history of these rules will weigh heavily in determining their character as customary law. The evidence that ordinances of war dating from the Middle Ages prohibited pillage and protected women goes far beyond the Hague Regulations or the Lieber Code in establishing the customary law roots of these rules.

It is often claimed that the Peace of Westphalia (1648) which introduced a system of modern nation-states and international relations governed by sovereign equality resulted in the end of laws of war of the late Middle Ages. Such assertions are buttressed by the emphasis many scholars place on the role of Grotius as the father of modern international law.[4] Despite the tremendous importance of the new political order established by the Peace of Westphalia and the magisterial work of Grotius, the truth is that the evolution and adaptation of the core rules far outweighed any discontinuity and rift. Grotius did not claim to

---

[3] The report notes: 'The law of armed conflict . . . with respect to collateral damage and collateral civilian casualties is derived from the Just War tradition of discrimination; that is, the necessity for distinguishing combatants from noncombatants and legitimate military targets from civilian objects. . . . [T]his tradition is a major part of the foundation on which the law of war is built.'
US Department of Defense, *Conduct of the Persian Gulf Conflict: An Interim Report to Congress Pursuant to Title V Persian Gulf Conflict Supplemental Authorization and Personnel Benefits Act of 1991 (Public Law 102–25)*, (1991), 12–2.

[4] I suggested elsewhere that it is only fair that Gentili share with Grotius the reputation as the founder of modern international law. Theodor Meron, 'Common Rights of Mankind in Gentili, Grotius and Suárez', 85 AJIL 110, 116 (1991).

create the law of war.[5] To a very large extent, both Gentili and Grotius drew and commented on the laws of war of the late Middle Ages, emphasizing continuity. Their works, as well as those of Suárez, are still used as entirely appropriate commentaries on many medieval norms. Grotius and Gentili shaped these norms in the light of their era, facilitating their adaptation to the new political order of co-equal and independent states. While undoubtedly some medieval norms were discarded or fell into desuetude, many others shed their feudal and chivalric gloss and gradually metamorphosed into rules of modern international law. The legacy of medieval norms is therefore important for an understanding of the sources of the modern law of war.

Because Shakespeare wrote about a medieval war during the Elizabethan Renaissance, it would be comforting to suggest that in the 179 years that elapsed between the Treaty of Troyes and the writing of the play the law had significantly progressed towards greater humanity. Unfortunately, major progress cannot be discerned. Consider, for example, the cruelty of the Thirty Years War (1618–48) which was soon to break out and was conducted without the constraints of chivalric rules.

The medieval umbilical cord connecting *jus ad bellum* and *jus in bello*, still conventional to the contemporaries of Shakespeare, was eventually cut, giving rise to the uniform and more equitable application of the law of war. But echoes of the medieval doctrine of just war still resonate in some theories of modern international law.

The principle of *respondere non sovereign* gave way to the much stricter modern concepts of attribution and responsibility, so essential to the effectiveness of international law. Although necessity has not been eliminated from the lexicon of the law of war, persons *hors de combat*, including prisoners of war, are now protected by clear rules of law from both reprisal and slaughter on the basis of military necessity, in contrast to the unfortunates at Agincourt. Protection of civilians—once limited to privileged categories—now applies to all civilians, as does the protection of prisoners of war. The grant of quarter has become a fundamental norm, from which no derogations or exceptions are allowed.

[5] Regarding the links between Grotius's writings and medieval law of war, see generally Peter Haggenmacher, *Grotius et ·la doctrine de la guerre just* (1983), 441–2, 602–5.

Although characterizing a conflict as international or internal is still difficult, at least the principal criteria for making a distinction have been established. Yet the applicability of modern international law to internal conflicts is less than half a century old. Although modern conventions governing civil wars provide for important protections, they are rarely respected. Even these treaties allow governments to try domestic rebels according to criminal laws of the land, including those defining and punishing acts of treason. In Henry's times, as is still true today, disrespect for the existing rules, rather than the absence of rules, was the principal problem.

Holinshed wrote about public affairs of state in which *jus gentium*, including the ordinances and proclamations of war of King Henry V, served an important role. It was therefore only natural that Shakespeare, an ardent student of Holinshed and a writer who had explored the law of the land in such non-historical plays as the *Merchant of Venice*, should take a keen interest in *jus gentium* in *Henry V*, a history.

Shakespeare's attention to historical detail and rules of law in international relations and diplomacy is truly impressive. A compelling example is his careful formulation of the ultimatum to France, which contains a statement of the claim, its legal basis, and the consequences of non-compliance. Shakespeare had a clear command of legal and chivalric phraseology and a good intuitive understanding of the rules. His descriptions of duels before courts of chivalry, for example, faithfully reflected their terminology and procedure. Whether knowingly or not, Shakespeare appeared to differentiate between English and Irish rebels and French enemies. This distinction was already made by the common law, but was still blurred in the *jus gentium* as reflected in the writings of the Renaissance jurists contemporaneous with Shakespeare. Shakespeare was distancing himself from the medieval and edging towards the modern law of war, which distinguishes between international and internal wars and demands a more humane treatment for those involved in the former.

In a few plays, and especially in *Henry V*, Shakespeare's heroes advocated resort to a just war. Like the more sophisticated jurists of his times, Shakespeare recognized that both parties might assert the justness of their causes. He alluded, in *Troilus and*

Cressida, to the difficulty that arose when both adversaries invoked a just cause for the war:

> TROILUS   O virtuous fight,
> When right with right wars who shall be most right.
>
> (Troilus and Cressida, III. ii. 167–68)

Shakespeare seldom glorified war and certainly was not a war-monger. Even in those few plays where he supported a war because it was just, and certainly in many others, Shakespeare's text is replete with references to the brutality, bloodiness, and horrors of war. Even the heroic, patriotic, and just war, which he favoured in his *Henry V*, ends with the Chorus's admission that it was both bloody and useless: the protector of the infant Henry VI 'lost France and made his England bleed' (Epilogue, 12).[6]

The play *Henry V* illustrated the underlying issues implicated in the law of war. While, for the most part, Shakespeare was faithful to Holinshed's version of the facts, he departed from that version in two major instances: the addition of Henry's admonition to Exeter at Harfleur to 'use mercy', and the favourable gloss put on the order to kill the French prisoners at Agincourt. There was no mention of 'mercy' in Holinshed. Yet Shakespeare not only highlighted it as the principal order issued by the King in Harfleur, but also passed over in silence the harsh measures taken by the English in Harfleur, including the deportation of its indigent population.

In these two deviations from Holinshed's *Chronicles*, the dramatist was probably simply trying to portray the heroic King to his best advantage. But, in so doing, Shakespeare aligned himself with the advocates of greater adherence to humane laws of war, whether medieval or Renaissance.

The importance Shakespeare attributed to mercy in *Henry V* was entirely consistent with the esteem the dramatist expressed

---

[6] Phyllis Rackin offers this explanation: 'We get not only two interpretations of the action but two accounts of the action, one in the discourse of the chorus and one in the dramatic representation staged before us; and the two accounts not only differ from each other but also insist upon each other's inadequacies. Moreover, instead of reconciling the two views at the end of the play or discarding one for the other, Shakespeare let both of them stand, directing our attention to the abyss at the center of the historiographic project: the impossibility of recovering the past or of getting behind the historiographic text . . . to discover the always postulated and never graspable fiction called historical truth.' *Stages of History* (1990), 69, 82–3.

for mercy in his other plays. Mercy was the highest attribute; it was God's quality, as it was that of kings, the brave and the noble. 'But mercy is above this sceptred sway. | It is enthronèd in the hearts of kings; | It is an attribute to God himself' (*Merchant of Venice*, IV. i. 190–2); 'Sweet mercy is nobility's true badge' (*Titus Andronicus*, I. i. 119).

In addition to frequent references to mercy, Shakespeare's plays are replete with references to honour, a concept central to the enforcement of chivalric rules in the Middle Ages. Honour and mercy, combined, formed potent forces for civilized behaviour in time of war. The medieval concept of mercy on which the dramatist drew evolved into the concept of obligations of humanity in the modern law of war. What, after all, are obligations of humanity if not legally binding progeny of mercy?

Index

Printed in the United Kingdom
by Lightning Source UK Ltd.
133863UK00001B/263/A